BUSINESS WEEK's
Guide to the Best
Business Schools

John A. Byrne
Associate Editor, BUSINESS WEEK

with a team of
BUSINESS WEEK Editors

McGraw-Hill Publishing Company
New York St. Louis San Francisco Auckland
Bogotá Caracas Hamburg Lisbon London
Madrid Mexico Milan Montreal New Delhi
Oklahoma City Paris San Juan São Paulo
Singapore Sydney Tokyo Toronto

Library of Congress Cataloging-in-Publication Data

Byrne, John A.
  Business Week's guide to the best business schools.

  Includes index.
  1. Business schools—United States.   2. Master of
business administration degree—United States.
I. Business Week (New York, N.Y.)   II. Title.
III. Title: Guide to the best business schools.
HF1131.B95   1990   650'.071'173   ‒   89-12611
ISBN 0-07-009327-X

    4567890   DOC/DOC   943210

ISBN 0-07-009327-X

The editors for this book were William A. Sabin and Barbara B.
Toniolo, the designer was Mark E. Safran, and the production
supervisor was Dianne Walber. The book was set in ITC Garamond
Light. It was composed by the McGraw-Hill Publishing Company
Professional & Reference Division composition unit.

Printed and bound by R. R. Donnelley & Sons Company

CONTENTS

CONTENTS

6. THE RUNNERS-UP / 138

7. ACCREDITED B-SCHOOLS . . . AND HOW TO SIZE THEM UP / 180

PREFACE

The origins of this guide go back to the phenomenally popular BUSINESS WEEK cover story of November 28, 1988, on the nation's best business schools. So taken was the public with the subject of graduate business education and a ranking of schools that the issue became an instant best-seller on the newsstands. Hundreds of letters flowed into the magazine's New York office. Newspapers and magazines worldwide reported the findings of the article.

The response from readers led us to the idea that BUSINESS WEEK should significantly expand its coverage of the B-school world with a comprehensive guide to the best schools. Our goal was to produce a full-fledged scouting report, something that went beyond merely listing the schools and offering a superficial description of their programs. The project won enthusiastic support within McGraw-Hill, Inc., publisher of BUSINESS WEEK. McGraw-Hill Publishing Company agreed to publish the guide.

A key to the cover story's success was a unique rating of the B-schools. BUSINESS WEEK ranked the top B-schools by surveying recent graduates and corporate recruiters. In the past, rankings relied primarily on the opinions of B-school deans, faculty, or top executives, who were asked to name the top programs—even though they often had only indirect knowledge of many of the schools.

For this guide, BUSINESS WEEK used its surveys of students and corporate recruiters as a starting point. Then the staff interviewed hundreds of students, alumni, recruiters, faculty members, and deans to draw out the strengths and weaknesses of the top schools.

We also tried to find out how the schools differ in their personalities, cultures, and extracurricular activities.

The result is a guide that reveals in depth the fascinating findings of our graduate survey of the Class of 1988. In addition to the Top 20 schools, BUSINESS WEEK also names and profiles 20 other excellent MBA schools that are often overshadowed by the top-tier institutions. And we add to this mix plenty of invaluable information on how to get into one of these elite schools.

The project was directed by Associate Editor John A. Byrne, who has covered graduate business education on a regular basis for more than six years. Author of *The Headhunters* and coauthor of *Odyssey*, the biography of Apple Computer Inc.'s Chairman John Sculley, Byrne initiated the original research. He also conceived and wrote much of what you'll read in the guide.

Monica Roman, a staff editor for BUSINESS WEEK's management department, made a major contribution in reporting and writing the B-school profiles. Celeste Whittaker, who played a key role in the research for the cover story, returned to this broader project to amass thousands of pages of information on over 200 top business schools. Assistant Managing Editor Mark Morrison supervised the project and edited the guide.

CHAPTER 1

WHY GO FOR THE MBA?

Wharton's new first-year students were lined up straight, listening in fear to the tough-talking drill sergeant. He marched by the erect recruits, telling them what to expect from their upcoming two years in graduate business school.

> *"Corporate America is a hellhole!" the sergeant barked.*
> *"It's work! It's sweat! It's stress! My job is to mold you into finely honed corporate tools. You slobs are soft, too weak to work grueling hours. Do you think you could work a 100-hour week?"*
> *"No sir," pipes a squeaky voice from the line.*
> *"That's right!" the sergeant smiles. "But by the time I'm finished with you, I'll have you working 100 hours a week and begging for more. I'll teach you to walk, talk, barter, bargain, deal, and dress like a Wharton MBA!"*

Although merely an opening scene from the 1989 Wharton Follies, the B-school's annual student show, the lines satirically capture the promise of a business school education: It's to prepare you for life in the corporate world, to give you a headstart against the competition, and to somehow make you stand out in the managerial crowd. Indeed, the right MBA can often lead to a more exciting career, a fatter paycheck. It can provide a foundation for an entrepreneur to launch a successful business. It can even be a ticket to a high-powered job running one of the largest companies.

These are all good reasons why so many people are rushing off to get an MBA these days. And few of them are disappointed by what they find at a top-ranked program. Many describe their two years of business study as the high point of their lives: meeting new friends, sharing new experiences, discovering horizons and careers they never knew existed. A good B-school education also imparts a level of confidence and maturity that years of actual work experience could never deliver. "It's like drinking from a fire hydrant," explains one Stanford University graduate. "There is so much intense learning and growing going on, both inside and outside of the classroom."

The MBA has emerged as a modern-day symbol of business success. The education teaches you to think and analyze. The experience fosters enduring friendships and business contacts with exciting, dynamic people. It opens doors to some of the most admired corporations in America. Some graduates gleefully report doubling their salaries after spending two years in a top B-school program. No wonder so much magic and mystery has surrounded what has become the most famous acronym in the vocabulary of business.

Yet because many prospective students don't do their homework, they end up wasting a lot of time and a lot of money. At the outset, they don't find out what an MBA can and can't do for them. They don't properly evaluate a particular school or program to find out what it can deliver. They don't adequately analyze the costs of going to a school against the likely benefits. As a result, many MBAs find that the rewards of a graduate degree in business are elusive. Much to their chagrin, the MBA fails to deliver on a better job, a bigger salary, and greater opportunity to climb the corporate ladder.

One reason an MBA can often lead to disappointment is that it's hardly unique to have one today. This year as many as 70,000 graduates armed with the degree will burst forth from campuses. That's nearly a 30% jump from 1980, more than a threefold rise from 1970, and almost a fifteenfold increase from 1960, when only 4814 got the degree. And more are on the way: Some 200,000 students are now studying for MBAs.

"It's hard to convince myself that the world needs 70,000 or so MBAs a year," says Robert K. Jaedicke, dean of Stanford University's B-school. "If you look at the growth rate over the past 25 years, you could come to the conclusion that everybody in the United States will have an MBA degree by the year 2010."

What gives? With visions of big promotions and heady salaries dancing in their heads, hordes of people have gravitated to the B-school world. Many of them felt disadvantaged at work without an MBA. Many others, particularly those with liberal arts backgrounds, felt they needed some business instruction to be successful in corporate America. Still others, trapped in careers they really didn't enjoy, saw the MBA as the ticket out.

For many, the so-called "Passport to the Good Life" became little more than a frustrating dead end. Oftentimes, the reason is that they received the degree from an institution that lacked either a national or regional reputation for quality. There were about 370 graduate business schools in 1974. Today, nearly 700 institutions offer the degree. Yet fewer than a third of them meet even the minimum standards of accreditation set by the American Assembly of Collegiate Schools of Business. "Many of these schools come very close to selling the degree," says Raymond E. Miles, dean of the University of California at Berkeley's B-school. Harvard University's B-school dean, John H. McArthur, has gone so far as to say that 97% of the schools that offer the degree admit "virtually anyone who applies."

That's not exactly true, but it gives you an indication of what has been going on in the B-school community. It also is a reason why BUSINESS WEEK published this guide. Not merely a listing of business schools, it's a scouting report on the best of the bunch. Too many schools jumped on the MBA bandwagon because it became something of a fad to offer the degree. Not only was it the degree to have, it was the degree to have to succeed. It's true that in some professions, especially consulting and banking, an MBA can be of critical importance. But its necessity in general business has often been overstated.

Indeed when BUSINESS WEEK and Louis Harris & Associates polled senior executives from major corporations in 1986, more than half of them said it wasn't important for an executive to have an MBA to get ahead in the company. Despite that belief, however, 56% of the executives agreed that when merit and abilities are equal, MBAs often get promoted faster than people without the degree. And when asked whether they would advise a son or daughter planning a career in business to get an MBA, an overwhelming 78% answered in the affirmative. A mere 17% of those surveyed said they wouldn't recommend the MBA.

The Promise of a B-School Education

What if you never really planned a career in business and are unhappy with what you currently do? Maybe you're a musician, artist, engineer, psychologist, doctor, lawyer, or teacher. Is the MBA a good investment for the career switcher? A degree from a top school can make the transition to the business world a lot easier. It will not only give you a taste of what business is all about, it may also provide the contacts to land a viable job when the educational experience is complete. Indeed, some MBA-recruiting companies like the different perspectives that someone from law or medicine can bring to business. If you're really tired of what you're doing, a quality MBA can be a pass to this new and different world.

There are other kinds of career switchers, too. These are people who already have good jobs in business, but don't want to stay in the same industry or career for the rest of their lives. An MBA degree is a tougher choice in this case. Indeed, don't expect any guarantees that the MBA will allow you to start fresh. If you have had valuable experience in an industry or a company, you'll find an MBA more worthwhile if you intend to build upon that previous experience—not reject it in the hopes of doing something completely different. "Let's take a guy who's coming from Merck and doesn't want to be a chemist anymore," says Ed Mosier, director of placement at Carnegie-Mellon's Graduate School of Industrial Administration. "After two years here, he may well return to the pharmaceutical industry, but in a business management position—perhaps finance or marketing. He is selling his industry background in addition to his MBA. Those who want to divorce themselves from their previous experience altogether face a tougher road."

There also is a new kind of MBA student, the would-be entrepreneur. Many now view the B-school as a useful "boot camp" in which you learn the nuts and bolts of business, make a slew of networking contacts, and get a corporate job where you'll spend your first three to five years before launching your own company. Responding to a growing interest in entrepreneurship, B-schools have launched a bevy of courses that make it possible to do your own thing sooner in life than you ever expected. Widely available courses instruct how to put together a business plan; raise money from venture capitalists and other investors; incorporate your company and produce, market, and sell a product. Dozens of businesses, in fact, have been started by recent MBA graduates. None of these courses confer immediate success, however. That's all up to you.

Why It's Crucial to Go to a Good School

Anyway you look at it, it's the graduate degree of choice among the corporate elite. Of the CEOs of the top 1000 corporations, 225 hold the degree. After all, an MBA from a top school can offer you entry into a brand-name corporation such as IBM, Procter & Gamble, Citicorp, General Electric, or Ford Motor—all big MBA recruiting companies that also boast outstanding business reputations as "academies" for senior management. Most of these companies consider the MBA to be something of a screen for the best and brightest young people in America. That's why they recruit so many MBAs and why they so willingly pay them handsome salaries. The combination of a top degree and an employment history with one of these companies can make a big difference on a résumé. Executive headhunters today say that their clients often specify that the MBA is a prerequisite for top management positions.

When should you go to business school, then? The succinct and difficult answer is when you can get into one that's good enough to make a meaningful difference to you and your career. With growing recognition that quantity-over-quality thinking has gotten American management into lots of trouble, a better idea is taking hold: the MBA is more crucial, or less, depending on which school confers it. "Today the term MBA doesn't mean that much," says Russell E. Palmer, dean of the University of Pennsylvania's Wharton School. "Now it's where you get it."

Little-known schools with small MBA programs that lack accreditation probably aren't going to give you either a quality business education or a hefty starting salary. If you want a worthwhile MBA, you have to get it from a school with a reputation for quality and/or prestige—whether it's known worldwide, throughout the United States, regionally, or only in your city or town. You might even want to ignore the big national schools if your goal is to take over the family business or simply become a kingpin in your home region. An MBA from a state university could turn out to be far more valuable than one from Harvard. Why? You'd make more relevant business and government contacts to further your career in the area.

Who exactly goes to B-school? When you count both full- and part-time programs together, you find that students range in age from 21 to the early 50s, though the biggest single age group is 28 years old. About one-quarter are at least 31 years of age, while only 7% are at least 40. Men easily outnumber women: at Columbia University fewer than one in three students is a woman; at MIT only one in five. Students are predominantly white. One recent study by the Graduate Management Admission Council found that only 8% of MBAs are black, 4% are Hispanic, and 5% are Asian. At any of the top schools, however, you'll still find lots of ethnic and foreign diversity. At Wharton, 21% of the students hail from foreign countries, 12% are minorities; at the University of Michigan's B-school, 21% of the MBA class is made up of minorities and 12% is foreign.

Most of the better schools prefer that MBA candidates have two or more years of full-time work experience under their belts before applying. (Sure, even Harvard accepts a few students direct from their undergraduate studies. But your chances of gaining admission to a good program fall significantly without work experience.) Many MBAs who lack experience say they regret not waiting before going to B-school. Having already earned a living gives you a reference point to use as you study business. It also makes your comments and insights in the classroom more valuable to a discussion. And work experience is often used by the better schools as an important consideration in whether you get into the school or not. The better the company and the experience, the more likely it will open the door to a quality MBA program.

Things to Consider in Deciding Where to Go

Of course, the MBA doesn't come cheap. If you're leaving a good job, you might have to give up $60,000 to $70,000 in salary over the two years you'll commit to most full-time programs. Expect to pay about $15,000 or more a year in tuition and fees at the best private schools that exude MBA prestige. Add a few thousand more for books and other expenses and the total cost will easily exceed $100,000. Quite a bit of money for a business education and a piece of parchment. That's why, in fact, so many top students flock to the world of investment banking and consulting: they pay graduates the highest starting salaries and that money can be sorely needed to pay off a pile of loans.

If you work the averages, however, you'll graduate into a job that should pay a starting salary and bonus of about $52,000 a year. Simple calculator mathematics will tell you that it might take a good number of years before you recoup your investment in lost earnings and tuition. In fact, some career counselors contend that on this basis it's simply not worth the cost. But those assessments often ignore an important consideration: the economic advantage you initially gain from the MBA is usually maintained throughout your career. And it's more likely to give you a better shot at attaining what most people want in their first job after B-school: interesting work, better chances for promotions, good pay, clear responsibilities, friendly coworkers, good job security, and challenging problems to work on. Besides, you can't feed into a calculator the increased confidence and psychological comfort an MBA might give you as a business executive or manager. One Harvard grad likened it to a vacation in Europe. "Can you justify its payback? No. But does it broaden your horizons, give you a new perspective on the world? Is it valuable? Of course!"

There also are ways, of course, to limit the cost of the degree. Students at state schools pay substantially less tuition than those at private schools. If you're a resident of North Carolina, for example, you could get a degree from the university's B-school at Chapel Hill for less than $2000 in tuition—over two years! That's one-fourteenth the cost of an MBA at neighboring Duke University. Even if you're not a resident of North Carolina, the tuition is only $4900 a year—compared with Duke's $13,500 bill. And sometimes nonresidents are eligible to pay only resident tuition in their second year of graduate study.

That's a pretty compelling argument in favor of the public university because few students want to graduate with $40,000 or more of debt on their backs. But also remember that the graduates of public universities seldom bring home the highest starting salaries. A Duke graduate, for instance, tends to earn on average about $4000 more out of the gate than a counterpart from the University of North Carolina. The MBA degree that has consistently garnered the highest starting compensation is from Stanford. In 1988, Stanford MBAs pulled down an average starting pay and bonus of $65,176—after paying about $14,100 a year in tuition and fees. The North Carolina MBA averaged $44,941 in starting salary and bonus.

Cost, then, certainly is one criteria in deciding whether you can go for an MBA and where you should go. What are other considerations? While a school's overall standing is critical to the value of its degree, you also should think about what you want to gain from an education. Do you want a job in finance? Marketing? Manufacturing? Human resources? Some schools have reputations for being the absolute best in a particular field. Take marketing. Northwestern, Duke, Texas, and the University of Southern California are known for their strong programs. Finance? There are Wharton, NYU, Carnegie-Mellon, or Chicago—schools heavy in financial theory and models. Among some other schools, MIT and Purdue are highly respected for their efforts to turn out students interested in manufacturing. For general management, the most logical picks are Harvard, Stanford, Amos Tuck, and Virginia.

Before applying to any school, you need to do some homework. Treat it the way an MBA would in a typical case study. "You should gather all the information about placement, the quality of the school, and do a business analysis of it," says Robert L. Virgil, dean of Washington University's Olin School of Business. "If you're investing two years of your life and a lot of money, I think you should visit the school when it's in session. Attend a class or two, talk to the students, grab a recruiter during a coffee break to find out what he thinks the place is like. Then, look at yourself in the mirror and see if you really match up with the school."

Before selecting which schools you might want to attend, it would also be helpful to chat candidly with recent graduates of the school. Why? If you already have your heart set on becoming a consultant at McKinsey & Co., it would be wise to find a McKinsey staffer who is an alumnus of the school you want to attend. Most alumni and/or admissions departments will help you locate recent graduates. Wharton goes so far as to send all applicants a directory of alumni who have volunteered to share their first-hand knowledge of Wharton by telephone. Applicants can call on Wharton MBAs by location, company, and undergraduate school from Alaska to Venezuela, from American Express to Yoplait, from Albright College to Wellesley College. Remember, however, when speaking to alumni, that graduate schools of business have changed so dramatically in recent years that alums who have been out of the school for five or more years may not have a good feel for the current MBA program. "We're changing so rapidly, they don't know what the school is all about today," says Donald Jacobs, dean of Northwestern's Kellogg School.

Consider, too, how a particular school's method of instruction suits your personality. "You will run into piranha (among your fellow students) in any of the top schools," says Colin Blaydon, dean of Dartmouth's Amos Tuck, "but the mode of interaction will be quite different." At Harvard, you could find yourself straining to make your voice heard in classroom discussions that account for most of your grade. If you're not good at scrambling for attention in a class of 90 very competitive students, you'll likely be better off at a school such as Amos Tuck. There's more emphasis there on how well you work in small teams and on cooperation instead of competition. On the other hand, if you're very aggressive and enjoy the thrill of a contest, you should go to one of the more competitive schools. (See Chapter 4 for BUSINESS WEEK's survey of top graduates and what they say about their schools.)

Above all, know that while most graduates of the top schools are fairly positive about their MBA experiences, some are pretty disenchanted about what they discovered. Some sample comments: "My greatest disappointment was that I spent two years learning to become an analyst, not a manager," griped one Duke graduate. "I can crunch numbers to death, but I didn't learn anything about managing, motivating, and leading people. My lasting regret is that I spent $40,000 to learn tools from academicians who never worked for a real business. Business school learning is too removed from the real world." Agreed an MBA from Wharton: "At no time in two years did any of my classes discuss organized labor, the role of government and business in society, the causes and possible solutions of the trade deficit, America's industrial decline, or any other issue that can't be solved in 80 minutes. We're taught that every human being is only a factor of production and every business a nugget of value to be bought, sold, or closed down based on return on investment alone."

The overwhelming majority of graduates, however, have little doubt that the time and expense of getting the degree were well worth it. They say they forged friendships and contacts that will endure through a lifetime; they linked up with new jobs that paid better money and offered greater opportunities for advancement than the positions they left. Some consider it the most important and formative decision they've made in their lifetimes. And they learned what the tough-talking Wharton sergeant promised: "to walk, talk, barter, bargain, deal, and dress like an MBA!"

CHAPTER **2**

HOW TO GET INTO AN ELITE B-SCHOOL

How tough is it to get into a top-notch B-school? Very—and it's getting tougher each year. Forget what you hear about declining applications. Some journalists have prematurely rushed to write obituaries for management education, reporting that after years of double-digit growth in applications, the number of applicants has finally declined.

Truth is, the best schools remain flooded with hopeful applicants and few of these prestige schools have witnessed any significant drop in applicants. In fact, many people who already have their MBAs from name schools wouldn't be able to get through the same B-school doors today. At Wharton, for example, 3761 applicants vied for only 767 seats in the class that entered the school in 1984. Four years later, 6163 applicants competed for even fewer spots — 760. In the past five years, applications to Wharton have grown by more than 60%.

The same holds true at many other schools with national reputations. In 1986, for example, Duke University's Fuqua School accepted 67% of those who applied. Last year, only 24% were accepted for admission. The most selective school in the country, Stanford University, accepts only 10% of those who apply. Not one of the BUSINESS WEEK Top 20 schools accepts more than 40% of those who knock on their doors. Most of them, in fact, reject three of every four candidates.

How do you get through so narrow and selective a door as that? B-schools generally look at academic factors such as your undergraduate grades and scores on the Graduate Management Admission Test (GMAT). They also consider leadership ability, special talents, background characteristics, motivation, work experience, and career interests. These factors are less tangible and it's harder to predict how they'll be weighed by admissions committees. But work experience can often tilt a decision in your favor. So could well-written essay answers or a good showing in a personal interview.

Above all, hedge your bets by applying to half a dozen or so schools—and try to apply early if you can. Most schools list their final deadline for admissions between March 1 and June 1. But you can be at a disadvantage if you mail in your application so late in the game. Ideally, you should try to get it in by early January to gain admission for the fall semester or quarter. Duke University's B-school admissions staff begins reading applications on December 1 and continues to admit students until the class is full. "Under that system, the earlier you apply the better off you are," says Michael Hostetler, director of admissions. By mid-May of 1989, he had 600 to 700 applications that had arrived before April 1, but only five seats left in the class. "It's just too late. They should have applied in January."

In contrast, Northwestern's Kellogg School tries to adjust its admittance rate in each of three admission periods. In the earlier periods, the school might admit as much as 10% of the pool, even though the admit ratio for the year is one out of eight or nine. So chances are that if you apply early, you'll still be better off.

How to Increase Your Score on the GMATs

No matter how you slice it, your chances of getting into a good school are very dependent on how well you score on the Graduate Management Admission Test (GMAT). Four times a year, in January, March, June, and October, thousands of people sit for three and one-half hours with number two pencils in hand, filling in answers that will largely decide what kind of school they can apply to. Every accredited B-school, with the exception of Harvard, which relies more heavily on work experience and essay answers, requires the GMAT as part of the admissions package.

If you manage to eke out only the average score of 475, from a range of 200 to 800, your chances of making it to a top school are pretty slim. You really need to score above 600 to seriously entertain the idea of making it into a Top 20 school. And you need to score no less than 550 to walk through the door of one of BUSINESS WEEK's Runners-Up schools—excellent graduate business institutions that tend to be overshadowed and therefore hidden from view by the frenzy to land a spot in the Top 20. True, Wharton accepted some applicants with GMATs as low as 570 and the University of Michigan as low as 370. But the average at the schools was 644 and 620, respectively.

If your test score doesn't quite measure up, don't surrender just yet. It's possible that you could be rejected from one school based on your GMAT score and be accepted by a Top 20 school with the same score. Why? Some schools, feverishly working to boost their reputations by appearing selective, will simply toss you out of their admit pool. They are using GMAT averages as a marketing tool to attract better candidates. Other schools, already assured of their quality reputation, might pay more attention to other parts of your application—work experience, essays, personal interviews, and undergraduate grades.

Many admission directors, too, look beyond the overall GMAT score to see how well or poorly you did on the quantitative and verbal sections of the test. Yale University's B-school, for instance, accepts students who on average fall within the 94th percentile on the verbal part of the GMAT. Yale's foreign students, however, typically score in only the 70th percentile. But their "quant" scores are so high it doesn't make much of a difference overall. The reverse is often true of American applicants who don't do nearly so well on the math.

Fewer than 10 out of the more than 269,000 tested ace the GMAT in any given year. Fewer than 2000 people score 700 or above on this test. A score in the low 500s would put you into the 60th percentile, while a score of 600 would propel you into the 89th percentile. So a difference of 100 points can move you up into elite school status. That's why it's important to spend some time gaining familiarity with the test before you take it. Most test-takers simply buy a workbook and use the sample tests in it for practice. One in four goes to the trouble of taking a formal preparation class.

Although you can take the test as often as you'd like, the schools to which you apply will see all your grades. So it's generally not a good policy to take the GMAT itself for practice. You don't send schools the rough drafts of your essay answers, and you don't walk into an interview with jeans and a three-day growth. If you're going to practice for the GMAT you should do it either in a preparation course or by buying some of the old tests from the Graduate Management Admission Council. This organization also sells *The Official Guide for GMAT Review*, which contains actual tests, for $9.95 and personal computer software to help study for the exam for $59.95. (The address is Graduate Management Admission Test; Educational Testing Service; P.O. Box 6108; Princeton, New Jersey 08541.) At the least, you need to get the *GMAT Bulletin of Information* to register for the test and gain essential information about it. (You can telephone GMAT at 609-771-7590 for the free bulletin.)

The GMAT looks like most other entrance exams. The math is tougher than you found on your old SATs, but the basic format of the test is the same. There are seven separately timed sections, each containing 20 to 25 multiple-choice questions. The quantitative sections of the test measure basic math skills and understanding of elementary concepts. They also are designed to measure your ability to reason quantitatively, solve quantitative problems, and interpret graphic data. The verbal sections aim to determine your ability to understand and evaluate what you read and to recognize basic conventions of standard written English.

Advice to up your score? Don't bother with coaching books that contain simulated GMAT exams. Get copies of the real things and practice with them. You need to become "fluent" in test-taking, knowing exactly what to expect when you step into the auditorium to take the exam. That's the goal in most prep courses. A key to this is attaining a level of comfort with the test itself. After a few practice tests, you'll be ready to approach the exam more systematically.

If you can rule out one or more of the five answers on the multiple-choice questions, you generally should guess. But be aware that your odds of guessing the right answer are not necessarily one in four or five. Each section of the GMAT typically flows from the easiest questions to the most difficult. "It doesn't mean that someone looked at a question, thought it was easy, and put it on the test as number 1," says John S. Katzman, president of the Princeton Review Inc., based in New York. "They gave them to a lot of people. If most people got them right, they put them up front. Whatever comes to your mind on those questions, do it. When you get to the end, whatever immediately comes to your mind is usually wrong. You should cancel your first choice and guess something else. If it were that easy it would be number 3, not number 20." Indeed, the percentage of test-takers who correctly answered the last five questions of a GMAT section are 19%, 36%, 26%, 15%, and 11%, respectively.

Decide in advance what score you're shooting for and pace yourself through each section. If you aren't dead set on going to a Top 20 school and are looking to hit only a 500, there's no need to answer the last couple of questions. "Question number 20 is there to separate the kids who get a 770 from those who try for an 800," advises Katzman. "Take more time on the easy ones and make sure you don't make mistakes. But if you spend any time on a question at all, eliminate what you can and guess."

Is it worth the money to take a prep course? Probably so. Princeton Review Inc. claims that its average students increase their GMAT scores between 85 and 93 points after taking its six-week review course. (That's the difference between what a student scores on the first diagnostic test and the final one given to them by the Review.) But if you take a course it makes sense to do it no more than two months before you sit down with the real GMAT. This is the equivalent of training for a race. You don't stop two months before the race.

A class will lighten your wallet to the tune of about $650—but both the Stanley H. Kaplan Educational Center, the nation's largest coaching service that offers an eight-week course, and the Review actually offer financial aid to offset the cost. You'll have to go to the trouble of filling out a financial aid form, but it can be worth it. Roughly 10% of those who sign up for the Review classes get some help (the average discount was $225).

The Review course meets in small groups once a week, in the early evenings or on the weekends. Instructors analyze typical mistakes made on actual GMAT tests and then work those areas to death. If you're weak in geometry questions, you'll get drilled on the subject. There also are workshops of six to eight people held on weekends, sometimes on Sunday mornings. Expect to spend about 24 hours in class and another 18 hours in workshops. A one-on-one tutoring service also is available for around $1000. To get more information on the Review courses, call 800-333-0369. To obtain more information on the Kaplan courses, call 800-KAP-TEST.

How to Score Big on the B-School Essay

Many of the best schools don't only evaluate test scores and academic records, they want to know the real you. That's why one of the most critical parts of the application process is the section of essay questions.

What can you expect? The University of Michigan's Business School hits you with four mandatory essay questions and gives you the the option of responding to a fifth one as well. Samples: "Describe personal achievements within the last five years which are good descriptors of your potential for a successful professional career." "What professional and/or personal goals have you tentatively established for the next five years of your life and how do you see the MBA helping you reach your goals?"

Those queries are pretty much straightforward. But the admissions directors at some schools almost seem to delight in thinking up unusual questions to ask applicants. One recently asked potential students to write a succinct description of how they handled real-life ethical challenges. Another asked applicants to describe the details of failures in their careers.

Applicants to the University of Pennsylvania's Wharton School found themselves puzzling over one of the more novel essay questions: "Please complete three of the five statements below. Each response should be between one-half page and one page in length. (A) Outside my job, I have demonstrated leadership ... (B) The area in which I have most tried to improve myself ... (C) For fun I ... (D) I have clearly demonstrated my interest in helping others by ... (E) People describe me as ..."

How should you answer such questions? Your essays should show how different you are, not how great you are. To stand out among countless applicants who all work capably in their jobs, tell how you have tutored underprivileged children. Discuss your Uncle Scrooge comics collection or your role as a guitarist in a rock band or a cellist in a classical quartet. "We pay a lot of attention to what people say about their lives outside the classroom or office," says Alice Brookner, associate director of admissions for the University of Chicago's B-school.

Accomplishments count, but schools also use essays to assess your personal goals and values. So discuss an accomplishment in terms of the obstacles you overcame to achieve it. Too frequent use of the word "I" and little use of the word "we" in recording your accomplishments can often put off some B-school admissions officers. Sensitive over criticisms that MBAs are too self-centered, many schools today emphasize teamwork and read essays with an eye toward ferreting out the egomaniacs.

Don't plan to knock off the essays in a single evening. Completing a set should likely take 20 to 40 hours of thinking, organizing, drafting, and polishing. On each essay, stick to the point you want to make. For an idea of what to emphasize, look over the school's brochures: they often contain clues about what kind of students are wanted. Those with managerial potential? Diversified skills? Play up how well you fit their bill.

"Most candidates tend to use a grab-bag approach, hoping they'll hit on something that clicks with us," explains Stephen Christakos, Wharton's director of admissions. "We don't want people to ramble on." Be succinct and to the point. Figure out the themes you need to fully answer a question or essay topic and don't wander or overwrite. Admissions staff, weary from reading through thousands of pages of this stuff, favor quality over quantity. Duke University's Fuqua School of Business was shocked when it recently received a four-inch-thick package via Federal Express from an overzealous applicant. The application materials were in a three-ring binder that included a table of contents, with charts detailing what the applicant had done so far with his life and where he planned to go. "We stood there and laughed for five minutes," says Michael Hostetler, director of admissions. "I have never seen or heard anything like this before. We won't immediately dismiss it, but to me one of the things I want to get out of an essay is the ability of the applicant to concisely deal with the questions without all the extra crap. To the extent they exceed the bounds of the question, they are penalized for it."

Honesty also is vital. "Don't play games," advises Karen Page, who runs a Learning Annex seminar for MBA applicants in New York. "Play up everything you've done for what it's worth, but don't cross the line to lie or cheat." Admissions staff aren't likely to check on your facts, but they've read through so many applications that they can sense when something doesn't quite add up.

If you know a graduate of the school, ask him or her to read your essays before you turn them in. What about attention-getting ploys like writing in crayon or sending a videotape? Some applicants are bold enough to try them. Rather than complete an essay, one UCLA applicant, an avid runner, sent a picture of himself with the headline: "How badly do you want to go to UCLA?" The picture showed him with a victorious smile, completing the New York Marathon in record time. That, too, drew a few laughs around the office. As a rule, most admissions directors dislike gimmicks.

To Interview or Not

In recent years, there's a new wrinkle in the applications process: a personal interview. Northwestern University's Kellogg School is the only B-school that interviews every applicant to its full-time program—4000 of them—in one-hour sessions in places as far-flung as Tokyo and Kuala Lumpur. The reason? Kellogg officials don't believe it's possible to assess a person's composure, articulateness, or leadership ability from test scores or past grades. Many observers believe that the reason Northwestern is a favorite among corporate recruiters is because it screens its candidates well, bagging the best of them.

Other top schools are giving more candidates the once over. In 1988, for example, Wharton conducted personal interviews with more than 2100 of the 6163 applicants, 23% more than a year earlier and more than eight times the number of interviews held five years ago. Duke University's Fuqua School of Business interviewed 60% of its applicants in 1988. Some schools allow alumni to interview and file reports on candidates; others prefer that only a select group of admissions staff conduct the questioning.

What should you expect? In general, interviewers want to try to evaluate leadership and communication skills. In foreign applicants, the schools are also looking to evaluate English-speaking proficiency. "I'm most interested in motives," says Steven DeKrey, director of admissions at Kellogg. "I'm after the whys and the decisions that brought the candidate here. Why this school? Why management? I'm looking for the individual who has made his or her own decisions. Someone who isn't aimed at me because of a boss or someone else."

Seek an interview if you think it would be helpful to plead your case in person—especially if you're articulate and think you can demonstrate some leadership qualities. "All we know about you is what you put on paper," reasons Michael Hostetler, director of admissions for Duke. "So it's the applicant's best way to make sure we have as accurate a picture of him or her as possible." Conversely, however, it could be the kiss of death. If you're not likely to do well in an interview situation, by all means avoid it. "Anyone who interviews poorly is a fool to do a nonrequired interview," admits DeKrey. A poor performance during an interview can cancel all your hopes for admission to a good school.

A Caveat on References

Most applicants don't give enough attention to the people they ask to recommend them for MBA admission. If you can get a successful alum to write a letter on your behalf, do it. A reference signed by a familiar name is always worth more than one from an unknown person.

If that's not possible, however, make sure that whoever you ask for a reference will give you a good one and will send it in on time. That's not as easy as you might think. Some B-schools ask particularly specific questions of recommenders and ask that they mail their questionnaires to the schools separately and in private. Harvard, for example, even requires them to rate you on a scale of "Unusually Outstanding/Top 2%" to "Poor/Bottom Third" on such characteristics as integrity, intellectual ability, self-confidence, maturity, and your ability to work with others. Make sure that your references have a positive view of your abilities and talents.

How to Get a School to Foot Part of the Tuition Bill

Getting into a good B-school is hard enough. It requires smarts, motivation, and maturity. It also requires money and lots of it. How do most full-time MBAs meet the staggering costs? One study showed that they borrowed half of the cost and squeezed a quarter of it from their parents. Scholarships account for only 11% of the total bill for male students, but cover 25% of the female MBA's bill. Minorities also are more likely to get a greater proportion of their tuition from scholarship funds.

The best way to get financial help is to ask for it and ask early. That means your application should arrive as soon as the admissions office begins to accept them. Ask the admissions staff and student aid office about the scholarships offered. Inquire whether work study or graduate assistantships are available. Most scholarships are based on either merit or need, so you have to prove one or the other—and it's best to provide evidence of both. It's also sometimes possible for a top applicant to gain greater financial aid from a second-tier school than a brand-name one. Why? B-schools that lack Top 20 status may dangle big bucks in front of strong candidates they otherwise might not be able to attract. Consider Nick Grasberger, who had three years of work experience with USX Corporation and a spinoff company, Aristech Chemical Corporation. Besides the solid work background, he was a dean's list scholar at Notre Dame and scored a 680 on the GMAT.

He was set to go to Wharton after gaining acceptance there, but then the University of Pittsburgh offered him a full tuition scholarship and a $250-a-month stipend even though he hadn't asked for any financial aid at all. Pitt hands out six of these "Associate Fellow" scholarships a year. "I had always had my heart and mind set on Wharton," says Grasberger, "but I may have had to borrow $50,000 to go there." He opted for Pittsburgh, graduating from the 11-month program in 1989 and joining H. J. Heinz.

"Top students really can't write their own tickets, but some can get full tuition and a fellowship to boot," says Robert L. Virgil, dean of Washington University's Olin School of Business. His school, anxious to attract high-caliber applicants to move it up in stature, has budgeted $1.25 million in MBA scholarships for the 1989–1990 year. What strategy should you employ? Virgil suggests writing the admissions directors and the deans of B-schools you want to attend. "Tell them which schools accepted you and plead the case for financial aid," he advises.

How much scholarship aid is available varies greatly from school to school. More than two-thirds of Olin's first-year MBA class in 1988 received some form of financial support from the school. The average MBA scholarship totaled about $5200, with a low of $1000 to a high of $17,450. About 40% of Olin's MBAs also had graduate assistantships, which on average paid $2000 during the academic year.

Of the 127 students in Carnegie-Mellon's Class of 1990 who applied for financial aid, 108 got scholarships that averaged $3887 each for their first year. At Northwestern's Kellogg School, 20% to 25% of the class gets some scholarship money. But there are very few full scholarships and most of those are for minorities. About 60% of the MBAs at Duke get financial assistance, half of them scholarships that average about $7000 a year. If you can't get a scholarship, try for a low-interest loan from the school. Some schools use a central application service such as the Graduate and Professonal School Aid Service. If that's required, you can write for a form from GAPSFAS, CN 6660, Princeton, New Jersey 08541. You'll need to complete the form and send it back to Princeton. The service will analyze your resources and send its analysis to the schools of your choice. Check with the admissions or financial aid office to find what they require. You might not like the idea of going into hock to pay for your MBA, but if it's the only way to pay the bills it might be worth it. In most cases, you won't have to worry about repaying the debt until after you graduate and get that lucrative job.

CHAPTER **3**

PART-TIME MBA PROGRAMS

Can't afford to quit your job and go to school full-time? Don't want to walk away—even temporarily—from a fantastic job with great opportunities for advancement? One way to have your MBA and your job too is to enroll in a part-time program. Up to 60% of the students currently studying for their MBAs go to schools during the evenings and weekends.

The hectic pace can take its toll, even jeopardizing your standing on the job and putting pressure on your family life. Still, you wouldn't have to forego two years of earnings as you would in most full-time programs. And, in many cases, your employer might foot part or all of the bill for the degree through a tuition reimbursement program.

The advocates of part-time programs are quick to boast of their other advantages. For one thing, you might find greater linkage between what's taught in the classroom and what you do at work. Applying classroom learning to the real world can give you a major advantage over colleagues on the job. For another, going to school at night or on weekends takes quite a bit of stamina and will make you stand out as someone who is highly motivated, ambitious, and hardworking. Those are traits that most employers prize highly in a manager.

Before you jump at the chance, however, consider the biggest problem with part-time programs: quality. Harvard and Stanford shun part-time programs altogether, in part because they believe that a full-time experience is far more valuable. Indeed, one of the most important benefits of an MBA—the people you meet and the networks the degree creates—can be missing from an evening program.

Whereas full-time applicants are likely to evaluate schools on the basis of their quality and prestige, most part-time applicants consider location and convenience first. "You obviously can't work in California and go to NYU's night program," says Edmund J. Wilson, who heads up Northwestern University's part-time program. "So the whole point of reference changes when you go to school at night. If you decide you're going to continue to work full-time, your job sets the tone and dictates where you will apply. People generally look around a 50-mile radius for a school. If you're in a small town in the northwest, you may be plumb out of luck. There may be no school around you with a night program."

The Quality Problem With Part-Time Programs

The emphasis on location—rather than prestige or quality—permits many schools, including those with fairly decent reputations, to offer so-so evening programs. Schools with both full- and part-time programs usually claim that the part-time program is identical to the full-time one except that it is delivered over a longer period of time. Some will offer and require the same courses, taught by the same professors. But that's not always the case. "Oftentimes very-well-known accredited programs offer part-time programs that are less than good," acknowledges Chuck Hickman, an official with the American Assembly of Collegiate Schools of Business. "Mainly the concern is faculty. You'll often see more adjunct faculty and fewer of the stars that teach during the day."

One of the nation's largest and best part-time programs is at New York University's Leonard N. Stern School of Business. Yet when a planning committee of the school recently sketched out a plan for its future, the group urged a reduction by one-third in its part-time enrollment. The reason? It believed that the large size of its part-time program harmed the school's reputation and credibility. "Academic programs based primarily on part-time attendance tend to be less than excellent," according to the report. "To a disturbing degree, part-time educational programs, including most part-time MBA programs, are little more than 'degree mills.'"

So many part-time programs have less than desirable reputations that when the University of Chicago offered a weekend MBA program three years ago, it attracted a spate of students from out of state eager to take advantage of the university's good name. Today, 30% of the students arrive from outside the Chicago area, flying in from New York, Detroit, Minneapolis, and Washington, D.C. Chicago even arranges to pick up students at the airport and whisk them in a van to its downtown location on North Michigan, across from the John Hancock Building. When the Saturday classes are over, the van returns the students to the airport. Courses meet once a week in three-hour sessions. You can take two courses a quarter, morning and afternoon. You can get an MBA in two and a half years if you study through the summers in this program.

Obviously, you have a greater shot at enrolling in a top-ranked school if you live in a major metropolitan area. Schools such as Chicago, Northwestern University, New York University, and UCLA offer outstanding evening programs. If the full-time program is highly acclaimed, a good deal of the school's prestige and quality will likely rub off on the part-time program, too. Five of the 10 largest part-time MBA programs are in the New York area. Two of them are based in Chicago. But there are plenty of weaker programs in the big cities, too. The Chicago metropolitan area alone boasts at least 17 schools that grant a part-time MBA. Only 5 are accredited by the American Assembly of Collegiate Schools of Business: the B-schools at University of Chicago, DePaul University, Loyola University, Northwestern University, University of Illinois at Chicago. Indeed, two of the three largest part-time MBA programs in the nation fail to have the accreditation seal. They are New York's Pace University and New Jersey's Fairleigh Dickinson University.

Biggest Part-Time Programs

(Fall 1988 Master's Level Enrollment)

(1) Pace University (New York, NY)	2764
(2) New York University (New York, NY)	2396
(3) Fairleigh Dickinson University (Rutherford, NJ)	2203
(4) Baruch College (New York, NY)	2040
(5) DePaul University (Chicago, IL)	1810
(6) Wayne State University (Detroit, MI)	1626
(7) Bentley College (Waltham, MA)	1528
(8) University of Minnesota (Minneapolis, MN)	1481
(9) University of Chicago (Chicago, IL)	1366
(10) Rutgers University (Newark, NJ)	1317

Source: AACSB.

One way to ensure you're getting a quality education is to make sure it is accredited. If the school has received AACSB approval then all its programs must pass muster. That's hardly the only way to make sure you'll get a good education, however. While on a few occasions the quality of a part-time program has been a concern, no schools have ever lost their accreditation over a scrap about a part-time program. So view the AACSB as a bare minimum necessity. Then, ask what percentage of the part-time courses are taught by professors who also teach full-time. If the overwhelming majority of teachers are poorly paid adjuncts, you have cause for concern. "Some evening programs have been viewed as second rate and have been staffed accordingly," agrees Harry Davis, associate dean at the University of Chicago's B-school where the same professors teach in all programs.

Also ask if there are different admissions policies for the full- and part-time programs. A quality part-time program will have roughly the same standards for admission as its full-time counterpart. In a recent quarter, for example, the average GMAT score for a successful applicant at Northwestern's Kellogg School was 625 for the full-time program and 620 for the evening program. The average grade point average was identical (3.4) for both programs. More often than not, however, the admission standards for part-time programs fall below those demanded of the full-time MBA applicants. The B-school of the State University of New York at Buffalo is excellent. Yet, nearly 60% of the applicants to its evening program are accepted, versus only 29% for the day program. The average GMAT scores for its night students are nearly 25 points lower than those of its day students. Some schools justify using lower hurdles for part-timers on the basis that work experience is more important than test scores.

The kind of answers you want to hear will roughly approximate what Wilson says about Northwestern's premier program. "We have taken a position that we have one school, one faculty, and one degree," says Wilson. "Our night students study under the same faculty; we even have courses open to day and night students to prove that there is equal quality. We would rarely admit a person to the night program who failed to pass the screen for our full-time program." For more information, write to the Graduate Management Admission Council for Wilson's excellent report on *Part-Time and Special Programs* (GMAC, 11601 Wilshire Boulevard, Suite 1060, Los Angeles, California 90025).

The Part-Time Grind

Even if you can find a quality program, it's unlikely that an evening MBA can approach the education received in a full-time program. Some B-school deans with flourishing evening programs go so far as to say they wouldn't recommend it. "I would not advise my son or daughter to go to a part-time program over a full-time one," says H.J. Zoffer, dean of the University of Pittsburgh's B-school. "For some people into the house, spouse, and Buick syndrome, it might be the only way. But you go to work at 8 a.m. until 5:30 p.m. and you get in your car, plump yourself down in the basement of the school for a sandwich for dinner and then you have to absorb the package in three hours from 6:30 to 9:30 p.m. You're tired and the faculty member may be in much the same condition. And this goes on for three or four years! You can't take advantage of the other programs in the school that are important to the MBA experience. It puts terrible stress on the marriage and the family. It's an incredible grind."

Just how heavy is the workload? At Chicago, you can gain an MBA in only two and one-half years in the evening program. The trouble is that you'd have to take 2 courses a term for 10 straight quarters to meet the university's 20-course requirement for graduation. That means attending classes twice a week from 6:15 to 9:15 p.m. Count on an additional 12 to 14 hours per week of study. You also, of course, can stretch it out to a more sustainable pace. But like most quality B-schools, Chicago has set a maximum amount of time in which to complete the program: five years.

The length of a program obviously varies according to the university's schedule and the rigor of the program itself. Some schools require more courses than others. And some schools are more flexible about allowing you to transfer to the full-time program should you decide to do so. Generally, however, if you're accepted as a part-time student, you remain a part-time student. If your company moves you to a new location, you're likely to find that few of your courses can be transferred for credit into a new program.

Most students put up with the grind because they simply can't afford to quit their jobs and go into a full-time program. While the cost of MBA education, whether full- or part-time, is hardly cheap, part-timers tend to pay far less of the actual bill than those who quit their jobs to go full-time. One study, in fact, found that employer tuition payments for part-time students paid for between 64% and 69% of the total cost. On average, part-timers footed the bill for only 28% to 35% of the costs of their MBAs. Full-timers, in contrast, ended up paying between 62% and 76% of their MBA bills—even after gaining scholarship money and qualifying for work-study assignments.

However, part-time MBA programs rarely provide scholarship aid and seldom hand out low-interest loans from university funds. Schools may try to provide financial help to students who aren't able to draw upon tuition-remission benefits, but loans are more likely to be offered than scholarships.

What About the Executive MBA?

Of course, there are part-time programs and then there are *part-time programs*. Part-time doesn't always have to mean classes in the evening. Many excellent schools offer executive MBA programs in which companies must sponsor you as an executive. You can apply individually or your company can nominate you, but in all cases you must have your corporation's support. Typically, these programs require a greater number of years of full-time work experience (generally 10 years or more) and a commitment from your company to pay the bill and give you time off. Like many B-schools, Northwestern has an alternate Friday and Saturday program. Your company must give you every other Friday off to attend the two-year program. The average age of a student in Northwestern's "Executive Master's Program" is 38.

One major advantage an executive MBA program has over the typical part-time program is quality: B-schools generally charge premium prices for these programs and put their best faculty into them. Indeed, these programs often steal from full-time programs the most outstanding professors at the school who would rather teach experienced professionals on the fast track.

Many of these programs also begin with a live-in week during which you'll get to know intimately your classmates and what kind of perspectives they bring to the program. These sessions also help ease the transition period from work to school. After all, most executive MBA students haven't set foot in a college classroom in well over a decade. Most graduates of executive MBA programs believe the most interesting part of the sessions is the interaction they have with fellow executives from different companies.

In recent years, B-schools have devoted time and energy to making executive MBA programs as attractive and innovative as possible, developing overseas trips, business-government ties, and other sidelights. At New York University, the executive MBA program features three 5-day residence sessions per year and a 10-day international session at such places as Insead in Fontainebleau, France, or Keio University or the University of Tokyo in Japan. Washington University in St. Louis begins its two-year program with a residential week at a conference center in late August and ends the first year in June by spending one week in Washington, D.C., where executives meet senators and congressmen, lobbyists, and other political players. The second year begins on campus with a week-long immersion in Tycoon, a management simulation game. The final week involves a study tour to a foreign country. (Japan seems to be the country of choice these days; executives visit such corporations as Nippon Kokan Steel, Mitsubishi Trading, Nissan Motor, and Sumitomo Corporation.)

Wharton's excellent executive MBA program also features a Friday evening executive speaker series at which leading CEOs and government officials address the group, from Pfizer Chairman Edmund T. Pratt, Jr., to Time President Nick J. Nicholas. At Wharton, you check in at 9 a.m. on alternate Fridays, spend the day in class, and attend the executive speaker series. Then you're in a review session at 9 p.m. The following morning, breakfast is served at 7 and classes begin at 9 a.m. You're free by 4 p.m., unless you want to study with your group. Wharton executive MBAs, too, spend their final week abroad. (Guess where the last two classes have trekked? To Japan, of course.) None of this comes cheap: the total cost of your degree at Wharton will run $52,000.

There's another major difference in an executive MBA program. Unlike the typical part-time MBA, you'll neither major in a subject nor are you likely to take many, if any, electives. Most executive MBA programs are general management programs. They cover the basic core courses of the MBA curriculum and then add a few advanced classes from each of the key disciplines. On the other hand, GMAT scores and undergraduate grades aren't nearly as important for admission as your performance on the job, your company's willingness to sponsor you, and your personal interview.

CHAPTER **4**

THE BEST B-SCHOOLS

What's the best graduate business school in the country? The chief executives of America's corporate behemoths say it's Harvard hands down. The business school deans give the nod to Stanford. Corporate recruiters point to Northwestern's Kellogg School, while the MBA graduates of the top schools ranked Dartmouth's Amos Tuck School of Business top of the list.

So who's right? It depends. If your interest is prestige, it's obviously hard to beat a Harvard degree. Indeed, more corporate chief executives hold a Harvard MBA than any other. Some 76 CEOs of BUSINESS WEEK's top 1000 U.S. corporations with the highest market value have an MBA stamped by Harvard—far above Stanford's 17 or Wharton's 16. If you're more concerned with academic research in the mix, you might pick Stanford. Either way, however, you're relying on the image of these two schools held by executives and deans, many of whom have limited direct experience with the schools.

A Guide to the Rankings and What They Mean

Based on an extensive survey of recent graduates and corporate recruiters, BUSINESS WEEK's ranking of the best schools found that Northwestern's Kellogg School, in Evanston, Illinois, has the best MBA program in the country. Kellogg captured the top spot in BUSINESS WEEK's rankings by emerging as the favorite of corporate recruiters and by garnering some of the highest grades from its graduates. That Northwestern beat out such powerhouses as Harvard and Wharton was not the only surprise. Cornell and Dartmouth made the top five.

Stanford and Chicago, usually near the top of conventional rankings, finished way down.

Until now, rankings have been based largely on the reputation of the schools' professors and their published work in academic journals. Typically, B-school deans or faculty are asked to list the top schools in order of personal preference. A school's academic prestige usually looms large in such ratings, and the deans and faculty members tend to give lots of weight to a school's reputation for academic research. There's no disputing that research is vital both to a school and to American business. But traditional surveys may not fully reflect a school's teaching excellence, its curriculum, or the value of its graduates to corporate America.

BUSINESS WEEK took a strikingly different approach, surveying both the Class of 1988 and corporate recruiters to determine the best business schools. The findings?

BUSINESS WEEK'S **Top 20 Business Schools**

	Full-time enroll- ment	Total MBA cost	Starting pay	Jobs by gradua- tion
1. Northwestern (Kellogg)	930	$30,804	$53,031	89%
2. Harvard	1,592	30,700	64,112	98
3. Dartmouth (Amos Tuck)	343	30,500	62,681	91
4. Pennsylvania (Wharton)	1,575	30,880	55,183	85
5. Cornell (Johnson)	420	29,800	52,339	95
6. Michigan	800	25,960	43,976	85
7. Virginia (Darden)	476	20,240	50,554	80
8. North Carolina	368	9,800	44,941	80
9. Stanford	654	28,188	65,176	80
10. Duke (Fuqua)	530	27,000	48,740	95
11. Chicago	1,011	31,000	54,772	95
12. Indiana	593	12,662	38,407	95
13. Carnegie-Mellon	399	30,400	49,109	85
14. Columbia	1,191	30,400	49,397	97
15. MIT (Sloan)	391	29,800	60,680	85
16. UCLA (Anderson)	969	15,022	45,378	96
17. California, Berkeley (Haas)	459	15,400	45,083	70
18. NYU (Stern)	1,173	28,452	47,037	92
19. Yale	370	30,350	46,455	87
20. Rochester (Simon)	330	27,000	39,990	85

In effect, the survey measures how well the schools are serving their two markets: students and their ultimate employers. The graduate poll was randomly mailed to about 3000 MBAs from 23 schools that regularly top traditional rankings. MBA grads were asked to assess such characteristics as the quality of the teaching, curriculum, environment, and placement offices at their schools. We received 1245 replies to the 35-question survey, a response rate of about 42%. The poll of corporate recruiters was mailed to 265 companies that have recently recruited at a third or more of the 23 most prominent schools. BW received 112 responses, a 42% rate.

How does this ranking differ from others? In 1986, when BUSINESS WEEK hired Louis Harris & Associates to poll senior executives on their beliefs regarding the best business school, they overwhelmingly named Harvard, followed by Stanford, Wharton, Chicago, and Northwestern. In 1987, the executive headhunting firm of Heidrick & Struggles Inc. asked the CEOs of the country's major corporations what they thought. The answer: Harvard, Stanford, Chicago, Northwestern, Wharton, Virginia, and Michigan (only seven schools were named). Another survey in 1987, capturing the beliefs of B-school deans instead of executives, found that the best schools were, in order: Stanford, Harvard, Wharton, MIT, Chicago, Northwestern, Michigan, Carnegie-Mellon, Columbia and University of California at Berkeley, Dartmouth and Texas (the last two groupings tied for ninth and tenth places).

The standing of each of the schools in these polls largely reflects the bias of those who are asked for their opinions. Senior executives and CEOs rank the schools based on what they "perceive" to be the best. That's partly a reflection of their personal dealings with graduates from the schools as well as how often they read about these institutions in newspapers and magazines. The deans are largely responding on the basis of their perceptions about the quality of the faculty, the academic research, and the articles published in scholarly journals.

How can the applicant use these rankings? Most people, of course, apply to several schools. If you're lucky enough to gain acceptance to a group of the best, don't simply go to the school that's highest on the list. Instead, try to pick a school where you're most likely to excel. All these top institutions have unique cultures just as their applicants have unique personalities. Most schools, however, fail to articulate these differences and differentiate themselves from the pack.

Applicants can make the best match by carefully looking over BUSINESS WEEK's graduate survey findings to see how these schools truly differ from one another. Would you work harder in a culture that emphasizes competition or cooperation? Would you rather have leading-edge professors at the top of their fields in research or simply the best teachers? The following tables will provide clues about these and many other critical factors. Keep in mind, however, that you are looking at the results for what most people believe to be the absolute best B-schools in the nation. If BUSINESS WEEK were to include a far greater number of more typical business schools, virtually all of these 23 institutions would look great.

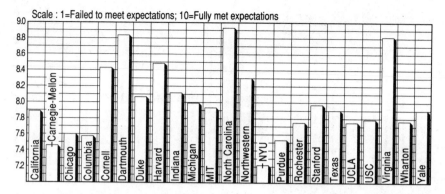

Scale : 1=Failed to meet expectations; 10=Fully met expectations

1. To what extent did your overall graduate experience fulfill or fail to meet your expectations of what a good business school should be?

Everyone arrives on the campus doorstep with a certain set of expectations. The better the student who gets through the door, the more likely it is that his or her expectations are going to be high. As a result, these answers nicely correlate with the quality of the graduates who gain entry into each program. Not one school failed miserably on this index. But North Carolina clearly tops the chart, followed closely by Dartmouth and the University of Virginia. At the bottom? New York University, Carnegie-Mellon, Purdue, and Columbia University.

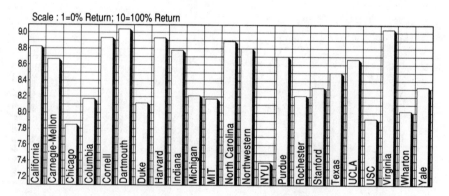

Scale : 1=0% Return; 10=100% Return

2. Do you believe your MBA was worth its total cost in time, tuition, living expenses, and lost earnings?

Business school isn't cheap. And most students at these top schools quit jobs paying between $25,000 and $35,000 a year just to attend one. Indeed, Northwestern's Class of 1990 has been dubbed the "$40 Million Club." The reason: each left a job paying $30,000 a year to attend the school at a cost of about $20,000 a year. The total cost: $100,000 times 415 students, which comes to more than $40 million. Dartmouth, Virginia, and Cornell grads think they're getting the best deal. MBAs from NYU, Chicago, and USC are less convinced it was worth it.

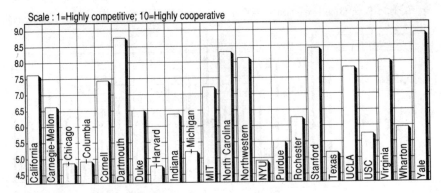

Scale : 1=Highly competitive; 10=Highly cooperative

3. How would you assess your business school's atmosphere?

In *The Big Time*, Ned Dewey of Harvard's famous Class of 1949 said about the recent crop of Harvard MBAs: "... I'd as soon take a python to bed as hire one. He'd suck my brains, memorize my Rolodex, and use my telephone to find some other guy who'd pay him twice the money." Despite the obvious hyperbole, it will come as little surprise that Harvard grads rate their school the most competitive. As for cooperation, it's Yale, Dartmouth, Stanford, and North Carolina—schools that foster teamwork, emphasize group projects, and frown on backstabbing.

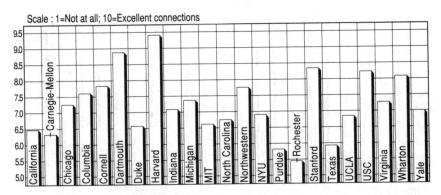

Scale : 1=Not at all; 10=Excellent connections

4. Do you feel that the business school has the connections that can help you throughout your career?

MBAs should graduate with not only a degree and a job, but with the contacts that will help them mount the corporate ladder throughout their lifetimes. While Harvard *students* may be the most competitive, Harvard *graduates* are among the most cooperative. No other school in the nation even comes close to having as large (35,900 MBAs) or as elite a network of connections as Harvard. Rochester, Purdue, and Texas come out on the end of this scale.

28

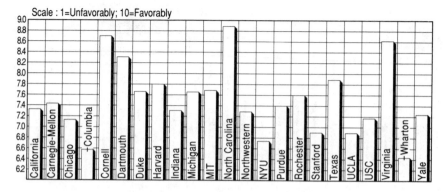

Scale : 1=Unfavorably; 10=Favorably

5. How did the teachers in your MBA program compare with others you have had in the past?

There's probably no more sensitive issue on the campus than this one: the quality of teaching. Even at the best schools, graduates tend to bemoan the uneven quality of teachers—particularly in the most important courses in the core curriculum. At some top schools, students gripe that they have difficulty understanding the lectures of some heavily accented professors from abroad. Truth is, the most experienced professors hate to teach those elementary courses. The best? North Carolina, Cornell, and Virginia. The worst? Wharton, Columbia, and NYU.

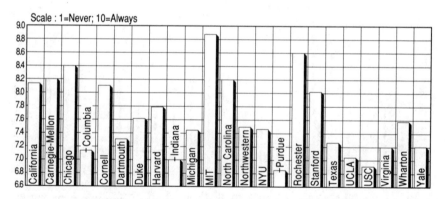

Scale : 1=Never; 10=Always

6. Did you have the feeling that your teachers were at the leading edge of knowledge in their fields?

Schools that rely too heavily on real business executives for adjunct faculty run the risk of putting a retired executive in front of a class to tell little more than old war stories. It's not only important to maintain a balance of the theoretical and the practical, it's also critical for a school to boast professors who are at the leading edge of thinking in management, finance, and marketing—people who know their stuff and know it cold. Grads felt this to be particularly true at MIT, Rochester, and Chicago. They were less certain of it at Purdue, USC, and Indiana.

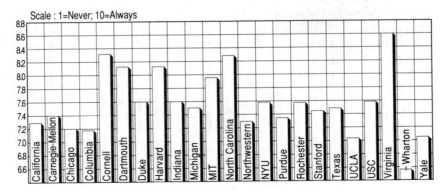

Scale : 1=Never; 10=Always

7. Did the professors convey enthusiasm for what they taught?

It's no secret that the best teachers know their subjects inside and out—and they're often passionate about what they are teaching. Professors who convey enthusiasm in the classroom more readily convey learning as well. They give students more than knowledge; they share with them the passion to learn. That's why enthusiasm is so important. MBAs rated Virginia—which places more emphasis on teaching than most schools—at the top, with North Carolina, Cornell, Dartmouth, and Harvard. Last were Wharton, UCLA, Yale, and Columbia.

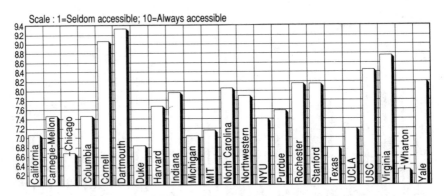

Scale : 1=Seldom accessible; 10=Always accessible

8. In classes taken with popular or distinguished professors, how would you rank their accessibility after class?

Distinguished professors at B-school are often in high demand. Corporations want them as consultants. Journal editors want them as writers of articles. Publishers want them as authors of books. And students not only want them in the classroom, they also want time with them after class. Whose star faculty seems to be most available to help students outside the scheduled class time? Dartmouth grads thought their profs were best in this department. The teachers at Cornell, Virginia, and USC also did extremely well. Wharton, Chicago, and Texas less so.

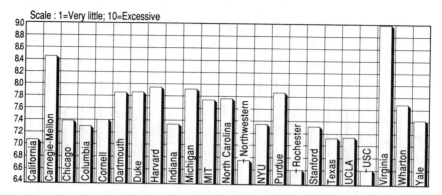

Scale : 1=Very little; 10=Excessive

9. How would you describe the amount of assigned work and reading?

Almost everyone who goes to B-school says they never thought it would be as hard as it was—particularly the grueling first year when schools load students up with the required core courses. Some schools, however, throw amazing amounts of work at students, partly because they want them to experience the heavy workload and pressure of life in the real world. That way, you're forced to figure out how best to manage your time. Grads felt the toughest "boot camps" were Virginia and Carnegie-Mellon. The "country clubs" were Rochester, USC, and Northwestern.

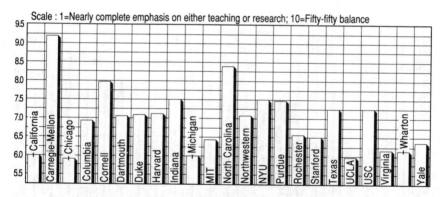

Scale : 1=Nearly complete emphasis on either teaching or research; 10=Fifty-fifty balance

10. Rate the importance that you believe is attached to teaching versus research by the faculty of the graduate business school.

What drives academia is research. Teachers are largely awarded promotions and tenure on the basis of their own research and publication thereof in scholarly journals. Much of it, however, is either meaningless or inaccessible to the average business executive. Few excellent teachers gain tenure if their research doesn't please colleagues; virtually all excellent researchers get tenure even if they can't teach. A 50–50 balance would be ideal. Grads say the schools that do the best job are Carnegie-Mellon, North Carolina, and Cornell.

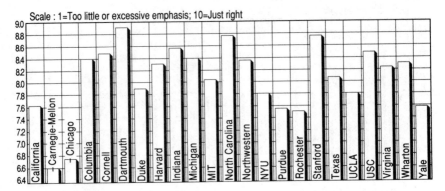

Scale : 1=Too little or excessive emphasis; 10=Just right

11. Overall, to what extent did the curriculum stress analytical skills?

All B-schools rightly attach a great deal of importance to teaching students basic analytical skills. These models and ways of thinking are critical to problem-solving and decision-making in the real world. But it's possible that a school can put either too little or too much emphasis on this part of the curriculum. More grads at Dartmouth, Stanford, and North Carolina thought the emphasis at their schools was just right. MBAs at Carnegie-Mellon and Chicago were more likely to think it excessive.

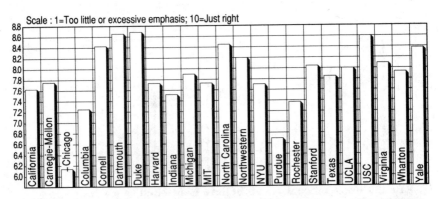

Scale : 1=Too little or excessive emphasis; 10=Just right

12. Overall, to what extent did the curriculum stress interpersonal skills?

When corporate executives are asked their views on MBAs, they typically talk about how bright and ambitious they are, but also how poor their interpersonal skills are. They complain that MBAs lack the sensitivity and personality to be true leaders. In recent years, many B-schools have launched major efforts to hone communication skills and teamwork. Some may even have gone overboard. Where do grads think the balance is just right? Duke, Dartmouth, and USC lead in this area. Chicago, Purdue, and Columbia don't fare nearly as well.

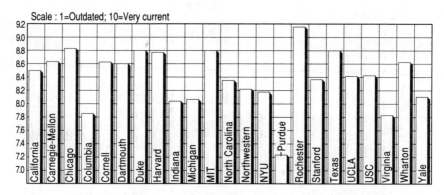

Scale : 1=Outdated; 10=Very current

13. How current was the material/research presented in class for discussion and review?

While a lot of the research that goes on in academia is rather esoteric, a good deal of it is vital to a school and to American business. Professors who conduct leading-edge research, however, should be able to transmit some of it to their students in the class. If that research work fails to filter down into the classroom, students can hardly benefit from it. Grads think Rochester does the best job of this, with Chicago, MIT, Texas, and Duke not far behind. At the other end of the scale are Purdue, Columbia, and Virginia.

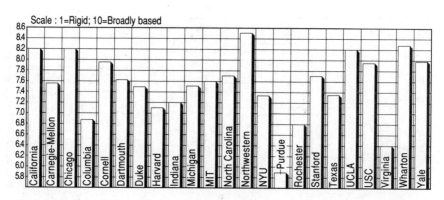

Scale : 1=Rigid; 10=Broadly based

14. Was the program broad enough to allow you to follow your interests?

The larger the school, the more course offerings and teachers it will have. That feature significantly broadens the opportunities for students to explore in depth the areas in which they have the greatest interest—but only if the schedule and the school permit it. Some make it hard to waive core courses even if you know the material well. MBAs from Northwestern, Wharton, UCLA, and the University of California at Berkeley believed their programs allowed them to follow their interests best. This was less true at Purdue, Virginia, and Rochester.

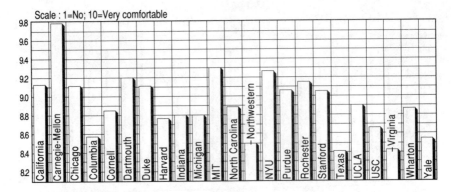

Scale : 1=No; 10=Very comfortable

15. Are you comfortable with your ability to deal with computers and other analytical tools that affect your ability to manage?

In what many call the "Information Age," managing data has become an important part of business. B-schools have responded to this challenge in different ways, but it's vital to learn how to use computers and other analytical tools to help you become a better manager. Carnegie-Mellon grads say they're most comfortable here—Carnegie makes available nearly as many personal computers in eight different labs as it has students in its graduating class. MBAs from Virginia, Texas, and Northwestern aren't nearly as comfortable on this scale.

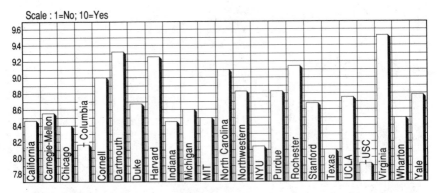

Scale : 1=No; 10=Yes

16. Were you given a way of thinking or approaching problems that will serve you well over the long haul?

One of the most important benefits of a good MBA program is to provide graduates with a systematic way to solve a business problem. When a manager or executive confronts a difficult decision, he or she should have a framework or way of thinking available to weigh the pros and cons. At the very least, B-schools should give you that tool to bring to the real world. Graduates think that Virginia did the best job in this department, followed by Dartmouth, Harvard, and Rochester. MBAs were less satisfied at University of Southern California, Texas, and NYU.

34

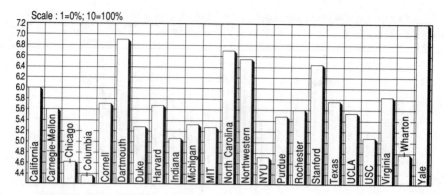

Scale : 1=0%; 10=100%

17. What percentage of your classmates would you have liked to have as friends?

Call this the BUSINESS WEEK friendliness index. It's mighty important to find a campus where you're likely to make lasting friendships and really feel at home. No school does better at this, according to its own graduates, than Yale, whose program heavily emphasized teamwork, group projects, and intimate relationships. The same is true of Dartmouth, North Carolina, Northwestern, and Stanford. Least desirable on the friendship index? Columbia, Chicago, NYU, and Wharton—all large schools, some with older antiquated facilities.

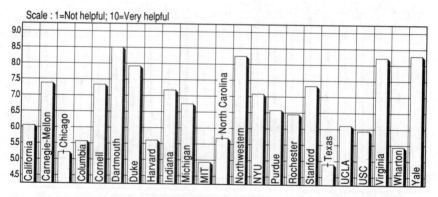

Scale : 1=Not helpful; 10=Very helpful

18. If you needed financial aid, how helpful was your business school?

How readily available is financial aid? Many schools say they will provide financial aid to virtually all accepted applicants who ask for it. But that promise usually includes loans and work-study programs. Grads think Dartmouth, Northwestern, Yale, and Virginia are the most helpful. Texas, MIT, and Chicago are the least. But if you attend Texas, you might not care about financial aid. After all, even an out-of-state student can get a Texas MBA for under $10,000—that's less than a third of the cost at most private schools.

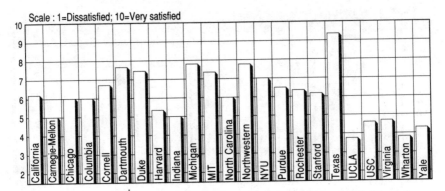

Scale : 1=Dissatisfied; 10=Very satisfied

California, Carnegie-Mellon, Chicago, Columbia, Cornell, Dartmouth, Duke, Harvard, Indiana, Michigan, MIT, North Carolina, Northwestern, NYU, Purdue, Rochester, Stanford, Texas, UCLA, USC, Virginia, Wharton, Yale

19. If the school provided housing for you, how satisfied were you with it?

Most schools have at least some kind of housing available to MBA students. Some, like Dartmouth, put all first-year students together in a dorm. Others put them up in over-all graduate living quarters. Still, the majority of MBAs at most schools tend to live in privately owned apartments or homes off campus. Schools often give you a list of these student rentals so you can go off and find what's best for you. When housing is provided, MBAs were most satisfied with Texas. Least? UCLA, Wharton, and Yale.

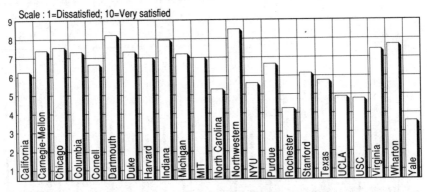

Scale : 1=Dissatisfied; 10=Very satisfied

California, Carnegie-Mellon, Chicago, Columbia, Cornell, Dartmouth, Duke, Harvard, Indiana, Michigan, MIT, North Carolina, Northwestern, NYU, Purdue, Rochester, Stanford, Texas, UCLA, USC, Virginia, Wharton, Yale

20. Are you satisfied with the number and quality of firms recruiting on your campus?

You'd think that if nothing else, the halo effect of Yale University would bring a great array of corporate recruiters to its business school. But students complained that few manufacturing companies bother to come to Yale. Many students interested in non-profit and public enterprise say they see too few of those organizations coming to recruit at Yale despite the fact that 15% of Yale's graduating class typically goes that route. The best: Northwestern, Dartmouth, Indiana, Wharton. The worst: Yale, Rochester, USC, and UCLA.

CHAPTER **5**

THE TOP TWENTY

The schools on BUSINESS WEEK's Top 20 list offer the best MBA education you'll find in the world. But that may be the only common thread that holds these schools together. Like the differing personalities you'd find in any group of people, each institution boasts its own culture and style. Each has strengths and weaknesses. Each promises students vastly different educations and experiences.

Which one is best for you? Read through the profiles to find out. They start with a snapshot view of the school that tells you something about its size, diversity, cost, selectivity, standing in the polls, and how much its graduates command in the marketplace. There are other interesting statistics here: not only how many applicants are rejected by the schools, but how many of those who are accepted reject the school that accepted them.

Most applicants hedge their bets when they apply to B-school, so if they get into more than one program, they have to turn down some schools. Indeed, when you try to settle on the "best" choice, a clue is how many candidates turn down the B-schools that invited them in. Harvard may only accept 12% of those who apply, but Harvard enrolls 86% of those it agrees to admit. More than half the people accepted into Duke and Carnegie-Mellon decide not to go.

The average starting pay of a school's MBAs includes sign-on and guaranteed bonuses. BUSINESS WEEK culled this data from its graduate survey rather than relying on figures provided by the school's placement office. An asterisk indicates a BUSINESS WEEK estimate.

1. Northwestern University

J. L. Kellogg Graduate School of Management
Leverone Hall
Evanston, Illinois 60208

Recruiter ranking: 1
Enrollment: 2130
Women: 30%
Foreign: 13%
Minority: 9%
Part-time: 1200
Average age: 26
Applicants accepted: 19%
Accepted applicants enrolled: 60%

Graduate ranking: 5
Annual tuition: $15,402
Room and board: $6230
Average GMAT score: NA
GMAT range: 580 to 670 (50% of class)
Average GPA: NA
GPA range: 3.1 to 3.6 (50% of class)
Average starting pay: $53,031

Application deadlines: November 15/January 6/March 15 for fall

Donald Jacobs has raised eyebrows in academic circles for years. When he took over as dean of Northwestern University's Graduate School of Management in 1975, he brashly declared that he wanted to push the perennial also-ran to the very top of the business school heap. Rival deans winced at how openly competitive Jacobs became. Some university officials scoffed at his dream of building a $6.9 million executive seminar center as part of his strategy to invigorate the MBA program. Even close friends scratched their heads in disbelief. "They thought I was crazy," says Jacobs.

But in recent years, the doubters are taking him and the Kellogg School a lot more seriously. The corporations that recruit MBAs rave about the Kellogg program and the kind of MBAs it produces. Only the University of Pennsylvania's Wharton School comes close to the flattering reviews Kellogg gets from the recruiting community. And the graduates of this school are enthusiastic advocates of its MBA program.

That wasn't always so. When Jacobs, a finance professor, became the reluctant draftee as dean, the school had just inched its way into top-10 listings in some academic journals. The school's undergraduate business program had been axed in the mid-sixties to enhance the quality of the full-time MBA program. Jacobs built upon this base by campaigning for a center with a dormitory and classrooms for executive seminars.

He got his wish in 1979 when the James L. Allen Center opened for business. As business executives flocked to the large, modern building on the shore of Lake Michigan, the school's visibility and credibility with the corporate world soared. So did the quality of his students, assisted in part by the dean's insistence that every applicant to the school pass a personal interview. (Kellogg is the only major B-school that interviews all its applicants to assess their leadership abilities and communication skills.) "The students became older and more experienced in terms of having had work experience," says Jeanne Brett, a Kellogg professor.

Jacobs also built upon the marketing foundation of the Kellogg School, named after the champion of breakfast cereals. While other B-schools may boast superb marketing departments, none come close to Kellogg's outstanding reputation in the field. Philip Kotler, the school's marketing superstar, is widely quoted and admired, as are

Sidney Levy, an authority on consumer attitudes, and Brian Sternthal, Kellogg's advertising guru. Yet, like most major B-schools, the strength of Kellogg may well be the breadth and depth of its offerings. A faculty of 25 people in finance rivals the size of the marketing department. Policy and environment, the third most popular major at the school after marketing and finance, is yet another strong area.

Then there's an array of other programs, including concentrations in hospital and health services, international business, public and nonprofit business, transportation, and real estate. The latest wrinkle: the B-school has joined forces with the university's Technological Institute to offer a two-year Master of Manufacturing Management degree. Applicants must have an undergraduate degree in engineering or science or three years of work experience in manufacturing. The program's main classroom and laboratory is at the institute, about two blocks north of the B-school. Jacobs helped to developed the program, which includes a manufacturing internship in the summer, with an industry oversight committee of the heads of manufacturing at 20 companies.

By numerous accounts, the workload at Kellogg is not nearly as severe as it is at many other top B-schools. "The order of the day was to enjoy yourself in every way, whether in class or interacting with other students," says Marc Landsberg, who graduated in 1989 and now works in advertising for Leo Burnett. "The biggest surprise was that the culture and environment here were incredibly cooperative and supportive."

Kellogg classes, which meet twice a week for an hour and 40 minutes, are scheduled on a quarter basis (with three quarters a year). No classes are scheduled on Wednesdays, a good day to sleep in, take a swim in the university rec center, or go out of town for interviews. You need 23 courses to graduate. You can waive out of core courses, but must replace them from the more than 200 electives and advanced classes offered. Most Kellogg MMs (instead of the MBA, grads here receive the Master of Management degree) major in 2 of 13 areas, from marketing to MEDS, shorthand for managerial economics and decision sciences, the Kellogg equivalent of the quant jock. Four courses are required in any given major.

Group work is pervasive at Kellogg, reflecting Jacobs's belief in the value of teamwork. It's rare when a project in a class is assigned only to an individual. Instead, professors encourage groups of four to six students to work together to come up with ideas and solutions to problems. So often is this done that some grads gripe that group work borders on the excessive. Still, students say it breeds an open, cooperative environment and long-lasting friendships among a rather cosmopolitan group drawn from virtually every state and 30 foreign nations. So many Kellogg students speak a foreign language that the school's placement office has added a foreign language fluency index to its résumé book: 133 of the 585 second-year students in 1989 were fluent in at least two languages.

If there's a problem at Kellogg, it's clearly in the teaching. Some students take Dean Jacobs to task because they feel he hasn't taken seriously their complaints about inconsistent teaching quality. As one 1988 graduate put it, "Some of the best teachers I have ever had were at Kellogg, as well as most of the worst." The problem became something of a cause célèbre in 1989 when the student-named teacher of the year, Robert Bies, was denied tenure. Bies teaches the popular Power and Politics course.

Jacobs counters that each year about 10% of his faculty is new, so everyone may get some weak teaching, but not much of it. "We post their teaching evaluations on the bulletin boards, and if you have a big ego, you don't want to be at the bottom of any list," he says. Clearly, students need to consult these ratings and avoid the teachers who, as one graduate asserted, "could not communicate their ideas to a kindergarten class." If not for the qualms over teaching quality, Kellogg would have gotten a much higher rating in BUSINESS WEEK's graduate poll than number five.

At the top of the teaching list, however, you'll find some excellent teaching. Robert Dewar's Organizational Design, Dan Siegel's Futures Markets, and Aharon Ofer's Financial Decisions have won each of these professors the top teaching award in recent years. Several grads also sing the praises of Lawrence Lavengood's Management and Environment, which features several weeks of theory and debate on business ethics. Gushed one fan: "This course was by far the most thought-provoking and rewarding portion of my education."

Stuart Meyer's Small Business Management brings groups of students into contact as consultants to small, local businesses. One team recently took apart Zigz Dogs, a hot dog joint on Howard Street in Chicago. After studying the restaurant's finances, the students recommended that the place be shut down. The reason: it sold a tasty hot dog, but had a poor location. Zigz Dogs is no more.

Highly praised is Entrepreneurship and New Venture Formation, an elective centered around writing a business plan for a start-up company. Students work in teams of two to five people, outlining their dream company's basic strategy, defining its market and product concept, developing projected financials, and making a final presentation. "It's much more hands on and you're applying much of the theory you've learned in other courses," says Jennifer Steans, a 1989 graduate who works as a consultant for Touche Ross. Throughout the class you get lectures from venture capitalists and lawyers who tell you what it's really like. Some of the latest ideas: Distinctive Desserts, a specialty food store; Indoor Golf & Grill, a combo indoor course and restaurant, and ABC Corp., which stands for "a better condom corporation."

The center of MBA activity is Leverone Hall, a six-story building in the heart of the university. A Living-Learning center, renovated in the early 1980s, houses a third of the students who vie for a spot there on a lottery system. Students jokingly refer to the place as the Loving and Lusting Center. The famous Allen Center is two blocks away.

Every Friday afternoon in Leverone's second floor lounge, a keg gets tapped at 4:45 for the weekly TGIF session. Tapping the keg had been delayed here because students were sneaking out of class early to get first in line. In the spring, the TGIF adjourns to the meadow directly in front where Frisbee flinging is the sport of choice. After a few brews, students tend to form groups and hit the town for dinner and fun. There's plenty of downtown pub crawls, beer and pizza fests, Chicago Cubs games, and museums, too. Evanston is a $12 cab ride from downtown Chicago. MMs particularly favor Howard Street's Tally Ho and P.M. Club, known for its jukebox loaded with Sinatra tunes.

There's never a time when there's just nothing to do at Kellogg. More than 50 student clubs, from the Asian Management Association to a flying club, keep every day busy. "The social calendar was fuller than my undergrad fraternity calendar," says Landsberg. There are international dinner parties and an annual event in which grads dress in black tie and boxer shorts or Reeboks. In 1989, the dinner's $15,000 in proceeds went to benefit battered wives and children. Students keep track of happenings by glancing at "Felix the CRT"—two screens that scroll the day's activities—and reading *The Merger*, Kellogg's student newspaper.

Kellogg takes placement very seriously—indeed, some students say too seriously because it siphons off a good deal of educational time. The placement center boasts 11 full-time staffers and 10 work-study students. It works hard to cultivate close relationships with recruiters, sending top recruiters a pair of tickets to the annual Special K-Revue, Kellogg's version of the student follies. There's even an annual recruiting day in mid-May when the school puts on a student panel to advise corporations on what makes for a successful interviewing process.

In 1989, some 312 companies came to campus to conduct about 12,000 interviews. Each Kellogg student gets 20 to 25 interviews on campus. The office also posted 687 job offers via correspondence. Carting away the largest groups of Kellogg students in 1988 were McKinsey (10); Citibank (9); Booz Allen & Hamilton (7); Hewlett-Packard (7); First Chicago (6); LaSalle Partners, Procter & Gamble, and Touche Ross (6). One in every five students go into marketing jobs. Another 20% head for the consulting firms. Wherever they go, they tend to stick close to the marketing roots of the school that Dean Jacobs made famous, singing the praises of the Kellogg School for a long time to come.

Contact: Steven DeKrey, director of admissions, 312-491-3308

Prominent alumni: Robert Beeby, CEO of Frito-Lay; James Bere, chairman of Borg-Warner; Edward Campbell, CEO of Newport News Shipbuilding; Donald Clark, chairman of Household International; Raymond Farley, CEO of S.C. Johnson & Son; Thomas Fey, president of Godiva Chocolates; Edwin Gage III, president of Carlson Cos; James McManus, chairman of Marketing Corp. of America; John Meinert, CEO of Hartmarx; William Smithburg, chairman of Quaker Oats Co.

Kellogg MBAs sound off

The level of fraternity at Kellogg was astonishing. The range and depth of extracurricular activities and facilities were exceptional. The people make this school. They are as interesting, well-rounded, diverse, and capable as they come.—Corporate marketing assistant

Some professors were excellent teachers, easily accessible, enthusiastic, and still on the leading edge of knowledge in their fields. Others could not communicate their ideas to a kindergarten class and spent all their time doing research.—Assistant finance manager

Kellogg's greatest strength is the diversity of the program, especially the variety of approaches taken to teaching. The students are not extremely bright, but they are team oriented and earnest. The greatest disappointment is the complete lack of attention to quality of teaching. It is painfully obvious that the administration gives only lip service to teaching without demonstrating any commitment to improving the situation. This is not to say that Kellogg lacks outstanding teachers, merely that the typical professor does not put anything other than minimal effort into teaching.—Corporate marketing assistant

I was extremely impressed with Kellogg students. The emphasis on teamwork was critical in helping to develop many of the individuals as good *team players, leaders, and organizers as opposed to a single purpose of individual stardom. I believe that this is key to being a successful manager today. My only complaint was the overwhelming emphasis placed on research versus teaching quality by our dean. Although there were teachers who clearly loved to teach, there were too many who appeared to be in the classroom only to fulfill a teaching requirement so they could conduct their research.—**Marketing brand assistant***

Overall, I could not imagine a more positive experience than the one I received in my two years at Kellogg. Most importantly, it is much more than a résumé builder. Kellogg has given me the skills and tools I need to be successful in my career on a day-to-day basis. Best things about the school: quality of faculty, caliber of students, emphasis on group projects, and teamwork. Worst things: too much time spent on job search.
*—**Assistant product manager***

Kellogg did a great job of providing personal attention, prior to enrolling, as well as throughout the two years of school. You felt wanted, appreciated, and well cared for. They were very helpful in finding my wife a job at the school, so she could be as much a part of the program as I was.
*—**Manufacturing analyst***

2. Harvard University

Graduate School of Business Administration
Soldiers Field
Boston, Massachusetts 02163

Recruiter ranking: 3	*Graduate ranking:* 6
Enrollment: 1592	*Annual tuition:* $15,350
Women: 27%	*Annual book costs:* $1500
Foreign: 16%	*Room and board:* $5050
Minority: 13%	*Average GMAT score:* Not required
Part-time: None	*GMAT range:* NR
Average age: 26	*Average GPA:* 3.5
Applicants accepted: 12%	*GPA range:* NA
Accepted applicants enrolled: 86%	*Average starting pay:* $64,112

Application deadline: November 14 to March 27 for fall

Six times a year the magazine flops into mailboxes around the world with a thud. Thicker than BUSINESS WEEK, it's no ordinary publication. The *Harvard Business School Bulletin* is the alumni magazine of the biggest, the richest, the most prestigious, and the most powerful of all the B-schools. And every other month it tells you more about the magic and influence of owning a Harvard MBA than all the hundreds of thousands of words written about the cathedral of American capitalism.

The first 50 to 60 pages are filled with the kind of academic news you'd expect to see: accounts of seminars on management problems, interviews of leading business executives and politicans, news of professors and course changes. Then come the Class Notes—anywhere from 150 to 180 pages of them—informal reports from the field on how Harvard MBAs are faring in the world of finance and industry. They are, as the *Bulletin* reminds its readers, "unique for their quality, quantity, and degree of alumni involvement in their preparation."

They inevitably begin in the early 1900s with reports of strokes, open-heart surgery, and retirements, and they end with jokes about how quickly new graduates are abandoning their first jobs. There's a marvelous continuity to these informal and chatty reports filed by alumni around the world. There's also the overwhelming sense that a Harvard MBA is the entry ticket to the most privileged and invaluable fraternity in business, a pass to an elite network of contacts in consulting, investment banking, industry, and government. Of the top three officers in the 500 largest industrial corporations, a remarkable 20% are Harvard MBAs. Twenty-five years out of school, one-third of them boast the title of CEO, managing director, partner, or owner.

In the red-brick, neo-Georgian buildings on the Charles River in Boston, you'll find more superstar professors than work at all the other top B-schools combined. They teach in modern, tiered classrooms with state-of-the-art audiovisual equipment. So rich in resources is Harvard that the students now have their own fitness center with whirlpool, sauna, and steam rooms. After all, most B-schools could fit into Harvard's Baker Library with room to spare.

The facilities are striking, yet what most students find surprising about Harvard is their classmates. "I had some pretty rigid preconceptions about what they'd be like: arrogant, one-dimensional, destructively competitive," says Keith Hammonds, a 1986 grad and now BUSINESS WEEK Boston bureau chief. "My first-year sectionmates impressed me in three ways: (a) The breadth of their experiences and interests was remarkable; (b) they were the most self-motivated people I'd ever seen; and (c) they managed to balance strong senses of individualism with compassion and group spirit."

Hammonds recalls that on the first day of class, all new students stood up and publicly introduced themselves. Like other newcomers to Harvard, he discovered a good number of accountants, consultants, and bankers and no shortage of finance jocks. "But we also had a pro baseball player and a hockey player who had negotiated for the NHL players' union. One guy had spent several months living with, and reporting on, a rebel tribe in Afghanistan; a woman had spent the last year consulting in a Nepalese village; another had been an independent filmmaker. Several had already started, and sold, their own small businesses. About 15 in my section of 90 were foreign students. Sure, there were some jerks. Some of the best students in my section were either really arrogant or really boring, or both. And it's not like they were the most intelligent, deepest-thinking people in the world."

While most arrive here thinking they'll discover savage competition, many are surprised that it's not as competitive as they first imagined. Even so, a forced grading curve in which 10% of the students receive a grade of 3, the equivalent of a low-pass, sometimes fosters rivalries among students. There's always the danger of, in Harvard MBA parlance, "hitting the screen," or flunking out. If 45% of your first-year grades are low-pass, you're effectively put on probation. Roughly 3% of first-year students and only 1% of second-year students meet this fate.

With classroom participation accounting for 50% or more of your grade, there can be a considerable amount of game-playing among the 90 students in a single class. When critics bemoaned the lack of teaching of ethics a couple of years ago and Harvard became sensitive over the issue, some students invoked the issue in discussions just to garner "air time" in class. "Chip shots"—short, easy comments that require little or no preparation but win points at the expense of a classmate—are not uncommon. Some make remarks geared to fit neatly with a professor's known theory or perspective to gain higher grades.

Against this competitive backdrop, you'll find the tension mounts with the immediate workload. There's a curious imbalance to the MBA program at Harvard. The first year is hellishly intense—not because it's heavily quantitative or academically rigorous, but because the school loads you up with hundreds of pages of case study reading each week. Virtually all the instruction is via case study, which requires students to analyze and debate brief, problem-oriented company reports or cases in class.

The typical first-year week consists of thirteen 80-minute classes, each requiring the preparation of a case study that might take two to three hours per case. Add in time with your study group and you're apt to work until 1 a.m. or 2 a.m. most weekdays, only to get up the next morning for an 8:30 class. Several grads figure that at least 75% of the learning is crammed into those first two semesters. Then, the workload and competition ease considerably. About 20% of the work gets piled into the first semester of your second year, while the the remaining 5% takes up the last semester. As one grad put it, "The second year is a good time to do intense job hunting, in-depth work in a chosen field, to relax and enjoy intramurals, or plan an extended summer vacation."

In the first year, Harvard divides the class of 800 into nine sections of about 90 students each. Each section goes through the required 12 first-year courses as a group. Harvard recently added a three-week, seven-session ethics module to this core. There are no exceptions and no waivers. In the second year, the sole required course is Management Policy and Practice, which focuses on vicariously acquiring top management perspective by assuming the role of a decision maker in case studies. You also must take 10 electives out of more than 60 offered at the B-school or a limited number from the university's other graduate schools and departments. There's plenty of freedom to do what you want because no formal concentration or major is required at Harvard.

The quality of teaching from Harvard professors ranges, as one grad put it, from "God-like to God-awful." Many of the first-year courses are taught by newer professors. Each student seems fated to have as many washouts as superstar professors in the first year. While friction typically exists between research and teaching at most B-schools, at Harvard this seems to be a minor issue. A more tangible tension exists between teaching and consulting. There are so many faculty stars here that they are in high demand as consultants. Some students grouse that the faculty isn't nearly as accessible as they would like. Indeed, some grads find Harvard professors "generally distant and cool."

The same is true, they say, of Dean John H. McArthur, a beefy man who favors short-sleeve shirts. One grad complained that the first time the dean addressed the Class of 1988 was at its graduation. Yet, McArthur has dramatically added to the quality of Harvard's stars by proving more willing than predecessors to hire from the outside. In recent years, he has lured to the school some of the leading academicians in business today, from Robert S. Kaplan, a specialist in management accounting systems, to Rosabeth Moss Kanter, who consults on organizational issues with many top corporations.

And in a faculty of more than 200 teachers, where teaching is in fact emphasized, there are many exceptions to the "distant and cool" rule. Jay Light's and William Fruhan's second-year courses in Investment Management and Corporate Financial Management are favorites. So are David Hawkins's Analysis of Corporate Financial Reports and John Quelch's Consumer Marketing. Douglas Anderson's Business Policy is a highlight in the first year, just as Michael Porter's more advanced strategy course is in the second. Other good bets: John Gabarro for Power and Influence, Janice Hammond for Business Logistics, and Abraham Zaleznik for Social Psychology of Management.

Separated from the rest of the university, the Harvard B-school is a total community unto itself. On the 61-acre campus you'll find four restaurants, a branch of the Harvard Coop, a grocery, a post office, and even a barber shop. Almost everyone eats lunch at Kresge, the main dining hall, or at the snack bar in Gallatin Hall—especially on Mondays, Wednesdays, and Fridays, when there's still a 1 p.m. class after lunch. The Pub at Gallatin is always full on Wednesday nights and Friday afternoons. Off campus, MBAs favor The Boathouse (bar); Shay's (wine bar); Border Cafe (Mexican); Charlie's Kitchen (a bar, with cheap double cheeseburgers).

More than half the first-year students live in the B-school residence halls, which are nicely appointed, like little Sheraton rooms, but so small you can literally lean over your desk chair and fall into bed. Even so, you can wake up at 8:20 and still make an 8:30 class. Not many consider this an advantage that's worth it because only 20% of second-year students live in the dorms. They prefer to live off-campus in rented homes or apartments, or in the fairly expensive student apartments at Soldiers Field Park, adjacent to the school.

Whether or not you stay on campus, you'll never want for things to do at Harvard. First-year sections have regular keg parties or ice cream "study breaks" on Wednesday nights and during exams. There are weekend barbecues at a local beach, ski trips, baseball games, and organized trips during vacations, from Florida to China. Besides the more than 35 student clubs on campus, there's a lot of emphasis on sports, from rowing on the Charles to intramural rugby. HBS also is very big on black tie. If you belong to the right clubs, you can end up going to two black-tie dinners or parties a month. The European Club tends to be the champion of black-tie galas at various Boston and Cambridge landmarks, most notably, the end-of-year bash at a Newport mansion.

Because nearly a third of Harvard B-school students are married, there's a very active support group for spouses called Partners. It organizes such things as pot-luck dinners and night classes with spouses' professors. More importantly, the group provides an informal network for couples who tend to spend more time with each other and less time with sectionmates as the two years wear on, until it's time to pack up for that new, lucrative job.

You'd expect an embarrassment of riches when it comes to placement. But many firms avoid Harvard simply because its grads demand too much money and are too eager for promotion once hired. In 1988, however, 347 companies sent recruiters to the school to conduct more than 6150 interviews. In the wake of Wall Street's crash, nearly 29% of MBAs headed off into the world of consulting where the average starting salary hit a record $65,000 without bonus. Some 27% went into finance, 18% into marketing, and 10% into general management.

How long Harvard MBAs stay put is another matter. As one 1988 grad joked in a recent issue of the *Bulletin*: "Stay tuned for the next Section E chapter entitled 'Meandering MBAs.' It seems that Section E could set new records for the average life cycle of an HBS MBA's first job. The current average is 18 months. Our sources indicate that at least five Section E-ers have abandoned their first jobs within three months." No doubt they'll someday find their niche and the *Bulletin* will be there to report it.

Contact: Laura Fisher, director of admissions, Morgan 102, 617-495-6000

Prominent alumni: James E. Burke, chairman of Johnson & Johnson; Howard Love, CEO of National Intergroup; William G. McGowan, CEO of MCI Communications; Colman M. Mockler, Jr., CEO of Gilette; Robert H. Malott, CEO of FMC; Harry E. Figgie, Jr., CEO of Figgie International; Rueben Mark, CEO of Colgate-Palmolive; Frank A. Lorenzo, CEO of Texas Air; Drew L. Lewis Jr., CEO of Union Pacific

Harvard MBAs sound off

*The secret to the success of the Harvard Business School lies in its tight admissions policy. If you collected the same group of motivated, intelligent people and taught them fingerpainting, they would still go out and be successful.—**Director of operations***

Harvard is a paradox: excellent and mediocre; sensitive and confrontational; open to new ideas as well as rigid and inflexible. Students with

little/no quantitative backgrounds are not drilled in quantitative analysis, which leaves them unprepared to tackle complicated tasks upon graduation. The joke is, "If we need numbers to be crunched, we'll hire someone from Wharton or MIT." It's a big picture school, not a down-in-the-trenches school.—**Real estate leasing agent**

The biggest problem with Harvard is its emphasis on class participation rather than fundamental skills. Grades are determined by what you say in the classroom, rather than how well you do on projects, papers, and exams. In the real world, managers are evaluated by what they do, not on what they say. Harvard seems to have gotten this mixed up. The result: students spend most of their time preparing for class trying to think up "chip shots" to say, rather than on mastering the skills and techniques being taught.—**Assistant product director**

HBS is not the competitive, cut-throat place everyone on the outside likes to think it is. The people are friendly, the classes challenging, the environment exciting and fun. It's a great place.—**Finance associate**

I never truly expected to be accepted at Harvard. But for me, the experience was incredibly enriching and extended far beyond the classroom. It was not Utopia. We were demanding of Harvard, because it's supposed to be the best, the same reason it was demanding of us. The impressive placement statistics of HBS graduates don't tell the whole story. Behind them is a very arduous and painful job hunt, full of interviews, which often end in rejection and demoralization. Just having a Harvard MBA isn't enough.—**Marketing consultant**

Harvard gives lip service only to a lot of important trends and issues. These include: team play and the role of people in business, corporate responsibilities, individual creativity, computers and technology, manufacturing competitiveness, entrepreneurship. Things that are wrong: class size is too big, it's too expensive, and you have a rigid learning approach and environment. Even so, the bottom line is that HBS was the best move I've ever made.—**Director of business development**

After years of rigorous medical training and two years as a practicing physician, I thought that I had seen it all. Wrong again! HBS was the most exciting and challenging experience of my life. A whole new world has been opened for me—I will be forever indebted.—**Vice president of operation**

3. Dartmouth College

The Amos Tuck School of Business Administration
Hanover, New Hampshire 03755

Recruiter ranking: 15
Enrollment: 343
Women: 26%
Foreign: 13%
Minority: 8%
Part-time: None
Average age: 26
Applicants accepted: 15%
Accepted applicants enrolled: 43%

Graduate ranking: 1
Annual tuition: $15,250
Room: $2750 to $3100
Meal plan: $1950
Average GMAT score: 648
GMAT range: 510 to 790
Average GPA: 3.31
GPA range: 2.3 to 4.0
Average starting pay: $62,681

Application deadline: April 16 for fall

Whoever said that a good B-school is supposed to encourage cutthroat competition didn't have in mind Dartmouth College's Amos Tuck School of Business. Maybe it's Tuck's remote locale in a small New Hampshire town. Maybe it's the school's relatively small size. But what seems to impress most graduates is the esprit de corps among the school's students and faculty. That's the major reason Tuck ranked first in BUSINESS WEEK's poll of graduates.

On the opening day of classes, professors hand over their personal phone numbers and invite students to call if necessary. Second-year students host dozens of welcome parties for new students. The second-year folks even get up early on Saturday mornings to serve their new brethren breakfast in the mess hall before exams. One professor tells of how his students sent his wife flowers and a gift certificate to a restaurant because he had to work weekends to accommodate an overload of students in a popular class.

"The emphasis is always on constructive competition instead of you versus me," says Jonathan Jodka, of the Class of 1989. "One classmate of mine who was good in statistics gave a four-hour review session for the class the night before our final exam. He knew the material inside out and wanted to help anyone who needed it."

It sounds almost too good to be true, particularly at a top business school. But only one other business school—Yale's School of Organization and Management—scored higher in having a cooperative campus in the BUSINESS WEEK sample. "This is sort of like joining the Moonies," quips Rich D'Aveni, an assistant professor. "The Tuck culture is very rah-rah and homogeneous. If you're not the kind of person who joins up and goes along, it might not be the best place for you."

For one thing, it's small and compact—each Tuck class of about 170 students is less than half the size of one at UCLA and a mere fifth of Harvard. The full-time faculty numbers only 40, less than the tenure-track faculty at Wharton's finance department alone. "Occasionally, there is a fishbowl feeling," says Bill McNamara, of the Class of 1990. "It is tough to hide here. At a school with very large classes, it's easy to sulk in the back. If you're in the back row here, you're only 20 feet from the professor."

For another, it's pretty isolated. Only prop planes can fly into the tiny airport in West Lebanon, six miles south of Hanover. When the weather turns bad, you face a white-knuckle flight onto the short landing strip that's carved into a mountainside.

Boston is a two-hour drive away. Sleepy Hanover rolls up the sidewalks fairly early. The only time people are out late is when they're coming out of the Nugget Theatre on the main street or attending something at the Hop, Dartmouth's impressive performing arts center.

The business school sits on the edge of the Dartmouth campus, bordering the Connecticut River. The cluster of five brick Georgian buildings that make up the B-school is like a private 13-acre encampment at the end of a private road appropriately named Tuck Drive. Underground tunnels and glass-enclosed halls—dubbed Habitrails—connect all the buildings so students needn't venture outside to attend class during the bitterly cold winter months. You could trek from your Woodbury Hall dorm room to a class at columned Tuck Hall in your slippers. Still, the winters are harsh. One student from Los Angeles remarked that he'd like to fly the whole campus to L.A. for a few weeks during the winter.

Yet, the snow-covered campus makes for a pastoral setting. Students can hear the bronze bells of Baker Tower sound off each hour with such ditties as "Heigh Ho, Heigh Ho" and "Yellow Submarine." Tradition abounds. Founded in 1900, Tuck is the world's first graduate school of management. Mr. Chips would feel particularly welcome in the dining room of Stell Hall with its cathedral ceiling and carved heavy oak interior. Over the fireplace hangs a fading, formal portrait of old man Tuck, a lawyer and Congressman for whom the school was named in 1900. "You can imagine a row of 25 kids with beanies eating there at the long tables," jokes Sam Lundquist, director of admissions.

While MBAs tend to congregate every night for drinks and grub at Raphael's Cucino or Bentley's on the main drag in town, the number one diversion at Tuck is the outdoors. Skiway, a small ski resort some 20 minutes away in Lyme, is the downhill run of choice. And there's hiking on Mount Moosilauke on the edge of the White Mountains National Forest, rowing and canoeing on the Connecticut River, or a slew of intramural sports from ice hockey and rugby to basketball and squash.

Tuckies tend to be outdoorsy, exceptionally self-assured, and somewhat preppy. They generally lack the arrogance and cockiness of their brethren at some other top schools. MBA candidates here also tend to be less narrow, less functional, and broader in their outlook, a consequence of the program's design.

Tuck offers a general management program, with the emphasis on how different functional areas come together. People who are looking for hard-core functional and theoretical experiences probably want to avoid Tuck, which discourages overspecialization. Indeed, Tuck is the only prestige B-school without a Ph.D. program in business, a fact that leads some academics to pooh-pooh the intellectual rigor of the place. Truth is, it discourages narrow thinking, too. Students take four courses during each quarter (with three 10-week quarters a year in the fall, winter and spring) for a total of 24 required courses. Classes meet twice a week for an hour and a half each session.

Unlike other schools, Tuck discourages students from waiving out of the 13 core courses that make up the heart of the program. The reason? The school believes that nonaccounting types can benefit from having CPAs in the same classroom. Besides, more of the work in these courses is applied, rather than theoretical. It's also not easy to take nonbusiness courses at Dartmouth College because the college is on a different class schedule than Tuck, which offers about 60 electives a year.

Most B-school deans talk a lot about teamwork these days. But few really immerse their students in it like Tuck. "One of the reasons teamwork works here is because there is student pressure against backstabbing," adds a faculty member, who earned his doctorate at Columbia University. "At Columbia, students would hide books in the stacks so that they wouldn't be available to others for key projects." Tuck students perform a huge amount of their classwork in groups. In the first quarter alone, MBAs do four major team projects in Managerial Economics, Management Communication, Marketing, and "Dec Anal," Tuck slang for Decision Analysis. Virtually all first-year students live together in Woodbury Hall, so foreign students can't gather in subcultures here as they might in other places." People are thrown together 24 hours a day, seven days a week, and they have to rely on each other," says Dean Colin Blaydon. "You couldn't simulate this in an urban university where students are scattered in apartments all across a city."

Team projects dominate the Tuck experience. One of them, a major event of the year, is the Tycoon Game. Part folly, part learning experience, the contest is played out by second-year students each October. Classes are cancelled for the week-long, 24-hour-a-day marathon. The second-year class is divvied up into four worlds, each with two teams. Teams of six students each start off with about $25 million in cash and then must bid for one of eight companies in the same industry that they will manage over a compressed eight-year period. A professor plays god over each world, while student tycoons—trained on computers—are tapped to oversee the team strategies in each world.

Even though you play with funny money, this is hardly Monopoly. No one wants to get "looped," a low pass grade, so everyone works hard to make their company the top performing one in the game. Students devise strategies, trying to make savvy investment, production, and marketing decisions that will make their companies the most profitable. A typical decision: whether to sell your clocks abroad. If few companies invest in the foreign market, you could make a fortune overseas. But if everyone else jumps into the foreign market, the competition could cost you your shirt. Advertisements that hail the virtues of different clock companies—the industry of choice—inundate the campus.

While second-year students play tycoon, the capstone event for first-year MBAs is a major consulting project that begins in late November. Students are assigned real clients with real problems, mostly small local businesses, town governments, and school districts. They have to meet with the client, study his or her problem or opportunity, and produce a report of recommendations as part of the Managerial Economics class. They then present the final results of their work in an oral presentation to clients, outside consultants, and Tuck faculty as part of the Management Communication course. In the past, Tuckies have tackled marketing and distribution for Catamount Brewery, a local microbrewery, completed a feasibility study to help Plymouth, Massachusetts, lure new business to town, and worked on a report for Vermont Yankee's nuclear facility.

For those longing for an international adventure, Tuck recently launched a management program with the International University of Japan. As a Tuck MBA, you could spend a second-year term enrolled in the school as an exchange student. There's also a formal exchange program with the London Business School or Escuela Superior de Administracion in Barcelona, Spain. And there's even the possibility of doing a quarter at Insead in Fontainebleau, France, arguably the best non-U.S. business school in the world.

Whether you take off for foreign environs or not, there are some can't-miss professors and courses at Tuck. J. Brian Quinn leads the list of "star" faculty. His Organizational Design class is highly recommended. So is Richard J. Rogalski's course in securities and debt markets and Leonard Greenhalgh's Executive Power and Negotiation. Rogalski brings practical Wall Street experience to bear, having created a couple of debt market products for Morgan Stanley. Greenhalgh advises how to manage in an organization, neatly packaging the functional knowledge gained in core courses with executive suite savvy.

Tuck also boasts an unusual Executive-in-Residence program that welcomes up to 10 business leaders each year for three-to-five-day periods. They live in a two-room suite in Chase Hall, attend classes, eat lunch and dinner with students, and participate in discussion groups at night. Recent visiting executives have included Louis Gerstner, now chairman of RJR Nabisco, John Byrne, chairman of Fireman's Fund Corporation, and Marina von Neumann, chief economist of General Motors.

Also popular are the recently started book discussion groups on Sunday evenings. Small groups of students meet in Morse Lounge in Tuck Hall to chat about a book assigned by different professors for the discussion. Dean Blaydon recently held forth on Gore Vidal's *Lincoln,* dissecting the relationships the book explored between President Lincoln, his friends, and rivals. Like many ideas at Tuck, the discussion group evolved out of student interest.

Overall, the faculty wins plaudits from students for its accessibility, quality, and enthusiasm. When courses are oversubscribed at other schools, students are typically told, "Tough luck. Try next time." At Tuck, teachers with popular courses are often expected simply to add to their workload by offering extra sections if the students want them. "Student interests usually take precedence over the faculty," says one Tuck professor. "The first-year program is set up so that students can take all their classes in the morning and go skiing in the afternoon. If you have a 7:30 a.m. class, you might have to get up at 4 a.m. to prepare for it and get to school. The bottom line is that the students prefer that schedule, so it won't be disturbed."

Faculty accommodation occurs even after graduation. As one graduate noted, "I have talked to two professors about two different business questions—free of charge!" Second-year students often host dinners in their apartments for professors. When graduates return to campus, they frequently stay at the homes of faculty members. No wonder, then, that graduates gave Tuck's distinguished professors the best rating for accessiblity after class in the BUSINESS WEEK survey. They also awarded the school high marks on teaching quality, the friendliness of their classmates, and the overall preparation the program provided for a career in business.

So why does Tuck rank only fifteenth in BUSINESS WEEK's corporate poll? Fewer recruiters visit the school because of its small class size and remote location. In 1989, 124 companies recruited on campus, conducting 3172 interviews. Another 263 job opportunities were posted via correspondence. That's fewer than half the companies that Northwestern's Kellogg draws, and little more than a third of the job opportunities that arrive via mail.

During the tense weeks when students await word of job offers, a tension-relieving exercise gets played out. When an MBA opens a "ding" or rejection letter, the student rings a ding on a hanging bell in the mailroom. While virtually everyone gets a chance to ring the bell, each student has on average about three job offers—roughly the same as those at Kellogg. And Tuck MBAs last year garnered the highest

51

starting pay packages after only Stanford and Harvard. Who cares how many "dings" you get, if the final offer is one like that.

Contact: Samuel T. Lundquist, director of admissions, HB 9000, 603-646-3162

Prominent alumni: John W. Amerman, chairman of Mattel Inc.; Richard M. Bressler, chairman of Burlington Northern Inc.; Anthony M. Frank, postmaster general; E. John Rosenwald, Jr., vice chairman of Bear Stearns & Co.; Andrew C. Sigler, chairman of Champion International Corp.; Philip E. Benton, Jr., executive vice president of Ford Motor Co.

Tuck MBAs sound off

*My fellow classmates were outgoing, athletic and well-rounded. Internecine competition was almost unheard of. There was no back stabbing during recruiting season. We were confident that we would all get the sort of jobs we desired.—**Managing consultant***

*My only caveat: prospective students must be outdoors oriented, willing to take advantage of Dartmouth's New England location, and kindly disposed toward the social isolation of a rural setting. There is a lot to do, but it all centers around the Dartmouth community.—**Corporate finance associate***

*The professors were conscientious, knowledgeable, and willing to spend time with students who showed a genuine interest in their subjects. They also provided careful guidance in field projects. I think Tuck assigns more field projects than most schools (I did five in my second year), and I found these projects to be the best formal preparations for my current job. —**Management consultant***

*I was less than satisfied with the number and quality of recruiters on campus. The same firms tend to come year after year with very few additions or deletions. Recruiters tend to be concentrated in investment banking and consulting. We had some consumer goods companies, fewer high-tech companies, and very few small companies recruit at Tuck. —**Marketing manager***

*I could have gone to any of the top business schools, but I chose Tuck because of its size, mix of theory and case study, and Tuck's emphasis on team projects. I wasn't disappointed. The Tuck curriculum was rigorous, but professors and fellow classmates were eager to help those who were struggling. Tuck's placement office is very aggressive and helpful, too. Overall, I enjoyed my business experience and found that I was well prepared to meet the challenges of management.—**Project analyst***

*One of my professors came up with a good synopsis of what people should look for in a business school. He said that 20 years ago 40% of what MBAs studied can now be done on an HP 12C calculator. But things like leadership and personal-relationship building don't fit on the chip. And that's what Tuck does really well.—**Insurance analyst***

4. University of Pennsylvania

The Wharton School
102 Vance Hall
Philadelphia, Pennsylvania 19104

Recruiter ranking: 2
Enrollment: 1575
Women: 27%
Foreign: 21%
Minority: 12%
Part-time: None
Average age: 26.5
Applicants admitted: 21%
Accepted applicants enrolled: 65%

Graduate ranking: 13
Annual tuition: $15,440
Room and board: $9400
Average GMAT score: 644
GMAT range: 570 to 720 (80% of class)
Average GPA: 3.34
GPA range: NA
Average starting pay: $55,183

Application deadline: April 15 for fall

> *We're Wharton MBAs, we're uptight and we're mad.*
> *We interview for jobs, but they take the Harvard grads.*
> *Got an ethics code. We disclose our grades.*
> *Still they take those Stanford grads for corporate raids.*
> *What a cruel twist of fate.*
> *I thought I applied to Penn State.*

Hardly! The cast of Wharton's 1989 Follies can easily afford to sing those self-deprecating lines because they can rest assured that the name on their diplomas does indeed open doors. Even if Wharton grads can't command the high sums paid Harvard and Stanford MBAs, they're not far behind in either the pay or prestige sweepstakes.

In the world of MBAs, Wharton may very well emerge as the "preeminent" business school of the twenty-first century—the dream and goal of Dean Russell E. Palmer, perhaps the most aggressive and dynamic B-school dean today. Wharton denizens, parading on stage in the follies, may joke about how often the word "preeminent" slips from Palmer's lips, but he's not kidding. He *is* transforming the school, founded by Philadelphia industrialist Joseph Wharton in 1881, into a powerhouse.

Recruited in 1983 from accounting firm Touche Ross International, where he was chief executive, Palmer has racked up impressive gains in almost every area: from fundraising to luring "matinee-idol" faculty to the school. He's also helped to redirect the school, making it more practical and real-world than ever before. "When I first got here," he says, "I'd go around, look at the blackboards and see lots of formulas on them. I think we've changed a lot." Wharton has added courses in communications, organizational behavior, government relations, labor, and service industries. And there's a strong international flavor to the entire program.

It's something you can appreciate as soon as you walk through the campus. You'll hear plenty of accents in the air as you stroll past the life-size bronze statue of an imposing Ben Franklin reading a newspaper on a park bench. Wharton itself is housed in four buildings. MBAs spend most of their time in Vance Hall, an American version of the industrial-looking Pompidou Centre in Paris. Some professors decry the factory architecture as moronic, complaining that the building is hot in the summer and chilly in the winter because of all the glass. If Vance has the appearance of a modern factory, Steinberg-Dietrich Hall, home to faculty and administration, seems more like a corporate headquarters. Then there's the Steinberg Conference Center, for executive education programs, and the career planning office next door.

The first thing to know about Wharton is that it's not a business school: it's a business university. Wharton's 180 tenure-track faculty outnumbers the graduating class of MBAs at such leading business schools as Amos Tuck and Carnegie-Mellon. And only Harvard turns out more MBAs each year than Wharton. The options of both academic and social life are bewildering. Wharton offers 200 courses in the MBA program alone (more than Harvard, Chicago, or virtually any other graduate B-school in the world). More than 90 different student clubs on campus compete for attention. The school also sponsors 26 research centers that study everything from entrepreneurship to real estate. "There are so many goodies," says William Pierskalla, a Wharton professor for over a decade, "that it's hard to choose the best things. The breadth of the place can overwhelm people."

Sure, everyone knows about Wharton's strength in finance. Some 41 tenure-track faculty are in the school's finance department, and some of the nation's leading financiers have Wharton in their backgrounds, including indicted junk bond guru Michael Milken, of Drexel Burnham Lambert. In fact after several Wharton grads were indicted or subpoenaed in various Wall Street investigations in recent years the investment banking club has jokingly adopted the nickname "The Unindicted."

But the focus on finance often overshadows excellent faculty and programs in Wharton's other departments. Palmer claims that 9 of the school's 10 departments have faculty that rate in the top three, while the remaining one is in the top five. With 40 tenure-track faculty in the management department and 20 in marketing, Wharton is able to offer extraordinary strength throughout its program. The school even boasts 9 faculty members in a public policy department.

Two years ago, David Reibstein, a Wharton vice dean, was teaching a market research course at Stanford. "In that quarter, it was the only marketing course taught there," he says. "There were probably 10 to 12 marketing courses at the same time at Wharton. The net effect is that a student comes out of Stanford saying he's a finance major or marketing genius after having two to four courses in an area. Here you're forced to take a major—a minimum of five courses in a functional area. So you get breadth through the core and depth through the major."

As a student, you have a greater choice not only because of the larger number of courses, but also because you can waive out of core classes. At Harvard and Stanford, you may have to sit through an introductory accounting course even if you're a CPA. Wharton students require 19 courses to graduate: 9 form the core education (unless you replace some of them with more electives), 5 are required in your major, while another 5 are free electives that can be taken anywhere in the university. The last semester, you take only 4 courses to give more time to job hunt.

Wharton boasts one of the more innovative international programs through its Joseph H. Lauder Institute. A joint venture between the B-school and the university's School of Arts and Sciences, the 24-month program requires a greater commitment than Wharton's typical MBA program. For one thing, the group of 50 students arrive in May instead of September. After spending a month on campus, they're shipped overseas to countries in which their chosen foreign language is spoken (a second language is required for admission into the program). While there, they'll tour the facilities of a dozen corporations and take in lots of cultural activities, from plays to museums. They return for the start of the school year in September, only to go back for 12-week internships with both foreign companies and the overseas affiliates of U.S. firms, including Procter & Gamble in Japan. They then return to campus to complete their studies. Though the Lauder program is relatively new, grads show incredible enthusiasm for it.

If you're keen on the international business scene yet unwilling to sweat through a full 24-month program, Wharton also offers foreign exchange deals with schools in The Netherlands, France, London, Spain, Italy, Stockholm, and Tokyo (only NYU has a larger exchange program). During each spring break, two group travel programs take faculty and students to Japan where they spend a week visiting the Tokyo Stock Exchange, a Nissan auto plant, the headquarters of Nomura Securities and Fujitsu, and the Japanese outposts of P&G and Exxon. Last spring, there were 260 applicants for the 41 student slots. The trip costs an extra $1000 per student. All the interest in international business led more than 17% of the Class of 1988 to accept jobs with non-U.S. companies or with the international divisions of U.S. corporations.

Wharton students are sharp, ambitious, and surprisingly diverse. "I expected to see a lot of Ivy League people and investment banker types here," says Neil Burns, who graduated in 1989. "But there really are a lot of different backgrounds. We've had musicians, lawyers, doctors, pro-football players, and even a former skater from Follies on Ice." They're also hotly competitive—particularly in the first year when everyone is trying to prove just how good he or she is. A grading curve imposes a good dose of pressure on everyone. About 5% of each class typically gets an "NC"—a grade of no credit for either failing a course or not completing one. Some 15% of the class lands the distinguished grade, while 20% receive an "HP," or high pass. Everyone else simply gets a "P" for pass. If you pile up four distinguished grades in a semester, you're on the "Director's List"—Wharton's equivalent of Harvard's Baker Scholar—that is published in *The Wharton Journal*. "There's a tremendous concern about grades and why people get graded down," says Ian MacMillan, who teaches entrepreneurial classes.

If the grading is tough for students, it's just as tough for the faculty. No graduates in the BUSINESS WEEK poll were more critical of their professors' teaching skills than those at Wharton. Students grouse that too many Wharton professors are interested in their own academic research or in consulting stints rather than teaching. Two-thirds of the faculty at Wharton are actively consulting. And some Wharton professors privately concede that getting the "Teacher of the Year" award from the students is equivalent to the kiss of death. Says one ex-Wharton professor who received it: "The chairman of my department told me I should be careful because now the faculty wouldn't take my research seriously."

MBAs do get some help in steering clear of the worst because student evaluations of teachers are posted on bulletin boards in the corridors of Vance Hall. Despite the dismay over the uneven quality of teaching here, you'll also find some excellent instruction. Grads say not to miss Harbir Singh's Mergers and Acquisitions, William Tyson's Securities Regulation, and Jamshed Ghandi's Theory and Structure of Capital Markets. The latter may not be for everyone. Ghandi can be intimidating. "He works you hard, but you learn so much," says a student. "Attend a few classes before you commit." Singh is no pushover, either. He assigns 1300 pages of readings for his course, but grads like him for being on the leading edge of knowledge in his field and for deftly wrapping up each class with a set of lessons you can take away. Howard Kaufold also gets good grades for his introductory finance course. He begins the class with the question, "How many people know how to spell finance?" Anita Summers in public policy has a reputation as one of the more caring faculty members.

Before you leave Wharton, you're expected to overcome one final hurdle in the form of the dreaded "ASP"–an advanced study project that might involve anything from a consulting assignment with a nearby company to a 100-page study on an issue approved by a faculty advisor. One Class of 1989 grad, for example, did a study on how Japanese-owned corporations in the United States treat their American managers and employees. A marketing major mapped out a strategy for how Wharton's alumni magazine could attract more advertising.

Grads have complained that Wharton's size makes it difficult for them to gain a sense of camaraderie with each other, particularly because most students were scattered in apartments and homes all around the campus and Philadelphia. Many MBAs live in either center city, a 10-minute ride by bicycle, or West Philadelphia. Wharton has set aside 12 floors of Grad Tower B for MBAs alone and dubbed it the "Living Learning Center." Now 350 students reside in the building, two blocks from Wharton, making it easier for them to organize in study groups, get advice on courses, or simply find a companion for a late-night snack. Since 1987, first-year students also are divvied into 12 "cohort" groups of 60 each—with names such as "Killer Bs" or "Special Ks." Each group is together for core classes. "With a graduating class of 750, I expected this place to be a factory," says one grad. "But the cohort system had the effect of breaking up the place into smaller sub-schools."

The friendships forged in a cohort often carry through the rest of the program and into the plethora of Wharton's social activities. "Socially," says Burns, "there's too much to do." Every Thursday at 4:30 it's happy hour in the MBA pub in Steinberg (for Reliance Group chairman and undergraduate alum Saul) Conference Center. First-year MBAs tend to prefer Murphy's, a joint with a great jukebox seven blocks west of the campus. The favorite local rock band is Daves which often plays at North Star in center city. Then there's a big celebration once every semester called "Walnut Walk." After mid-terms, grads don a combination of formal attire and shorts and begin the bar crawl on Second Street and make their way through up to 20 bars, ending up at a 3 a.m. breakfast. Wharton MBAs also show a remarkable interest in charitable causes. Among many fund-raising events is "Christmas in April" in which 250 students team up with about 100 skilled laborers and repair homes in West Philly that belong to the handicapped or indigent.

The "wailing wall" in the Leonard A. Lauder Career Center is an important part of campus life. Students flock to the bulletin board to learn if they've landed a spot on an interview schedule with a potential employer. Some 315 companies came to Wharton in 1988 and conducted about 100,000 interviews. Another 500 job opportunities flowed in via correspondence. In 1988, Touche Ross got the largest single contingent of Wharton grads (31), while McKinsey was next with 17, Bankers Trust 14, Citicorp 12, Booz Allen 11, and Hewlett-Packard 10.

If there's a major concern here, it's Dean Palmer. He intends to resign at the end of the 1990 academic year. Whoever succeeds him will have to carry on Palmer's dream of making Wharton the "preeminent school."

Contact: John W. Enyart, director of admissions, 102 Vance Hall, 3733 Spruce Street, 215-898-3030

Prominent alumni: Frank Cahouet, chairman of Mellon Bank; Robert L. Crandall, CEO of American Airlines parent AMR; John L. Kelsey, managing director of Paine

Webber; Yotaro Kobayashi, president of Fuji Xerox; Edmund T. Pratt, Jr., chairman of Pfizer; Charles S. Sanford, president of Bankers Trust; John Sculley, CEO of Apple Computer; Laurence A. Tisch, chairman of CBS

Wharton MBAs sound off

The quality of the education provided at Wharton is excellent. I was especially pleased with the finance department; before entering Wharton my financial knowledge and analytical skills were minimal. I left with a much better understanding of finance. Moreover, the emphasis is on learning, not competition and grades. The career placement office needs to strengthen and make a bigger effort to help those students not interested in working in the tri-state area or anywhere in New England or the Northeast for that matter. This would only strengthen Wharton's international and national reputation. **—Financial analyst**

Personally, I would like to see much more emphasis put on better teaching. I was terribly disappointed to spend $50,000 and two years of my life (in time and lost salary) to get "stuck" with professors who were at best marginally interested in teaching. To the school's credit though, I learned a tremendous amount from my fellow colleagues. But does it make sense to pay someone else for the opportunity to teach each other? Wharton does deserve high marks for a good mix of theory, case history, group study, and field study. **—Management consultant**

The Wharton School has a diverse group of intelligent, fun-loving and cooperative students. Spending two years with these people was very educational. Unfortunately, I cannot say the same about the professors, who range from excellent to lazy, stupid, and useless. Academically, the school is run as departments, rather than as a cohesive curriculum, which is too bad. That said, I'm very pleased with my current job and know that I could not have gotten it if not through the school. **—Management consultant**

When I applied to Wharton, I understood that the school was less for learning and more for grooming, polishing, and developing connections. I also understood it was a money machine for the University. My assumptions were not false. However, having had a career before I entered Wharton, I wasn't looking for a father figure to explain the mysteries of the Universe. I was more interested in gaining the skills and connections that would allow me to play hard ball in the big league. I got what I paid for. **—Real estate manager**

Some students were highly competitive and aggressive, while others were quite friendly and team oriented. As far as intensity or workload is concerned, one could really make what he/she wanted to with it. There was more than enough work to keep you busy continuously, but you could also prioritize and work on what was more important or what had the biggest impact on the final grade. **—Management consultant**

5. Cornell University

Johnson Graduate School of Management
Malott Hall
Ithaca, New York 14853

Recruiter ranking: 11	*Graduate ranking:* 3
Enrollment: 420	*Annual tuition:* $14,900
Women: 23%	*Room and board:* $5290
Foreign: 15%	*Average GMAT score:* 620
Minority: 6%	*GMAT range:* 590 to 800
Part-time: None	*Average GPA:* 3.2
Average age: 26	*GPA range:* 2.9 to 4.0
Applicants admitted: 27%	*Average starting pay:* $52,339
Accepted applicants enrolled: 49%	

Application deadline: March 1 for fall

Lots of B-schools promise to show students the ropes, but how many teach them to scale mountain peaks? In the summer of 1988, a small group from Cornell's Johnson Graduate School of Management traveled to the Colorado Rockies. There they spent a week rock climbing, rappelling, and orienteering that culminated in a night of camping solo. In typical B-school fashion, each day the half-dozen students and three professors sat around analyzing their exploits and figuring how they could have done it differently.

Not all students will have to prove themselves in such rugged terrain, but the Colorado wilderness experience says a lot about the Johnson MBA program. It's innovative, intimate, and challenging. Tucked away in New York's Finger Lakes region in Ithaca, Johnson's small class size of 210 fosters unusually close relationships between students and faculty—whether they're climbing mountains, debating an issue in class, or competing against each other in sports.

Indeed, one of the true annual events at the school is the battle between the Frozen Assets, the female MBAs' hockey team, and a group of professors. When the professors trounced the Assets in 1989, students spread the malicious rumor that the school considered hockey experience a prerequisite in hiring new faculty. It didn't prevent faculty and students from competing against each other in the eight-mile Joe Thomas Invitational Run. Despite heavy teaching and research loads carried by many Johnson teachers, they seem to make available plenty of time for students. "The most impressive part of JGSM (Johnson Graduate School of Management) is the accessibility of the faculty," says a 1988 graduate. "Their offices are in the same building as classes, and their doors are always open."

The school, named after Samuel C. Johnson of Johnson's Wax fame, is no bargain when it comes to tuition. You'll get better bang for the buck at the University of North Carolina, Berkeley, or UCLA. But it's hard to beat Johnson for personal attention, a flexible curriculum, and faculty involvement. The school's pastoral setting is great for studying and enjoying outdoor, especially winter, sports.

Given Cornell's scenic location—the campus is nestled between two gorges and overlooks Cayuga Lake—it's not surprising the Johnson school sells itself as an academic respite from the rat race of big city life. A slick brochure advises prospective

B-school students, "In Ithaca, you aren't likely to be wakened from your sleep or startled from your studies by screaming sirens and gear-grinding tractor trailers. You'll find that you have the necessary peace and quiet to do the kind of intense concentrating that graduate management study demands." While true, you'll also discover it's a place that few can easily escape—the nearest major airport is an hour away in Syracuse while New York City is a tedious five-hour drive.

The isolation helps spur a common spirit of enthusiasm, and the combination of a small student body and an involved faculty gives Johnson the freedom to be bold and experimental. It often forges links with other Cornell schools to develop unusual programs, encourages team teaching by professors from different disciplines, and creates novel international programs.

At the same time the group was climbing mountains in Colorado, another team of Johnson faculty and students was piloting a 30-foot boat equipped with oars and sails off the coast of Maine. Surprisingly, the Johnson school picked up the tab for both trips. Even when students disappear off the campus and into the corporate world, they find a rather generous alma mater. Johnson funds a Lifelong Learning Program, a series of free lectures for alumni held in major cities such as New York, Boston, and Chicago.

Although the B-school building, Malott Hall, is crowded, Curtis Tarr, the former dean, has been plowing millions raised from alums and corporate donors into programs, not facilities. Like MIT and Berkeley, Johnson wants to prepare students to manage in a global, competitive marketplace. The B-school has drawn on the strengths of the university by creating joint degree programs in Asian studies and engineering. Through the Cornell Manufacturing Engineering and Productivity Program, students with an undergraduate engineering degree and professional experience can obtain master's degrees in engineering and management in two years. The program also allows Johnson MBAs who concentrate in manufacturing management to sign up for engineering electives.

The Johnson School has won international recognition for two programs that teach MBAs about Japanese language and culture. The first is a three-year program leading to master's degrees in management and Asian studies. This option includes 12 months of intensive Japanese language classes and a summer internship in Japan with firms such as the Industrial Bank of Japan, Nippon Telegraph and Telephone, and Mitsubishi's chemical unit. The second is a two-year MBA course with a concentration in Japanese business that includes a summer of intensive language classes, Japanese classes throughout the year, and a summer internship in Japan.

These rigorous Japanese business programs are more than something for Johnson MBAs to put on their résumés or talk about during job interviews. For students with the requisite talent and commitment, they often lead to lucrative management jobs with American companies in Japan. After earning master's degrees in management and Asian studies, Jim Latimer of Johnson's Class of 1989 recently landed a job with Corning Glass's Japanese subsidiary. Latimer will help supervise the transfer of technology from a Kentucky plant that manufactures liquid crystal display glass to a new Corning production facility in Japan.

Before he came to Cornell in June 1986, Latimer had never spoken a word of Japanese. After earning an undergraduate degree from Georgia Tech, he had worked for robotics manufacturer Cincinnati Milacron for several years. "If you decide you want to learn Japanese as an adult, Cornell is one of the few places you can take the language for 12 months straight. The FALCON (Full-Year Asian Language Concentration) program is designed for people starting from scratch," he says. Other B-schools such as Michigan, Berkeley, and Wharton allow MBAs to simultaneously earn a master's in Asian studies, but few offer as innovative a program as Cornell's.

In addition to the joint degree programs in Asian studies and engineering, Johnson allows students to earn an MBA and a doctor of law in four years, instead of the five required to earn each degree separately. The B-school is also working with Cornell's College of Agriculture and Life Sciences to develop a joint degree program in management and agricultural economics. "What makes us unique among B-schools is how we've taken advantage of other schools at the university," says Curtis Tarr, who for the past five years has guided the school to its leading position. "Some of the major concerns of business have to do with regulation, liability, and environment. At Johnson, we expose students to these areas." That policy is expected to be continued under the new dean, Alan G. Merten, recruited from the University of Florida at Gainesville. Tarr remains at Johnson teaching Business Ethics.

For the run-of-the-mill MBA, there's unusual flexibility and variety, including one of the largest choices of electives of any B-school. Johnson MBAs may take up to 15 credits—or about 5 of the 20 courses required for an MBA—in other Cornell top-notch schools, including the College of Architecture, Art and Planning, the School of Hotel Administration, the School of Industrial and Labor Relations and the College of Human Ecology, which offers courses in health administration. To earn an MBA from the Johnson School, you'll need to spend four semesters in Ithaca and earn 60 credits. There are 10 courses equal to 30 credits in Johnson's core curriculum, 5 of which are taken in the first semester and 4 in the second semester. These include financial accounting, statistics, microeconomics, marketing, organizational behavior, management information systems, finance, macroeconomics, and operations.

During the second year, students take one core course, Business Strategy and Policy, and design their own programs of elective courses. Johnson provides "road maps" or lists of suggested classes for students pursuing a specific career track, but does not require students to concentrate in any particular area. The choices available to Johnson students through Cornell's Center for International Studies are staggering, including concentrations in international economics and trade, international management, and United States international public policies and issues.

In addition to the two programs in Japanese business, Cornell offers exchange programs with the London Business School, two universities in Belgium, and an institute in France. However, space in these programs is very limited and cannot satisfy demand to study abroad. Cornell, for example, can only send one student to the London Business School each year.

Like any Ivy League institution, Cornell puts a lot of emphasis on research. But the Johnson School prides itself on good teaching. Associate Dean Tom Dyckman and Professor John Elliott bring accounting alive in the classes that they team teach. Joe Thomas's Business Logistics Management class helps students vividly understand how raw materials are turned into products. Richard Conway's expertise in manufacturing information systems is also much sought after by Johnson students.

The External Environment of Business, a lecture course featuring Cornell professors from areas such as history, law, economics, and agriculture, has proven a big hit among students and has garnered recognition among academics. Professor David BenDaniel's Entrepreneurship and Enterprise class has even spawned a few small businesses, including a limousine service started by one MBA that runs between the Syracuse airport and Ithaca. If you're interested in international management, grads say you shouldn't miss Business in Japan, an elective taught by T. J. Pempel.

Think you've got what it takes to be a trader? You'll find out soon enough in Seymour Smidt's Trading class. Smidt, who worked as a foreign exchange trader before coming to the Johnson School, combines theory with hands-on training in the class, an approach that helped Cornell beat out seven other B-schools in a week-long foreign exchange trading simulation sponsored by Chase Manhattan Bank in 1988.

Like the Simon School at the University of Rochester, Cornell's Johnson School attracts a good number of finance types who recharge their batteries and beef up their credentials before returning to commercial and investment banking jobs in New York. In between their studies, Johnson MBAs ice skate at the university's rink and play golf on a school course when there's no snow on the ground. In 1988, B-schools from all over the country sent teams to Ithaca to the first of what will be an annual Invitational Golf Tournament. Johnson MBAs are dedicated athletes and like to play hockey, lacrosse, and volleyball. There's even a men's hockey team dubbed the Puck Bunnies. You guessed it: another of the year's big events is the matchup pitting the Assets against the Bunnies.

Since many graduates of Cornell's hotel school decide to stay in the area, there is no shortage of excellent restaurants and bars in Ithaca, including the famous Moosewood Restaurant, which has produced several best-selling cookbooks. When it's time to relax, Johnson MBAs often head to the Chapter House for a few beers.

Because it's off the beaten path, the Johnson School has to work harder to find students jobs. The managing director of Bankers Trust, a Cornell MBA himself, recently conceded to the student-published *Malott Times*, "Even I resent going there in the snow to recruit . . . ." Since corporate recruiters aren't wild about coming to Ithaca, the B-school brings students to them by holding job fairs in Boston and New York. Although nearly 90% of MBAs have jobs by graduation, students say the placement office focuses too much attention on New York firms in finance and consulting, a complaint heard at many B-schools. Chase Manhattan hired seven MBAs from the Class of 1988, sent a dozen recruiters to campus to interview the Class of 1989, and recently donated $100,000 to the school. Through its alumni, Johnson has had good success at placing graduates in international jobs and summer internships, particularly in Japan.

Johnson students say their biggest problem is that the rest of the world doesn't know just how good the school is. Instead of mountain-climbing and sailing, maybe Johnson MBAs should spend the summer knocking on doors in corporate America to spread the word.

Contact: Mariea T. Noblitt, director of admissions, 800-847-2082

Prominent alumni: Charles F. Knight, chairman of Emerson Electric; I. MacAllister Booth, chairman of Polaroid; Robin Mills, president of Glenbrook Laboratories; Kenneth T. Derr, CEO of Chevron; Lewis Eisenberg, partner of Goldman Sachs; Jeffrey P. Parker, CEO of Technical Data International; H.L. Tower, chairman of Stanhome; Albert Fried, Jr., New York Stock Exchange specialist

Johnson MBAs sound off

Cornell's Johnson Graduate School of Management is one of the best-kept secrets of American business schools. The atmosphere is down-to-earth, and excellence abounds in all academic aspects. Students graduating from JGSM are better prepared, in my opinion, than any other students for entering the real-time business world. —**Market analyst**

What most impressed me about the Johnson School from the beginning of the admissions process through graduation was the friendliness and openness of the staff and faculty. They took an interest in me as an individual. I can't speak highly enough of the faculty. In addition to staying on top of their teaching and research loads, they would always come out to social and sports events with us. —**Securities analyst**

The placement office focused entirely on career opportunities at large organizations, primarily located on the East Coast. It did a poor job for those who preferred to locate on the West Coast, although it actively recruited West Coast students, and an equally poor job for those who sought positions at small organizations. —**Research associate**

The school has an excellent faculty that is very accessible and friendly to students. In my job I have spoken with MBAs from other schools who had told me that it was impossible to find a professor after class. This was definitely not the case at Cornell. One real advantage Cornell has is the flexibility of its program. The university as a whole offers studies in a vast variety of areas. As MBA students we were able to take advantage of this since we could take a number of elective credits in other schools. This allows you to tailor your MBA curriculum toward your own career interests. —**Banking associate**

The administration was very receptive to students. For instance, several times in our second year, several other students and I arranged meetings with the dean on very short or no notice to discuss concerns we had with the school's approach to students from the West Coast. Not only did we meet with the dean, but action was taken and policies were reviewed. In many areas, not all, students are truly treated as consumers, which is about the highest compliment that can be made. —**Banking associate**

The most disappointing aspects were the career services office, the number of interviewing companies, and the school's indifference to the development of computer skills. I would estimate that more than half my graduating class is not proficient in spreadsheet fundamentals.
—**Assistant marketing manager**

6. University of Michigan

School of Business Administration
Ann Arbor, Michigan 48109

Recruiter ranking: 5
Enrollment: 1600
Women: 25%
Foreign: 12%
Minority: 21%
Part-time: 800
Average age: 26
Applicants admitted: 30%
Accepted applicants enrolled: 40%

Graduate ranking: 12
Annual tuition: nonresident—$12,980
         resident—$7136
Room and board: $5040
Average GMAT score: 620
GMAT range: 370 to 770
Average GPA: 3.2
GPA range: 2.0 to 4.0
Average starting pay: $43,976

Application deadline: March 1 for fall

You can easily mistake the University of Michigan's MBA program for one at a private school—in both the quality of the education and the number of bucks you need to fork over to get it. Your tuition bill at Michigan would be the highest of any state school and more than twice that of Indiana and North Carolina, other public universities with top-ranked B-schools. In fact, an out-of-state student at the University of Texas' MBA school pays roughly the same tuition as a resident of Michigan pays here.

Yet, without an Ivy League reputation to fall back on, Michigan couldn't charge top dollar without giving students a lot in return. They receive what is widely recognized as one of the best graduate educational experiences in the country. And MBAs don't waste time waiting in line to use computer workstations or to find a quiet place to study. While many B-schools have outgrown their existing facilities, Michigan recently tripled the size of its school, adding modern classrooms and lecture halls as well as a state-of-the-art computing center and business library.

The seven-building complex housing Michigan's B-school is by no means separate from the university's vibrant academic community. Some people decide to get their MBAs from Michigan simply because they want to be in Ann Arbor, which rivals Cambridge as one of the nation's leading college towns. As long as you don't mind cold weather, it's hard to beat Ann Arbor's combination of big-city culture and small-town charm. Its collegial atmosphere has made it a popular place for entrepreneurs and retirees to settle—so much so that the monthly rents can be steep because construction of new housing hasn't kept pace with demand. Michigan does provide limited housing for MBAs but space fills up quickly. Some students spend nearly as much as New Yorkers for apartment space, up to $800 a month for rent.

Ann Arbor's quaint, village-like atmosphere is far removed from Detroit's gritty, urban character, but Michigan may be the only B-school in the world that sends more MBAs to the car business than to the world of consulting. Last year, 16% of the graduating class drove off into a career with the auto industry. The organization charts at Ford, General Motors, and Chrysler are heavily salted with Michigan grads. Chairman Roger Smith, one of nearly 9000 MBAs at GM, got his MBA from Michigan. Allan D. Gilmour, the man many believe will become the next chairman of Ford, is also a Michigan alum. The school's faculty even boasts an auto historian, David L. Lewis, who is working on a commissioned history of Ford, and an auto industry manufacturing guru, Robert E. Cole. Just last year, students launched an Automotive Industry Club to mix engineering and business students with a penchant for Motor City. Articles on the car business, including a column called "Car Talk," are sprinkled through the pages of *The Monroe Street Journal*, the student-run weekly. One recent issue, noting the twenty-fifth anniversary of Lee Iacocca's Mustang, featured a lengthy historical look at the sporty car.

A Michigan MBA may be the ticket for future auto industry executives, but the B-school downplays its ties to Detroit for fear of being branded a regional program. Dean Gilbert Whitaker is trying to boost Michigan's national standing by emphasizing research and executive education. While such image-building enhances the value of a Michigan degree, some students complain that professors are too busy writing journal articles or teaching executives to give MBAs personalized attention. Whitaker says Michigan MBAs benefit from executive education because it generates revenues for the B-school and exposes faculty and students to real-world problems through contact with executives. As part of its five-year, $15 million construction program, Michigan built a new executive education center, which shares the same building as the computing center, and an executive residence.

Unlike many B-schools, Michigan does not have majors, which makes it ideal for students who do not know exactly what they want to do when they graduate. Although the MBA program prepares students to be generalists, they can specialize in areas such as accounting, finance, marketing and organizational behavior. "Our program is diverse," says Accounting Professor Paul Danos. "You can stay general if you want, but there are many opportunities for specialization. There are plenty of faculty members with in-depth knowledge."

There are 10 courses in Michigan's core curriculum covering quantitative methods, managerial and financial accounting, organizational studies and behavioral sciences, computer techniques, finance, marketing, corporate strategy, operations management, and business economics. Students can waive required courses by exam, allowing them to take additional electives.

At Michigan, you get to choose from more than 130 elective courses—15 each in such areas as accounting, business economics, and organizational behavior. In advanced OB seminars, students prepare cases on corporations involved in dramatic change. Then the corporate executives—from Unisys's Michael Blumenthal to Whirlpool's Jack Sparks—arrive in the class to critique their presentations. "Must" courses that grads highly recommend include Mike Ryan's Industrial Marketing and Susan Chaplinsky's Corporate Financial Policies. Students claim that Allen Spivey actually makes statistics fun.

One of the hottest courses during the 1988–1989 academic year was Failure 101. On the first day of the course, students were required to produce their most outrageous laugh in front of the class. Another assignment was to build something out of Popsicle sticks and sell it on the street in Ann Arbor. The point of these exercises was to teach students how to deal with humiliation and overcome the fear of failing. The course was taught by Jack Matson, an engineering professor at the University of Houston, who won Michigan's Zell-Lurie Competition in the Teaching of Entrepreneurship. The winner of the contest teaches at the B-school for a year and receives relocation expenses, regular salary and benefits, as well as a $25,000 cash prize.

One way Michigan competes with private MBA programs is to draw on the resources of the university as a whole. Business school faculty are encouraged to undertake interdisciplinary research with professors in other parts of the university. Joint degree programs have been established to allow MBA students to specialize in subject areas such as forestry and engineering. In addition, all MBA students can take up to 10 hours in other areas of the university such as the Program in Hospital Administration, the Institute of Public Policy Studies, or the School of Social Work.

Students with an interest in international business can apply to participate in an exchange program with a number of European business schools, which Michigan offers through its membership in the International Management Program. Between two and six Michigan students are chosen for each of the six international schools. They study abroad during the first term of their second year, unless they go to West Germany, where the exchange takes place in the summer between the first and second years. In addition to the European schools, the U of M is exploring exchange programs with B-schools in Asia and Latin America.

Michigan MBAs believe in balancing hard work with lots of social fun. "It's important to have good quality of life while you're going through the hell of business school," says Kathryn Hay-Roe of the Class of 1989. The University of Michigan Business School Association does its best to ensure that B-school students—undergrads, MBAs, and Ph.D.s—have fun. The group might start a semester off with a party at Good Time Charley's, a favorite bar, where B-school students will try to consume as much beer and pizza as possible. Later in the year, Charley's comes to the aid of B-school students by redeeming rejection "ding" letters for beer.

Michigan does not hold classes on Fridays, which students consider to be an advantage over Northwestern's Kellogg School, which gives students Wednesdays off. At the U of M, the weekend starts Thursday night with beers at Dominick's, the unofficial MBA lounge. Pizzeria Uno on South Michigan is famous for its deep-dish pizza and the Brown Jug is the place to go in the wee hours of the morning.

Sports is an obsession at Michigan and MBAs aren't immune to the mania. In the 1988–1989 year, sports frenzy reached an all-time high as the Michigan Wolverines won both the Rose Bowl and the NCAA championship. The UMBSA purchases blocks of tickets so that B-school students can sit together at football and basketball games and sponsors pre-game tailgate parties. Intramural sports, including touch football, team racquetball, soccer, and innertube water polo, are also popular among MBA students.

Like several other B-schools, Michigan has an annual follies where students spoof themselves, their professors, and business in general. The 1989 version featured a skit on the "Wizard of Biz," where Dorothy and Toto got blown out of Kansas by Hurricane Gilbert (also the first name of B-school Dean Whitaker) and landed at the Michigan Business School.

The stereotypical yuppie who wears a Rolex watch and drives a BMW doesn't get a warm welcome at Michigan. "Maybe it's because of the strong liberal tradition at the university itself, but the MBAs here don't like to be perceived as moneygrubbers," says Jeff Jezerc, who graduated in 1989. "They want a job that satisfies them, but they also want a happy life at home. They know the advantage of getting to know people and enjoying life."

Not that they aren't also known for their willingness to roll up their sleeves and get to work, an image most of the Midwestern B-schools cultivate. "The Michigan MBA is willing to work hard to prove himself," says placement director Margaret Carroll. "He doesn't expect the world to be handed to him on a silver platter." Although many students are aggressive, especially when it comes to dominating team projects, they are not prima donnas.

Nor do they tend to be investment bankers. Unlike other top 20 schools such as Wharton, Columbia, and NYU, Michigan is not a magnet for those high-paying, fast-moving jobs. "When Wall Street crashed, there was no hysteria at Michigan," adds Carroll. Many of the school's grads with an interest in finance are more keen to work in the field at General Foods or Ford than at Morgan Stanley or Goldman Sachs. The percentage of Michigan MBAs who found jobs in investment banking peaked at 11% with the Class of 1987.

While there is no well-worn path between Ann Arbor and Wall Street, financial services was the top industry chosen by 1988 graduates of Michigan's MBA program. Nineteen percent of the class found jobs in banking and financial services. One of the big surprises: the re-emergence of manufacturing as the employment area of choice for Michigan MBAs. In 1988, 53% of them headed for work in manufacturing, while 47% got jobs in the service sector.

Although it is a state school, Michigan draws blue-chip corporate recruiters found at Harvard, Stanford, and Wharton. Last year, 500 companies trekked to campus to recruit Michigan MBAs, including Hewlett-Packard, Chase Manhattan Bank, American Airlines, GM, and Ford. A lot of national corporations come to Ann Arbor specifically to hire for their Midwest operations, but then many grads prefer to remain in the Midwest. Maybe that's the reason why Michigan's average starting salary trails all other major schools except Indiana and Rochester. Michigan's prestige and tuition cost may rival that of private schools, but the paychecks of its graduates sure don't.

Contact: Jane Lieberthal, associate director of admissions, 313-763-5796

Prominent alumni: Roger Smith, chairman of General Motors Corp.; Roger Fridholm, president of The Stroh Brewery Co.; Philip L. Smith, former president of General Foods Corp.; Thomas F. Keller, dean of the Fuqua School of Business, Duke University; L. William Seidman, chairman of the Federal Deposit Insurance Corp.; Martha R. Seger, member of the Board of Governors of the Federal Reserve System; L. D. Thomas, president of Amoco Oil Co.

Michigan MBAs sound off

*Everything in the program has been well thought out and works very well. The number one objective of the U of M Business School is to upgrade its reputation. It is working very aggressively on several areas: physical facilities, executive education, placement, research, etc. Overall, this has a positive effect on the MBA program, but the current students sometimes question the benefits to them that some of these actions provide—research focus at the expense of teaching, the executive education program drawing off much of the school's top talent, etc.—**Product planning analyst**

The atmosphere, ethos, and course content of the business school is heavily biased toward the corporate sector. Although there may be sound strategic reasons for this policy, its emphasis upon eventual employment with large*

multinational firms tends to ignore the entrepreneurial and small-enterprise nature of U.S. society. The large "corporate-world refugee" faction of the class is particularly conscious of this tacit attitude.
—Management consultant

*Michigan has a very good mix of teaching methods and extremely good facilities. Unfortunately, the faculty is rewarded based on research and publishing and consequently put a lot of their efforts in that direction. The executive education program also steals some of the best faculty away from the full-time MBA program. Otherwise, I am extremely satisfied with the program.—**Career path unknown***

*Michigan is a very geographically centered school. The majority of students came from the Midwest and took jobs in the Midwest when they graduated. Likewise, the majority of firms that recruit on campus are from the Midwest and the national firms recruit for their Midwest offices. For students desiring to move to the East or West Coasts upon graduation, Michigan may not be a great choice. Even though it is a "Top 10" business school, it lacks the recognition that the other schools have, especially on the two coasts.—**Systems analyst***

*My goal was a career in finance or marketing with a basic manufacturing or high-tech firm. I selected Michigan because I felt that it would meet those expectations and I was not disappointed. Some of my classmates, seeking Wall Street or East Coast consulting jobs, were disappointed that Michigan did not fit their needs for these jobs. Great jobs with great salaries were available if you worked hard for grades and interviews. However, some people viewed business school as a pass-through process, with the degree as the more important goal rather than development of long-term career goals. A running joke at Michigan is "twenty Bs for fifty Gs." It tends to sum up the attitudes of some.—**Marketing intern***

The U of M is very heavily weighted with people either working for car companies or people who had quit one to go to school. This led to too many GM-mindset types in class, which was pretty frustrating at times. It's interesting I should say this, especially in light of the fact that I chose GM!
—Product planning analyst

7. University of Virginia

Darden Graduate School of Business Administration
P.O. Box 6550
Charlottesville, Virginia 22906

Recruiter ranking: 14
Enrollment: 476
Women: 26%
Foreign: 11%
Minority: 12%
Part-time: None
Average age: 26.5
Applicants admitted: 20%
Accepted applicants enrolled: 50%

Graduate ranking: 4
Annual tuition: nonresident—$10,120
             resident—$4640
Annual room and board: $6000
Average GMAT score: 630
GMAT range: 540 to 700 (80% of class)
Average GPA: 3.2
GPA range: 2.3 to 4.0
Average starting pay: $50,554

Application deadline: March 15 for fall

The telephone call came from an applicant who had the enviable distinction of being accepted to both the Harvard Business School and the University of Virginia's Darden School of Business. Over the years, Darden Dean John W. Rosenblum has become accustomed to such calls. But this one was unusually blunt.

"Tell me why I would even want to go to Virginia," the caller challenged.

"Why don't you call John McArthur (Harvard's dean) and ask him the same question," Rosenblum retorted.

"He won't answer the phone," the applicant complained.

"Well, there's one big difference.".

There are a lot of other differences as well. Like Harvard, Darden is a "case study" school that offers graduates a general management education. But it's also a dramatically different place, with a culture far removed from that of Harvard. The differences start with the intimacy that allows an applicant or a student immediate access to Dean Rosenblum. While most MBAs have little if anything to say about the deans of their schools, Rosenblum gets high marks from them for his candor and availability. "He is not only a great educator, but a spirited leader who serves as a true role model for us," remarks one student.

You'll find Rosenblum every weekday morning at 9:30, along with the entire faculty and student body, in the lobby of the B-school building where everyone meets for coffee and talk. When you attend one of the core courses, you'll find yourself in a class with 60 students—a full third smaller than Harvard's classes. Students obviously get more "air time" to voice their opinions in class. With class discussion accounting for 50% of your grade, that's a critical consideration. It's also possible to know most fellow students in a class of 240—not really in the cards in a Harvard class of 790.

At Darden, you're also less likely to be the victim of a "chip shot"—a cutting remark by a classmate made to score points with a professor. "When it happens, you'll see someone swinging an imaginary golf club to make it clear to everyone that it was a chip shot," says Richard M. Paschal, of the Class of 1989. Without Harvard's forced grading curve, there's no disadvantage in contributing to the learning of a classmate. People actually speak of a "Darden community."

The Charlottesville area doesn't come close to offering the cultural attractions of

Boston, but it's a quaint and rich environment. As part of the University of Virginia, Darden is an academic village in the country. Looming in the background are the foothills of the Blue Ridge Mountains and the Shenandoah Valley—land idyllic enough to attract a slew of "Beautiful People" from actress Jessica Lange to Sissy Spacek. MBAs go to The Barracks, a popular stable about five miles from the grounds, for horseback riding in the mountains.

Within view of the campus is Thomas Jefferson's Monticello, an architectural masterpiece that greatly influenced the look of most of the university buildings. Within this classic environment is the Darden School—a rectangular three-story building that some say looks like a modern textile mill. Across a tree-lined courtyard sits the university's law school.

More subtle differences between Harvard and Darden exist in the curriculum. There's more of a programmed feel to Darden's curriculum. "Our courses go for three weeks, stop, come back for another three weeks," says Rosenblum. "It's more of an integrated, shuffled deck kind of experience. There's a flow of learning that goes through the core curriculum." Academics have another name for it: a "lock-step program." Translation: one that is less flexible and more rigid. You can't waive out of any of the core courses. CPAs must sit through accounting; manufacturing types must attend the first-level operations class. The first year contains 10 required courses, including what is likely the only graded, 20-session class in ethics at a major school. There's also a course in written and oral communication in which students must make eight speeches to small groups, write business memos, and learn group presentation skills.

While most B-schools are still grappling with how to incorporate ethics into their programs, Darden is a pioneer in the field. In addition to the required course in ethics for MBAs, it blends the subject into courses in accounting, marketing, and operations. A 20-year-old Center for the Study of Applied Ethics also creates teaching materials, tracks scholarship in business ethics, and sponsors seminars in the subject for executives.

In the second year, there are three more required courses, including an independent research project with an assigned faculty member. Students get to choose from more than 45 electives as well. Best bets? Grads strongly recommend Sherwood Frey's Bargaining and Negotiation, R. Edward Freeman's Great Books in Management, Brandt R. Allen's Management Accounting and Control and Derek A. Newton's Sales Force Management. Animated and dynamic, Frey makes negotiation among classmates 40% of your grade. Freeman, a black-bearded man with a penchant for the satirical, extracts managerial lessons and styles from such farflung books as *The Great Gatsby* and *Madame Bovary*. Allen makes numbers easy for nonaccountants, while Newton's course is always oversubscribed.

There's another surprising difference between Harvard and Virginia: Darden is probably tougher. Indeed, its graduates rated the school's program the toughest of them all in the BW survey. So intense is the experience in the first year that 65 to 80 hours of study per week is the norm. Students who routinely got As as undergraduates found it difficult to achieve top grades at Darden. "The workload reaches a point at which students are unable to give anymore due to exhaustion and burn-out," says a Darden student. "At the overload point, the relationship between effort and learning breaks down and students are merely going through the motions."

One result: between 5% and 8% of those who enroll in the program fail to complete it. That's the highest attrition rate of any major prestige school. Many of those who survive the grueling pace, however, remain enthusiastic about their educational experience. The frenetic first-year workload brings people together like nothing can. And there is a sense of having survived the near impossible that makes Darden grads think they can climb any corporate mountaintop.

Not that this is a "survival of the fittest" culture. Students get help—and lots of it. When candidates are admitted to Darden, the admissions staff might suggest an accounting or statistics course over the summer. The school also invites some students to Darden a week before classes for tutorials and seminars designed to ease the transition. For international students, there's a special orientation week to help them bone up on English and debating skills—bonus: a trip to an American supermarket. On day one, second-year students guide group discussions of case studies to show the newcomers how it is done. On the first weekend, all students and faculty gather for a schoolwide picnic to get to know one another. Rosenblum hosts students at a series of four receptions in his home during the first month of school. Every Darden student is assigned a faculty advisor and a big brother or sister.

Sensitive to complaints that the first year amounts to academic "boot camp," Rosenblum has made several recent alterations. First-year students will now prepare 25 fewer cases than earlier classes. And they won't have to endure Saturday exams or Saturday deadlines for turning in papers for the required communications course. Not too many years ago, Darden actually held classes on Saturdays, as well.

When in the classroom, students aren't likely to find too many bumbling professors. The quality of the teaching here is superb, partly because the culture demands it. Says Freeman, a winner of several teaching awards: "You could be the best researcher in the world, but you can't get tenure here if you aren't a good teacher. Teaching is equally important or maybe more important than research at Virginia."

The case study approach to learning often requires excellent teaching to work. Few Darden grads have any misgivings about having gone through a case study school, though some think the school's commitment to one teaching method is limiting. Typically, students must prepare for three different case discussions every class day—except Wednesday, when they have two. Truth is, Darden students are likely to find that case study teaching doesn't take 100% of class time. The first half of an accounting course may even look a lot like one taught at Chicago, which boasts more traditional teaching methods. "If you did an analysis of the percentage of classroom hours that were case-oriented at Chicago, you'd probably find it to be 30% of the class hours," figures Rosenblum. "At Darden, it would be 70%." Even so, some graduates say that the shy are likely to have trouble here.

Some administrators describe Darden as "the liberal arts school of the B-school world" because it values a multidisciplinary approach to learning. "We have teachers from the arts and sciences, from education and from the law school, and all of them are welcome here," says Karen O. Dowd, director of placement. Students armed with undergraduate degrees in liberal arts account for roughly 30% of Darden MBAs. (In contrast, only 7% of the MBAs at Carnegie-Mellon hold a liberal arts degree.)

Among several joint-degree programs, Darden boasts a unique MBA/MA in Asian Studies that can be earned in three years. The program features customized foreign language courses and six months of independent study in either Japan or a Chinese-speaking country. One major caveat: that third year adds another $30,000 to the cost of the regular MBA program. Darden hopes to launch similar programs in Europe and Latin America over the next couple of years.

When these joint-program MBAs return to campus, they're likely to bemoan the quality of the food in the cafeteria next to the B-school, jokingly dubbed "Café Death." All the more reason, MBAs say, to order a pizza from Pizza Movers in Charlottesville, winners of the marketing club's "Brand Challenge" in 1988. When Darden MBAs work up a thirst, they're apt to stroll down to Sloan's, the bar of choice only a three-minute walk from school.

Most MBAs live in private housing within walking distance of the university because Darden lacks dormitory facilities. In Charlottesville, you can still rent a spacious two-bedroom apartment for little more than $400 a month. Some MBAs even live out in the country in cabins during their second year. Students' working spouses may find it rough to get a job in town. Sure, Pizza Movers's ads in *The Darden News*, one of the better MBA newspapers, offer delivery–driving jobs that earn up to $12 an hour, but the professional opportunities that would exist in New York, Boston, or Chicago simply aren't there.

On the other hand, there is a greater sense of camaraderie among students, spouses, and faculty than is possible at a large urban school. Professors and students team up to play on intramural sports squads, even fielding a softball team, the "Darden Old Guys," in the Charlottesville town league. Every Friday at 5, MBAs trek to the Graduate Happy Hour that brings together 300 to 500 graduate students from all over the university. The social event of the second semester is clearly the "B-bar Ball"—so named for the B minus grade students must gain to avoid probation. (If you get three C grades in the first year, you're on probation.)

Darden may be the only B-school in which recruiting companies outnumber job-seeking graduates. In 1989, 218 companies conducted 4243 interviews on campus with only 204 second-year students. Another 200 jobs were available via correspondence—which accounts for 7% of all Darden placements. Last year Digital Equipment Corp. pulled six Darden MBAs off the grounds. General Motors Corp. and Trammell Crow got five each, while American Express, Arthur Andersen, and Chemical Bank each took four.

These big companies know a Darden grad when they see one. As Paschal notes, "If you interview with a major corporation, you're fine. But if you're interviewing with smaller companies in places west of the Mississippi, Darden is an unknown commodity. People don't know the name and they lump Darden in with a thousand other MBA programs across the country."

What Darden obviously lacks is Harvard's greater brand-name identity, its vastly larger alumni network, and its diversity. That might be why Rosenblum wasn't able to convince the applicant on the phone to pick Darden over Harvard. But could he be the same student who told BUSINESS WEEK that the only time he saw Harvard's dean was at graduation?

Contact: Rosalyn Berne, director of admissions, 800-UVA-MBA1 or 804-924-7281

Prominent alumni: E. Thayer Bigelow, Jr., president of HBO; Terrence D. Daniels, vice chairman of W.R. Grace & Co.; George David, CEO of Otis Elevator Co.; Steven S. Reinemund, CEO of Pizza Hut Inc.; Linwood A. Lacey, Jr., chairman of Micro D Inc.; Betty Sue Peabody, president of Mellon Bank (East); S. Waite Rawls III, vice chairman of Continental Illinois Corp.; Thomas A. Saunders, III, managing director of Morgan Stanley

Darden MBAs sound off

*The Darden school, by reputation, may be the most demanding B-school of the best ones. I admit that although my undergraduate program was rigorous, I was unprepared for Darden's work load. The program is best suited to nonbusiness undergraduate majors. It offers no opportunity to use undergrad classes to get out of required classes. At Darden, surviving the first year is a certification of quality from the faculty. Although the program is very high-pressure, students were very cooperative as opposed to what I saw when visiting Harvard.—**Corporate product manager***

*The Darden experience will be a highlight of my life. It is hard to describe how strongly I feel about the people I have come to call friends, the professors who helped shape my thoughts, and the school and its ongoing mission.—**Bank vice president***

Darden is renowned for the extreme level of hard work demanded. We affectionately call it "Parris Island MBA" (after the famous Marine boot camp in South Carolina). The first year was especially grueling. But the faculty was also aware of the extreme pressure we were facing. They were supportive, even when we weren't quite as prepared for class as we should have been. They were always there to listen or help. Overall, Darden is unique among the top-tier management schools in its emphasis on both high individual performance and team process. The culture of Darden is quite unlike the other top schools, in that the atmosphere is one of support and mutual survival. Backstabbing is not tolerated by either students or the faculty. Honorable excellence is the emphasis here.
*—**Marketing consultant***

*After all the work, it's discouraging to return to the West Coast where not many have heard of the Darden school and its rigorous program. Often it is equated with less rigorous programs by those who are, quite simply, not in the know.—**Unknown career path***

*My two years at the Darden school have resulted in a quantum leap in my understanding and analysis of situations. I now look at life, not just business, on what I feel is a much higher level of understanding. I was pleasantly surprised by the amount of help my degree has been in my immediate position out of school. I find I use many of the skills gained at Darden everyday on the job.—**Corporate product manager***

*The case study method is the only way to go. By placing students in "real-life" situations, cases make learning a more practical experience that students respond to much more energetically. If I had to endure two years of lecture, I would have slept through the entire period. On the work load: Nobody works harder than Darden students in their first year of B-school! If you don't believe it, I challenge you to try it yourself. I liken the first-year work load to fraternity hazing. By sharing in common (often humiliating) experiences, students are drawn much closer and lasting relationships evolve.—**Corporate marketing manager***

8. University of North Carolina

Graduate School of Business Administration
Carroll Hall
Chapel Hill, North Carolina 27599

Recruiter ranking: 19
Enrollment: 400
Women: 35%
Foreign: 10%
Minority: 8%
Part-time: 91
Average age: 26
Applicants admitted: 25%
Accepted applicants enrolled: 51%

Graduate ranking: 2
Annual tuition: nonresident—$4900
resident—$980
Room and board: $5000
Average GMAT score: 605
GMAT range: 500 to 780
Average GPA: 3.3
GPA range: 2.5 to 4.0
Average starting pay: $44,941

Application deadline: March 1 for fall

When NCNB Chairman Hugh L. McColl Jr. came to speak at the University of North Carolina's B-school, MBA student John Hill picked him up at the airport and acted as host during McColl's visit to his alma mater. Hill's stint as tour guide led to a job as McColl's personal assistant during the summer of 1988 at the Charlotte-based superregional bank. When Hill graduated a year later, he was offered a permanent position at NCNB, but turned it down to work for Morgan Stanley & Co.

Not every North Carolina MBA student gets an exciting summer internship and lands a blue chip job on Wall Street, but the school's small class size of 200 gives students access to lots of top executives when they visit. And more executives are coming to North Carolina's Chapel Hill campus, thanks to Dean Paul Rizzo, former IBM vice chairman.

Some of the friends and business contacts Rizzo made during his 30-year career with Big Blue have been taking an active interest in North Carolina's B-school since he joined in 1987. IBM Chairman John F. Akers and Vice Chairman Kaspar V. Cassani came down for the school's 1988–1989 International Executive Series of lectures, as did S. Parker Gilbert, chairman of Morgan Stanley, where Rizzo is a board member. After being named dean, Rizzo formed a high-powered board of visitors that includes several of the nation's leading executives, including both McColl and Cassani.

Their involvement is good news for anyone wanting to come to North Carolina. Although Chapel Hill is renowned for undergraduate liberal arts education and basketball, the MBA program had been little heard of outside the Southeast. Former dean, John Evans, concentrated on internal developments, beefing up the quality of faculty and curriculum and boosting the academic research. Rizzo's focus has been more external. He's trying to bring an international flavor to the MBA program and enhance the school's image among prospective students and corporations. Despite its relative anonymity away from the Eastern Seaboard, North Carolina offers quality education at a bargain-basement price. At $4900 a year, its tuition for out-of-state residents is the lowest of any Top 20 school, while an MBA for state residents is a steal at $980 a year.

True, not many outside the Southeast would mention North Carolina in the same breath as MIT or Berkeley, but they will in the future if Rizzo's efforts are successful.

The three schools have a few things in common. For one thing, they all stand in the shadow of another prominent B-school. MIT plays second fiddle to Harvard while Berkeley tries to catch up to Stanford. North Carolina students suffer an inferiority complex in relation to their brethren at Duke, a highly respected private university that has invested heavily in the Fuqua School of Business. A management degree from MIT's Sloan School also is a ticket to a job in one of many high-tech firms clustered along Route 128 in Boston. Likewise, getting an MBA from Stanford is a surefire way to end up working at Apple Computer, Sun Microsystems, or one of dozens of other Silicon Valley startups. Like MIT and Berkeley, North Carolina's B-school also has a high-tech connection. Together with Duke and North Carolina State, North Carolina is part of Research Triangle, home to R&D and manufacturing facilities operated by IBM, GE, DEC, Mitsubishi, Burroughs Wellcome, and Glaxo. The state capital in nearby Raleigh brings government together with academia and business in Research Triangle.

Chapel Hill doesn't measure up to Cambridge, Ann Arbor, or Berkeley when it comes to diversity of people, restaurants, and political views, but it's still one of the nicest college towns in the country. Where else can you play golf 10 months of the year? B-school students plop down $7 to play 18 holes at North Carolina's Finley golf course. When they really want to splurge, they head over to Duke's course, which costs $18. If a fast-paced, demanding lifestyle is what you're after, better head off to a school in New York or Los Angeles. Life in the Southeast is more relaxed.

Research Triangle provides a stimulating, yet practical, environment for a B-school. North Carolina has traditionally been recognized for its marketing and finance departments, but its operations management area has been coming on strong the last few years. In addition to reading about new production techniques in a textbook, North Carolina MBA students can see them first-hand at nearby manufacturing facilities. An operations class recently visited the assembly line for IBM PS/2 personal computers to glimpse state-of-the-art American manufacturing. "We try to assign projects on issues such as just-in-time inventory and flexible manufacturing that are being faced by companies in the area," says William Perreault, associate dean of academic affairs.

Having major development and manufacturing activities in its backyard and the former vice chairman of IBM as its dean makes North Carolina particularly sensitive to the needs of business. Rizzo believes that "education needs to be more supportive of the business environment." Like several other B-school deans, he says that B-schools must prepare students to manage in competitive, global markets where the United States is no longer the dominant power.

One way North Carolina exposes students to international business is through the $8 million Kenan Institute of Private Enterprise, which brings together business, academic, and government leaders. Along with the B-school, the Kenan Institute co-sponsors an international executive lecture series and an executives-in-residence program. The head of the food and agriculture department at the Soviet Union's Academy of Sciences and the managing director of McKinsey and Company's Tokyo office were among the foreign speakers the Kenan Institute brought to Chapel Hill in 1988–1989. The institute also bankrolls five research centers spanning competitiveness and employment growth, international marketing, manufacturing excellence, human resources, and management and financial services.

Given Rizzo's background, you know that computers are widely used in MBA classwork, and all students are expected to be computer-literate on the first day of class. But there also exists an appreciation for liberal arts rarely found at a B-school. Part of this is due to the university's strong liberal arts tradition and part of it is due to Rizzo, a self-described "liberal arts bigot" who earned a bachelor's degree in business administration. Rizzo says that liberal arts provides a better preparation for managers than specialized technical training, which quickly becomes outdated in a rapidly changing business environment. More than 50% of North Carolina's MBA students majored in liberal arts as undergrads. Rizzo's goal for all students is to train managers whose responsibilities cut across functional areas.

During the first year of North Carolina's MBA program, everyone is required to take all 13 courses in the core curriculum regardless of previous academic or professional experience. This means that a certified public accountant must take introductory accounting. That may not sound too appealing to those with specialized training, but it guarantees everyone gets the benefit of one another's knowledge, too. It also goes hand in hand with North Carolina's team approach, which relies heavily on the case study method and class presentations. You'll also take a required communications course in the first year to hone written and oral skills.

At the beginning of the first year, students are assigned to study groups and asked to remain together even if personality conflicts emerge. The idea is to replicate the real world, where people with different levels of knowledge and experience are forced to work together whether they like each other or not. "If we didn't require everyone to jump through the same hoops, we'd lose the benefit of our team-oriented study approach," says Howard Rockness, director of the MBA program. "If we allowed people to opt out of organizational behavior or accounting, we'd be interfering with the philosophy that we build on people's strengths."

In the first year, you'll find yourself in a sequence of courses that start and stop at different intervals during a semester. "Students might start out with a course that is not necessarily a whole semester introducing them to accounting and also take Issues in Organizational Behavior, concurrent with that," Perreault says. "Halfway through the semester, they'll pick up a marketing course. It's an integration in terms of sequencing of components and developmental learning." The capstone of the first year is a course called Integrative Management, which brings together finance, marketing, operations management and quantitative methods.

During the second year, MBA students take four electives in a concentrated area of study. You can pick from an array of 67 elective courses. Whatever you choose, don't miss Gerry Bell's Power, Politics, and Leadership, which teaches students how to learn from their failures. Robert Eisenbeis wins plaudits for the way he weaves theory and current events such as the savings-and-loan insolvency crisis into his Regulation of Financial Institutions class. In his Futures and Options course, Richard Rendleman simplifies complicated trading strategies and explains why some of them work and others don't. If you're interested in operations management, don't leave Chapel Hill without having spent a semester in class with Bill Bearry, who wins praise for dynamically teaching the nitty gritty of operations.

North Carolina isn't as well-positioned geographically to draw foreign students and faculty as B-schools in New York and California, but Rizzo is committed to boosting the international content of the program. Whenever possible, international cases are being added to the curriculum and the school is selecting more students who can speak one or more foreign languages. North Carolina currently has an exchange program with the University of Manchester in Britain and is working to develop others with the London Business School and Insead in France. Rizzo is also encouraging faculty to take teaching assignments in foreign B-schools so they can start developing a global perspective.

Despite the perception that life in Chapel Hill is laid back, the MBA program is fairly demanding. But when they take a break from their studies, students here like to play intramural sports and take in a Tar Heels basketball game. First-year students wend their way to He's Not Here—even though the bar's name fails to acknowledge that women make up 35% of North Carolina's enrollment. In the second year, students tend to move on to Spanky's. The Spring Garden Bar and Grill is famous in these parts for its cheddar burgers.

North Carolina's dirt-cheap tuition, integrated curriculum, and quality of life wins high marks from students, who rate it No. 2 in the BUSINESS WEEK survey. But to remain a highly ranked B-school, North Carolina needs to invest in its physical plant. Carroll Hall, which houses both graduate and undergraduate business students, was built 20 years ago and is overcrowded. The facilities are merely "adequate," says John Hill of the Class of 1989, "but what we really need is a new building like Fuqua has at Duke." Rizzo is lobbying the state legislature for $15 million for a new building, but he's not holding his breath. He has used the occasion of the university's two-hundredth anniversary to kick off a major fund-raising campaign for the new building, more faculty and staff, and a substantial increase in the endowment.

Facilities aren't the only area where North Carolina is hurting. Students say the placement office needs to do a better job of attracting corporations to recruit on campus. Since more than 50% of graduates remain in the Southeast, corporations without operations in the region are reluctant to recruit here. Fortunately for grads who do not leave the state—about 33% of the total—there is steady demand for MBAs within Research Triangle and in the region's booming financial services industry. Nearly 35% of North Carolina MBAs find jobs in finance and many end up at NCNB, First Union National Bank, or First Wachovia Corporation, all aggressive superregional banks. Very few grads find jobs on Wall Street, which is one reason why the average starting salary for a North Carolina grad is a modest $44,941. In addition to financial services, marketing and consulting are the two other popular career choices of North Carolina MBAs.

North Carolina's small class size can also be a disadvantage in the recruiting sweepstakes. The number of companies recruiting at Chapel Hill—145—is only 55 less than the number of students in a single graduating class. To help make it worthwhile for companies to visit Research Triangle, North Carolina has been working with Duke to encourage corporations to recruit at both schools. That strategy has one drawback—it could lead to fights between the two schools over whose students get to pick executives up at the airport.

Contact: Ms. Anne-Marie Summers, director of admissions, CB #3490, Carroll Hall, 919-962-3237

Prominent alumni: Paul Fulton, president of Sara Lee Corp.; Richard H. Jenrette, chairman of The Equitable; Hugh L. McColl, Jr., chairman of NCNB Corp., Frank H. Dunn, Jr., president of First Union National Bank; Doug Martin, president of Tupperware

North Carolina MBAs sound off

*Unlike many programs, Carolina strives for balance. There are no letter grades. Most work is done in groups and you must work with others to survive and be successful. The MBA is the school's flagship degree and gets the best professors and resources. Unfortunately, it is a well-kept secret in many ways because our graduates tend to want to stay in the Southeast. In addition, our salaries are lower since we send so few grads to Wall Street.—**Territory manager for oil company**

*Overall, I am extremely pleased with my graduate education. Key factors include: emphasis on teamwork versus individual "stars," strong faculty with good student–faculty interaction, integrative curriculum (analytical, case analysis, comprehensive projects). Negatives include: placement office too small to effectively handle the number of students seeking job hunt assistance, especially during the first year.—**Marketing assistant**

*Overall, UNC has an excellent MBA program. The weak points include placement and external relations—the school does not do enough to sell itself. One point I feel is worth making is that UNC's teamwork approach is excellent training for the real world.—**Financial associate**

*The University of North Carolina is the best education for the dollar in the country. The quality of living in Chapel Hill is unsurpassed. My only regret is its poor placement services. However, that didn't stop me from getting a job on Wall Street even after the crash.—**Institutional sales associate**

*The program is underrated. The school pays a price for its insistence on several years of work experience in the majority of its students. But the payoff is impressive. The almost mandatory study–work groups (four to six students) to which you are assigned on the first day are a balance of experience, age, gender, and geographic location.—**Associate attorney**

*The integrative management courses in first and second year were great because they focused on a business as a whole and also looked at current events. I wish there were better facilities and a stronger administrative structure. If you had a problem it wasn't always clear who to talk to and how effective that person would be. The new dean may improve this area, but I got the impression he was not very accessible or visible to students, at least during his first year at Carolina.—**Attorney**

9. Stanford University

Graduate School of Business
Stanford, California 94305

Recruiter ranking: 7	*Graduate ranking:* 8
Enrollment: 654	*Annual tuition:* $14,094
Women: 27%	*Annual fees:* $1100
Foreign: 19%	*Room and board:* $8200
Minority: 11%	*Average GMAT score:* NA
Part-time: None	*GMAT range:* NA
Average age: 27	*Average GPA:* NA
Applicants admitted: 10.4%	*GPA range:* NA
Applicants accepted enrolled: 80%	*Average starting pay:* $65,176

Application deadline: March 28 for fall

Tucked in one corner, a beat-up jukebox blares out Aretha Franklin's "Respect." Silver duct tape seals the gashes in the bar stools. Black-painted plywood protects the windows when the crowd becomes unruly. Neon beer signs light the outside sidewalk, flashing the names Strohs, Michelob, and Miller into the busy street.

You'd expect to see a lineup of motorcycles outside the Old Pro on El Camino Real in Palo Alto. But on Tuesday nights, MBAs from the most selective B-school in the country, the same MBAs that draw the highest starting salaries in business, take over the joint. They even call the place Arjay's, after former B-school dean Arjay Miller, who lifted the school to number one in some rankings during his tenure.

Forsaking the myriad Yuppie bars of Silicon Valley for this watering hole tells you something about Stanford MBAs. They reflect the unique personality of the institution they attend: Not nearly as vocational as Harvard. Not nearly as theoretical as Chicago. Not nearly as specialized as Wharton.

Stanford is a pure and unadulterated general management program. No single group of faculty overwhelmingly dominates others. With the exception of health care, Stanford has resisted industry-funded centers of research, too, partly because they encourage specialization. "If I had enough money, I bet you I could find a business school that would produce a degree in the management of shoe shops," jokes James E. Howell, demonstrating his skepticism about the research centers so popular at other B-schools such as Wharton.

Yes, Stanford is different. The students are more cooperative than competitive, known for their diversity instead of their sameness. There's no grading curve at Stanford, and grades aren't publicly posted, either. Only at graduation is the top 10% of the class announced. The classes are smaller, too. And its location in California lends to its different approach. "There's an informality at Stanford," says Jeffrey Pfeffer, one of the most popular professors here. "It's partly the difference between the West and the East. And one of the caps on our enrollment is that our biggest classrooms hold only 66 people."

Students often refer to the campus as the farm—a throwback to when the campus was indeed a farm and racehorse-breeding ranch a century ago. Stanford boasts one of the most handsome campuses in the country. The B-school is housed in a four-story building in the center of Stanford's 8200-acre campus. It's a modern anomaly among the campus's arcaded quadrangles of Spanish-style buildings topped by red tile roofs. The newly opened three-story Littlefield Center, more in keeping with Stanford's architecture, houses the school's faculty. Not far off from the B-school looms the university's charming trademark, the Hoover Tower.

One in five Stanford MBAs turned down Harvard to come here and study amid the redwoods and palm trees. While they'll attend one of the best B-schools in the world, the program lacks the flexibility of many schools, including Wharton and Kellogg. Students can't waive any of the 13 required core courses. They're also required to take 14 electives. But without a requirement to major or specialize in any given field, students are free to take elective courses anywhere they want. In the 1988–1989 year, more than 20% of the MBAs enrolled in foreign language courses at the university. Mostly, however, they select from the B-school's own novel array of electives from Japanese Marketing to Managing Strategic Alliances. Stanford is known for innovating some of the most topical course offerings in business—more than half of the roughly 100 MBA electives are new every five years, including several of the 11 electives on international topics.

Many of these classes percolate from faculty research—in recent years, a rather sensitive subject at Stanford. The school seeks, in the words of Dean Robert Jaedicke, "balanced excellence" in teaching and reasearch—a balance that has proved elusive. Many grads say the scale is heavily tipped toward research at the expense of teaching. In 1988, Jaedicke, known as "Cowboy Bob" because his summers are spent herding cattle on a Montana ranch, absorbed a broadside of newspaper articles and other complaints from students unhappy about the quality of teaching in core courses.

One graduate described one of the key classes as "an indecipherable mishmash of confused thoughts; haphazardly taught and deathly dull." Some students said the teaching was so bad in one core class that they began walking out on the professor, migrating to another class on the same subject taught by a better teacher.

The complaints became so loud that Jaedicke felt compelled to publicly address the students on the issue. He also formed a task force to deal with the gripes, and Stanford has even put together a videotape of the do's and don'ts of effective teaching to help some lackluster teachers. For his part, Jaedicke pooh-poohs the ruckus. "I always want them to perceive that the teaching isn't as great as it should be," he says. "If they weren't saying that, I'd be afraid there wasn't enough innovative research going on."

Remarks like that, however, have given Jaedicke a reputation for being unresponsive to student concerns. The complaints carried over into 1989 when student leaders again maintained that the administration wasn't doing enough about the problem. The MBA association even launched a monthly teaching award to recognize the excellent professors and indirectly put pressure on the duds. Jaedicke has decided to resign as dean by August 31, 1990, or sooner if a successor can be found before then.

Stanford's sure bets? Any course by Richard Pascale or Jeffrey Pfeffer, two of the most dynamic teachers on the faculty. Creativity in Business, an exceptionally good team-taught course by Lorna Catford and James Collins, comes highly recommended. The course has been described as a study in self-introspection. H. Irving Grousbeck's Entrepreneurship: Forming New Ventures won him a distinguished teaching award from students. Said one: "He personifies the model businessman: He is intelligent, fair, ethical, and practical." Also winning plaudits are G. Peter Wilson and George Foster for, of all things, accounting. "Anyone who can keep you interested and involved in that subject at 4:30 p.m. on a Friday . . . may be a walking miracle," noted one grad on Wilson.

MBAs also have good things to say about Stanford's Public Management Program, perhaps the only real rival to Yale University's well-known program in public service. Designed for MBAs interested in the public and nonprofit sectors, the program attracted more than 100 students in 1988. MBAs seeking a PMP certificate must complete the regular B-school core, plus three public management courses from among 20 electives in the field. The emphasis on public management has another unusual twist: MBAs who land lucrative corporate internships over the summer months often pledge to donate some of their earnings to help subsidize classmates who work for nonprofit groups. There's also a loan-forgiveness program for students who take jobs in the public sector after graduation.

Many students enrolled in the program aren't headed for permanent jobs in the nonprofit arena, but want a sense of public policy issues. "This is a business school, after all," says James Thompson, the program's director. "The proof is not what they'll do immediately after getting the MBA. People will go to McKinsey or Hewlett-Packard and after a few years they may go to the nonprofits." In 1988, only 2% of the class assumed public service jobs directly out of school—half as many as did a year earlier.

The Wall Street crash had a greater effect on Stanford than most B-schools. MBAs who took investment banking jobs in 1988 fell to 8% from 21% a year earlier. Consulting supplanted the I-banks, taking the biggest share of Stanford MBAs by enticing one out of five students into their business. McKinsey & Company alone hired 16 MBAs, Bain & Company took 12, Booz Allen 8, and Boston Consulting Group 6. Other top recruiters included Hewlett-Packard (7), Apple Computer and Tandem Computers (4 each), Microsoft and Sun Microsystems (3 each). You'd have a difficult time picking a better B-school to penetrate one of Silicon Valley's high-tech companies.

Given Stanford's location, technology looms large. Many of the visiting speakers hail from the world of high tech, from Next CEO and Apple founder Steve Jobs to Intel's Andrew Grove. Many valley entrepreneurs make their way into the classrooms for lectures and discussions. Nearly 100 students spent the 1988 spring break touring electronics factories in Taiwan.

Stanford MBAs also engage in a broad range of extracurricular activities, from raising funds for the homeless to competing in every sport from dart throwing to soccer. Besides the Tuesday night ritual at Arjay's, Stanford MBAs enjoy Compadres for Mexican fare, though they clearly prefer the margaritas at Casa Real. For a pleasant dinner, especially when someone else is picking up the tab, MacArthur Park in downtown Palo Alto is hard to beat.

All the B-school news fit to print can be found in the biweekly *Reporter*, one of the better MBA newspapers around. Its attempts to publish humor sometimes rattle students and faculty alike. The newspaper generated a storm of howls in 1989 when a columnist jokingly referred to one of his professors as a "Julio Iglesias from some Third World country that can't even pay the interest on its debt."

Of course, Stanford MBAs tend to be passionate about things—whether it's the quality of the teaching, the wit in the student newspaper, or when someone threatens school rituals and traditions. A stir of sorts was caused in late 1988 when a group of first-year students brought a birthday cake to Arjay's to celebrate a classmate's birthday. The group even disrupted the Buddy Holly on the jukebox with a ragged rendition of "Happy Birthday." "What's next?" complained a second-year MBA. "Before you know it, Old Pro will begin serving potato skins and fried zucchini instead of peanuts. What will we throw on the floor then?"

Contact: Karen Nierenberg, director of admissions, 415-723-2766

Prominent alumni: David S. Tappan, Jr., CEO of Fluor; Donald E. Petersen, CEO of Ford Motor; H. Brewster Atwater, chairman of General Mills; John Young, CEO of Hewlett-Packard; David W. Kemper, CEO of Commerce Bancshares; Daniel C. Ferguson, CEO of Newell; Lloyd P. Johnson, CEO of Norwest; Scott G. McNealy, CEO of Sun Microsystems; James G. Treybig, CEO of Tandem Computers

Stanford MBAs sound off

*A decade of on-the-job training was packed into two years at Stanford. The professors are bright and experienced. They "know" business and they can teach it. The business school definitely "added value." Though the program is not perfect, I wouldn't hesitate to recommend it as one of the best possible educational experiences.—***Management consultant**

*I hesitate in giving an unconditional recommendation of Stanford, because several highly regarded teaching professors are leaving. The administration does not practice what the professors preach. If Stanford were a public corporation, I believe there would be a proxy fight to replace the "board of directors"—***Vice president**

*Stanford surpasses most of my expectations for a graduate business education. The program is balanced, both in terms of content and in teaching methods. The teaching quality was quite good, although some of my classmates felt otherwise. Expertise, enthusiasm, or accessibility were not issues. Delivery was what concerned some students. The administration did not respond to those concerns effectively.—***Consulting associate**

Two words characterize my experience at Stanford: opportunity and exposure. Access to brilliant faculty, world class speakers, exposure to a variety of new subjects, and brilliant classmates made it all worthwhile.
*—***Marketing product manager**

*From the perspective of someone who went back for an MBA after 11 years in business, I didn't find a lot of "value added" in the MBA educational experience. Much of the education focuses on basics that I picked up within my first years in management. The little bit of education that is "state of the art" is often highly specialized in its application. The sad truth for me is that the real value in an MBA from a "top school" is (1) its credential value for future employers and (2) the network of social contacts it provides access to.—***Management consultant**

The first year was excessive: too much work, too much theory, not enough time to absorb the material. A real boot camp experience. Stanford is not a dog-eat-dog place, but there were still a lot of unhappy folks in my first

year class because of all the stress. A tremendous number of Wall Street and consulting firms interviewed, but not many other types of firms. The Stanford name does help open some doors, but it does not get you the job.—Management associate

In two short years, I was transformed from a "jock" who took early retirement, into a person who is ready to step in and contribute at one of the world's top investment banks. I don't think I could've asked for much more! I could not imagine a more interesting, intelligent, diverse, and fun group of people. I know I'll keep in touch with many of them for a long, long time.—Investment banking associate

Many of my classmates will tell you that the specifics we learned (accounting, finance, etc.) were interesting and challenging, but that the biggest take-away was a sense of confidence—a realization that each of us can achieve what we want and can solve the business problem that we face. The problem solving we were taught will rarely involve turning to a page in an old text book and finding the answer, but understanding the process of teamwork and analysis that yields solutions.
—Management consultant

10. Duke University

The Fuqua School of Business
Durham, North Carolina 27706

Recruiter ranking: 10
Enrollment: 740
Women: 25%
Foreign: 11%
Minority: 9%
Part-time: 190
Average age: 25.4
Applicants accepted: 24%
Accepted applicants enrolled: 54%

Graduate ranking: 7
Annual tuition: $13,500
Room and board: $7200
Average GMAT score: 620
GMAT range: 390 to 780
Average GPA: 3.3
GPA range: 2.2 to 4.0
Average starting pay: $48,740

Application deadline: Rolling admissions

It was the first gathering of the board of visitors for Duke University's graduate school of business. Accounting Professor Thomas F. Keller had just been named dean of the four-year-old school and he was there to hear some pretty awful news from the corporate executives on the board in 1974.

"They told us, 'You don't have a business school. You have a management science department. And even that's not very good. And if you want to continue, you have to change.'"

Keller, of course, not only heeded the board's advice, he instigated something of a revolution in lifting Duke's B-school from one of more than a hundred also-rans into the ranks of the Top 10 in the nation. Keller ditched Duke's undergraduate business program, raised loads of money, recruited top faculty in finance and marketing, and built one of the most attractive B-school buildings in the country.

He also proved to be an adept marketer. Keller won widespread recognition for Duke's improvements, even before the school became selective enough to truly qualify for a berth in the top ranks. As early as 1985, for example, Duke was accepting 67% of those who applied for entry into the school—an acceptance rate far higher than any other Top 20 school. About 43% of the students then had no full-time work experience. Today, with full-time enrollment set at about 550, applicants stand a one in four chance of being invited to attend—making the Fuqua School of Business one of the choosiest. And 95% of the class has work experience.

It's hard for a visiting applicant not to be impressed by Duke and the Research Triangle Park area. Duke is one of four major universities in the triangle of Durham, Chapel Hill, and Raleigh. The mild climate, the rural yet progressive environment, and the modern-looking Fuqua school charm. The concrete and glass B-school building on the edge of the west campus of the university boasts an airy mall-like environment with trees, horseshoe-shaped classrooms, and a 500-seat auditorium. A new executive education facility—linked to the school by a bridge across a ravine—opened in May. It's a 10-minute walk to the Gothic-looking Duke Chapel, the heart of the university campus.

Fuquons and Fuquites, as Duke grads call themselves, have an unusual degree of latitude to do their own thing. They run and manage The Kiosk, Fuqua's snack bar and store. They sponsor several major conferences each year on such topics as entrepreneurship, marketing, and international services. And in 1989 they pulled off the first of a series of wacky games to benefit the Special Olympics. MBAs from different schools competed in such things as a corporate swimsuit relay and a briefcase throw. "There's a greater opportunity to play a role at the school," says Kurt Baumberger, who turned down Wharton and Harvard to come to Duke. "Everyone recognizes it is a young, growing school and things aren't perfect but you could have a big impact in what is going on here."

The Fuqua program is a simple four-semester curriculum. First-year students are divided into sections of about 65 each and then take all classes in a semester together. From the start, you'll find a heavy emphasis on communication and computer skills. Business Communication, a required course that meets once a week throughout the first year, attempts to enhance verbal and written skills through student feedback, one-on-one teacher critiques, and video tapings. In one assignment, students are given a bundle of raw data that they have to convert into a coherent and convincing executive briefing. The presentation is then videotaped and critiqued by the class.

All first-year students also take Computer Laboratory, a weekly course designed to get you up to speed on using computers as management tools. Every faculty member at Duke has a PC, and there are at least 85 PCs for MBAs to share. All of them are networked together so that a professor can do work on a problem in class and the students can later tap into the network to work on the same problem. Students use computers in 75% of their required courses and are even assigned homework on floppy disks they can check out of the school library. Duke, however, does not have a strong program in management information systems.

In the second year, students have only one required course—The International Environment. Otherwise, you pretty much craft your own program with the ability to take nine electives in your second year. No one is required either to major or to concentrate in a specific area. In addition to the nearly 65 electives offered by the Fuqua School, you also can take up to four graduate courses elsewhere in the university. Many students study a foreign language, government, engineering, or international law. You can increase your elective courses by waiving out of core classes by exam.

Fuqua administrators maintain they work hard to ensure that electives are available to all students. "If you are a second-year student and there is an oversubscribed elective you want to take, we'll create a new section instead of closing you out," says Michael Hostetler, director of admissions. "At other institutions, you can get crowded out." The average class size in the second year is about 33 students.

The strong points of the program are clearly finance and marketing. The largest single group of the 55 tenure-track faculty is in finance (12), closely followed by marketing with 10 teachers. Fuqua boasts one of the better groups of marketing faculty in the nation, having lured key people from UCLA, Carnegie-Mellon, and other top schools. A Marketing Workbench Laboratory takes scanned data from supermarkets and helps brand managers in consumer product companies better manage inventories. The research from the laboratory immediately filters into the classroom in such courses as Information Systems.

An annual student-run Marketing Symposium brings many corporate marketing executives to campus each year. R. Gorden McGovern, chairman of Campbell Soup, was the keynote speaker in 1989. A project course in marketing allows students to study a current problem faced by a corporation and formally propose solutions to management. Each year, the school features four to six "live case studies" as Dean Keller calls them. MBAs gather for a brown bag lunch during which brand managers from companies such as Mars, General Foods, Kraft, and Procter & Gamble describe challenges they are currently facing. The students break into groups of six or eight and, after lunch, they make their own presentations on what the company should do.

Like most other B-schools, Duke also draws heavily upon its own area—the Research Triangle—for guest speakers and lecturers. The 1988–1989 distinguished speakers series also attracted Edgar M. Bronfman, chairman of The Seagram Co. Ltd., and Koji Kobayashi, former chairman of NEC Corp. In 1989, Duke also boasted three full-time executives in residence for the entire year: William A. Sax, a former vice president of Unocal Corp., Richard B. Palmer, a former president of a Texaco subsidiary, and Nathaniel Lande, a former senior vice president from advertising agency BBDO. Whether it's dispensing career advice or telling old war stories, these former executives are helpful for their real-world perspective on business issues.

Student evaluations of teachers are not made public here. But grads highly recommend Valerie Zeithaml, a Fuqua Teacher of the Year winner, who has done pioneering research in consumer behavior. Campbell Harvey, who teaches finance courses, and William Boulding also gather rave reviews from students. First-year students can gain exposure to Boulding in their Marketing Management core course, while second-year students will find him teaching Marketing Strategy.

Fuquons read *Over the Counter*, the school's monthly newspaper, to keep track of campus happenings. Between classes, they also scurry to the Lakewood Shopping Plaza, a five-minute drive from campus, for drinks at Satisfaction or T. J. Hoops, the ultimate sports bar. At Hoops, grads gather to watch the university's basketball team on large-screen TVs and play pool on one of 15 tables. When the Duke Blue Devils are on the road, an alternate cheerleader often comes down to lead the crowd. Every Friday at 5 p.m., MBAs also get together in the atrium of the B-school or in the student lounge for beer and snacks.

Ever since the popular movie "Bull Durham," Fuquons have been trekking downtown to hoot and holler for the Durham Bulls, the professional baseball team upon which the movie was based. Like just about everything else in Durham, it's no more than a 15-minute drive away. Most MBAs live off-campus in privately owned apartments just a walk or bike ride away. If you have to drive to school, you'll be familar with 751, the nickname for the Fuqua parking lot about a three-minute walk from the school. The lot is so named because it's just off Route 751. About 15% of Fuqua students live in university-owned housing.

Duke's recent emergence as a B-school powerhouse has its disadvantages. The faculty is younger than most, so Fuqua tends to lack nationally recognized stars in their fields. "Teaching quality may suffer because they don't have a wealth of experience," says Richard Staelin, associate dean for faculty affairs. "The good point is that we have enthusiastic young people who care about their message and want to have an impact on the students."

As a relatively young program, the school also lacks a large and older alumni network of contacts. (The first class of 12 students graduated in 1972.) Duke University grads, however, show lots of loyalty to the school. Each of the last three graduating classes have donated $100,000 or more to the school by commencement day. Alumni have even put together an electronic bulletin board listing addresses of all Fuqua grads that can be accessed by a computer and modem 24 hours a day.

Fuqua's placement office has done well attracting top-flight corporate recruiters to campus. In 1989, more than 150 companies, including American Airlines, Coca-

Cola, Goldman Sachs, and McKinsey, came to interview students. Duke's placement operation is aggressive (some students complain that it is too aggressive). It even advises students on proper table manners because business luncheons are often part of a follow-up interview. In 1988, Unisys got the largest group of Fuqua grads, recruiting 10. Other top recruiters were Price Waterhouse, which took 6 graduates, Arthur Andersen and General Mills, which hired 5 each, and Coca-Cola, which took 4 graduates.

Dean Keller, meanwhile, shows no sign that he's complacent with Duke firmly established as a Top 10 school. In 1989 alone he opened the doors to the R. David Thomas Center for Executive Education, added a new research center in manufacturing and technology management, and launched an innovative program to bring Soviet managers to Duke to educate them about the business practices of market economies. No one could tell him he doesn't have a business school now.

Contact: Michael J. Hostetler, director of admissions, 919-684-5874

Prominent alumni: Benjamin W. Hill, president of Broyhill Furniture, Inc.; J. F. Harrison, vice chairman of Coca-Cola Bottling Co.; John D. Kearney, president of Robinson-Humphrey Co.; John A. Allison, president of Branch Banking & Trust; Kevin M. Twomey, senior vice president of Mcorp.; Thomas B. Roller, vice president of Carrier Corp.

Fuqua MBAs sound off

*Perhaps the greatest strength of the Fuqua School is also its most visible weakness: it's a very young program. Being young gave students the ability to impact the system immediately. At the same time, our youth hurts us in that there is a dearth of top-level alumni presently in the business community.—**Finance project manager***

*Duke is striving to be a finance school—so marketing majors beware! You will be forced to learn esoteric bond swap theory just so the big banks will keep coming to career day. My lasting regret is that I spent $40,000 to learn useless tools from academics who'd never worked in a real business. Business school learning is too removed from the real world. The best teaching tools Duke had were the CEOs who regularly visited. They knew what was going on outside, and they reminded us that we'd eventually learn to deal with it, too.—**Marketing account associate***

*The Fuqua School of Business is the best investment I've ever made, from both a personal and professional point of view. The program improved my communication and analytical skills. The school also allowed me the opportunity to manage several organizations, which enhanced my leadership skills. MBA graduates have been portrayed recently as ultra-competitive and money hungry. But the people I met at Duke had more character and integrity than any other group I've worked with in the past.
—**Finance associate***

The best aspect of Fuqua's program is its student body. They are exceptionally bright. Cooperation and teamwork are carried throughout the whole program from the first day. The broad range of management training I received during my two years of full-time business school was well

worth the time, earnings, and lifestyle I gave up to pursue a graduate education.—Consultant

Duke has a very underrated business school. It is an outstanding institution led by an enthusiastic faculty and administration. I don't think other schools have the vision the Fuqua school has, much as a result of the speed with which it has become nationally prominent. Once Fuqua has the alumni base of the other schools, there will be no stopping its rise into the top 5.—Assistant brand manager

I entered the program with no business background or knowledge, and two years later I walked out in the top 5% of my class. Fuqua taught me everything I needed to know and more!—Consultant

As an international student, the facilities extended to me and other foreign students were not up to par with those offered the Americans—only regards to placement and financial assistance. The placement office at Fuqua was, at best, apathetic toward international students. This is kind of unfair, given that these students form 25% of the student population. Summing it up, I'd say that Fuqua was worth only $25,000–$27,000 of the $40,000 that I spent.—Finance executive

The placement office was more interested in having students accept any job offer so that the school placement statistics would look good. No real attempt was made to help students find jobs that complemented their career interests. As a matter of fact, there was at least one incident where the placement director got wind that a student received an offer by a well-known investment firm, and proceeded to block his attempts to get on other interview lists. He was, in effect, trying to force this student to accept the offer, so that other students would "have a chance" at getting job offers, too. The school tried very hard to instill cooperative, team spirit values through extensive group projects. It really didn't work, though, as most students were only looking out for #1.—Corporate marketing associate

Academically, it was a great experience; socially, however, it was not. This is because I am a New Yorker, accustomed to big city life, while Fuqua lies in an isolated setting in North Carolina. I thought it to be socially stifling. Culture shock was indeed experienced. The lesson I learned is that I should stay in the big city in the future.—Career path unknown

*I am amazed at how my expectations of school and career changed while I was at B-school. I came there bound for Wall Street and left determined to work for a small entrepreneurial company, with a goal of running my own firm in five years. Business school ruined me for the corporate world. Seeing the excitement of small team cooperation and grappling with issues at all levels made me certain that being a junior executive again and climbing the corporate ladder would suffocate me. We had all the biggies—Procter & Gamble, Salomon Brothers, etc., but I had no interest in them. I was talking to clam farmers and software developers.
—Marketing entrepreneur*

11. University of Chicago

Graduate School of Business
1101 E. 58th Street
Chicago, Illinois 60637

Recruiter ranking: 4
Enrollment: 2275
Women: 23%
Foreign: 20%
Minority: 10%
Part-time: 1264
Average age: 26.4
Applicants accepted: 30%*
Accepted applicants enrolled: 56%*

Graduate ranking: 20
Annual tuition: $15,500
Annual fees: $210
Room and board: $6950
Average GMAT score: NA
GMAT range: 380 to 770
Average GPA: 3.0 to 3.5 (mid 50%)
GPA range: 2.1 to 4.0
Average starting pay: $54,772

Application deadline: May 1 for fall

The place reeks of tradition and academic excellence. Spires and gargoyles top the stone buildings. Gothic arches and tree-lined walks mark the stunning campus. "When you come here for the first time," says a student, "you almost get a shiver up your spine."

It could just as easily be Great Britain's Oxford or Cambridge. But no, this is the setting for the University of Chicago's Graduate School of Business. It is a haven for scholars and intellectuals, defying the image that many still have of an MBA institution as little more than a trade school. Since 1898, the school has turned more than 22,500 MBAs into the world.

Hailed in the late 1950s when most other business schools were vigorously attacked for being too vocational, Chicago's B-school has kept true to its academic roots. To this day, deans commonly view business schools on a scale that places case study based Harvard on one extreme as representative of the trade school mold and Chicago on the other as the lecture-based school that teaches business theory.

Yet, along the Midway Plaisance, the grassy expanse of lawn that cuts through the university campus, the Chicago B-school dean says it isn't so black and white. Indeed, these days Chicago seems almost defensive about such characterizations, wary of criticism that its business professors spend too much time conducting research in ivory towers and not enough time consulting in corporate offices. "I don't know that I would use the word 'theoretical,'" says Dean John P. Gould, "because it sounds like we don't apply the knowledge to real business. There was an imbalance. There wasn't enough emphasis on the applied, but we now offer a greater number of applied courses in marketing, general management, and finance."

That is true, but Chicago has hardly discarded its tradition or its roots. In the oak-paneled rooms of the B-school buildings, some students still jokingly refer to themselves as "digit heads"—a reference to the heavily quantitative nature of the program. You can overhear them in the halls and classrooms talking about the "free market system" and the "capital asset pricing model," ideas and concepts relentlessly drilled into Chicago MBAs. One graduate, assessing the worth of his MBA education there, laughs: "I'm not convinced that the present value of expected return exceeds the incremental cost of obtaining an MBA." Spoken like a true Chicago digit head.

So incoming students shouldn't be surprised that the required core curriculum of 11 courses is heavily laden with math and quantitative work. Some grouse that it's too much theory, too much academic pie in the sky. Others become strong advocates of the unique MBA education Chicago delivers. "The classes here teach you how to think and how to solve problems," says Paul Tashima, who will graduate with his MBA in 1990. "You base your solutions not on casework, but on a conceptual framework."

What does surprise many is the degree of flexibility built into the program. Chicago is one of the few B-schools that will actually allow you to waive every single course in the core if you already have mastered the material elsewhere. To get the MBA, you must complete 20 courses—whether you waive some or not. Most do it over six 11-week quarters spread out through two years. Yet it's possible to complete the program in a year and a half by giving up your shot at an internship and taking classes over the summer.

As a full-timer, you can also take evening courses in downtown Chicago with the part-timers. You can even enter this program in the summer instead of waiting for the fall. If your interests go well beyond business, you also can take up to 6 of the 20 required courses outside the B-school. Chicago offers MBAs a "concentration" if they complete three or four courses in one field or a "specialization" if they take at least six courses in one area. But neither is required for graduation from the program. "There's a lot of freedom here," says Lee Cunningham, director of admissions. "You can take courses anywhere in the university. So if you're interested in bolstering your proficiency in a foreign language, you can do that within the confines of the program."

But about those roots. No doubt about it, Chicago boasts outstanding academic researchers. A *Journal of Finance* report ranked the B-school first in the impact of its faculty's research in finance. Three leading academic journals are edited by B-school faculty. In 1982, the school's George J. Stigler, a specialist in economic sciences, became the first business school professor ever to receive a Nobel prize.

Research clearly takes precedence over quality teaching at Chicago, though you'll find some outstanding professors in the classrooms here. Garnering rave reviews from students are Kenneth French's Futures Markets from a Financial Perspective and John Deighton's Marketing Management. "They are dynamic and enthusiastic teachers, and they make you take the learning beyond the classroom," raves one graduate. "The subject almost rubs off on you when you're in their classrooms." Eugene Fama's finance courses and Robert Blattberg's advanced marketing offering also score highly with students.

Sensitive to charges that Chicago's curriculum is too theoretical, Dean Gould has been working to put a priority on applying more of the theory taught in class. He notes that one out of every five elective courses now consists of various applied field projects or case studies. For the first time, the entering fall class to graduate in 1991 is going through a leadership, education, and development program in which "softer" skills such as communications, ethics, and managerial leadership will be taught in a noncredit, albeit required, course. Then, the entire first-year class will take off for a weekend to a Wisconsin retreat to sum up the first quarter experience. The school is financing the trip to the tune of half a million dollars.

The school has also come up with several innovative programs to disprove the stereotype that Chicago is a hangout for digit heads and Ph.D. scholars. Consider the school's New Product Laboratory, in which teams of students work on new ideas and products for major corporations, from the *Chicago Sun-Times* to Zenith Data Systems. "We assign teams to work on the projects and try to maximize diversity on them so that a French lit major from Wellesley is on a team with an engineer from Cal Tech to generate new ideas for the client," says Harry L. Davis, director of the laboratory.

In 1989, more than 80 students signed up for the six-month course, worth 10% of the total MBA workload. Some 48 were accepted and divided into teams of a dozen each. Students sign confidentiality statements with clients and then roll up their sleeves. They run consumer research on the idea. They work with prototype developers on the new product and even consult with an advertising agency on communication issues and packaging strategy. At project's end, the teams make full-scale presentations and submit a written business plan, complete with the financials as well as advertising, promotion, and introductory marketing programs. Zenith Data Systems was expected to introduce a product dreamed up by the students in late 1989.

Another 45 students participate in the Argonne Chicago Development Corporation, in which they're involved in converting scientific discoveries into commercial products and new businesses. ARCH, an extracurricular activity by students, has already given birth to five companies. And within the last two years, two groups of 12 students each have worked with the National Aeronautics and Space Administration on the commercialization of products in space.

Chicago's B-school is a cluster of three classic buildings linked together: Stuart, Walker, and Rosenwald Hall on the 172-acre university campus in Hyde Park, about 12 minutes from the Loop on the subway. Students flip frisbees or bat softballs around on the Midway, which reaches to Lake Michigan from the campus. MBAs tend to hang out at Ida Noyes Hall, a block from the B-school. Many of them live at International House, the university dorm two blocks away, or in apartments or homes in Hyde Park, a residential neighborhood that has seen better times.

Once a week, between 8:30 and 10:30 a.m., students and faculty meet for coffee and donuts in Cox Lounge. Liquidity Preference Functions fill the calendar in the fall, when companies arrive for sessions to make their pitch for students and serve snacks and drinks after the presentation. There's also a fall dance and a winter carnival, a formal cruise on Lake Michigan and the annual Follies in the spring. *Chicago Business*, the student newspaper, keeps everyone well informed of the events—especially of visiting speakers and recruiting companies.

Chicago's reputation for imparting strong analytical and quantitative skills in students has a dramatic impact on who recruits U of C MBAs. A whopping 48% of the Class of 1988 took jobs in finance (versus only 27% at Harvard and 19% at Stanford). One in four Chicago MBAs became consultants, while 13% assumed marketing positions (that's roughly half the number rival Kellogg School sends into marketing jobs). In 1988, 273 companies came to recruit on campus. Arthur Andersen led the pack, taking 17 graduates alone, followed by Citicorp (16), Hewlett-Packard (11), Merrill Lynch (10), and Bankers Trust (8).

Wherever they go, they willingly or unwillingly bring with them that Chicago tradition for academic excellence. As Melzie Robinson, a 1989 graduate who now works in marketing at Amoco, puts it: "Students won't fully realize the impact of what they've learned here until later on. We're being exposed to a lot of leading-edge thinking that the business world hasn't picked up yet." And may never pick up.

Contact: Ms. Lee Cunningham, director of admissions, 312-702-7369

Prominent alumni: Charles Bowser, comptroller general of U.S. General Accounting Office; David Burke, president of CBS News; Ronald Frank, dean of Purdue University's Krannert School of Management; Melvin Goodes, president of Warner-Lambert; David W. Johnson, chairman of Gerber Products; Nina M. Klarich, CEO of Chicago Technology Park; Robert Nakasone, vice-chairman of Toys 'R' Us; Steven Rothmeier, chairman of Northwest Airlines

Chicago MBAs sound off

*Chicago is an excellent academic institution that has a reputation of being "very theoretical." This is misleading because students have the option and flexibility to take quite a lot of case-based courses. The true fact is that the U of C is the best school in the world for people who want to study on the high-powered theoretical level. Yet, what people don't understand is that it also offers individuals, like myself, the ability to take well over 50% of our courses as case study.—**Self-employed in finance***

*Two things stood out: one, from day one, everyone focused on getting a job: who they would work for and what they would be doing. Competition wasn't over grades, but about interviews, summer internships, and permanent positions. There was a lot of pressure not to be undecided about the future. Two, for a top-tier school, I expected more emphasis on leadership, decision making, people skills. Instead, the school was designed to create analysts, not managers or leaders.—**Technology associate***

*Chicago stresses economic fundamentals and problem-solving techniques. Professors don't rely on vague case study inferences; they teach analytical tools. In short, they treat business like any other academic discipline. If you want a guaranteed great job upon graduation, go to Harvard. If you want a real education, Chicago is the place to be.—**Law school student***

*Reading assignments were often excessively theoretical and numerical. It is doubtful that a person can retain that kind of information for a long time. Instead of emphasizing futures and options and mathematical deviation, the school could have invited dealers to a class to show how the theory relates to actual behavior.—**Corporate banking officer***

*At Chicago, there was little emphasis on competition in global markets or alternative ways to analyze problems. Instead, you received too much market efficiency dogma, with little emphasis on judgment and common sense. Students get little exposure to why Japan is beating U.S. firms routinely.—**Finance assistant***

*It's not what it's all "cracked up" to be. Some of the worst professors I've had in my life were at Chicago. Believe it or not, some of these instructors couldn't do simple mathematics!! I learned nothing from one of the most expensive MBA schools in the country. The only thing U of C has is its name. And even that is not all too known.—**Corporate finance trainee***

I feel I have learned more useful lessons outside of the classroom. Overall, I'm happy and pleased with my two years at Chicago, but feel that the ed-

ucation was not real world and will not be used for a long time (if ever). I believe most of my professors held students and teaching in low esteem. —Marketing brand assistant

I started my own company to market consumer products while in the Chicago program and found professors there very supportive of my plan for a start-up company. The marketing plan, pricing, etc. were all the basis of required projects for various courses. Professors supplied contacts, information, and acted as my sounding board for all aspects of establishing the company. Chicago has no official entrepreneurial course program, but you can design an excellent program on your own by taking certain courses and professors.—President

I felt that my experience could have been enhanced if there were fewer students in the program with no previous work experience and if there was more case study. At Chicago, 25% are right out of undergraduate school. (The university says only 6% of its MBAs come direct from undergrad studies.) The university also could have led the way to promote better relations amongst students. Instead, the university administration tended to be rather bureaucratic, cold, uncaring, and unconcerned about student needs.—Management consultant

12. Indiana University

Graduate School of Business
10th and Fee Lane
Bloomington, Indiana 47405

Recruiter ranking: 9
Enrollment: 612
Women: 27.5%
Foreign: 10.6%
Minority: 9%
Part-time: 19
Average age: 26.5
Applicants accepted: 34%
Accepted applicants enrolled: 48%

Graduate ranking: 11
Annual tuition: nonresident—$6968
resident—$2548
Room and board: $3323
Average GMAT score: 600
GMAT range: 350 to 730
Average GPA: 3.3
GPA range: 2.25 to 3.9
Average starting pay: $38,407

Application deadline: April 1 for fall/October 15 for spring

At Indiana University, the search for a job begins before the first class. During orientation week, new MBA students explore career options, polish up their résumés on personal computers, and learn how to find summer internships.

No other B-school spends more time helping its students find a job than IU's Graduate School of Business. Plenty of schools have an associate dean for alumni relations, but how many have an assistant dean for company relations? At Indiana, that position is held by C. Randall (Randy) Powell, one of the top placement directors in the country. He's the second person new MBA students meet, after Dean Jack R. Wentworth.

Ask anyone at Indiana what makes the MBA program unique and "placement" is often the answer. "The Indiana MBA is not that different from what you get at Michigan from an academic standpoint," Powell says. "We both have professors who have written textbooks. The difference between us and the other schools is that we care."

Last year, Powell and the 15 full-time employees in IU's business placement office brought more than 300 companies to Bloomington for recruiting. Powell helps nearly three-fourths of the school's 600 MBA students find summer internships and nearly all find a job after graduation. That's no small feat because the school is tucked away in southern Indiana. The nearest city, Indianapolis, is an hour away and it's hardly a mecca for MBAs.

With its rolling green hills and broad-branched trees, the campus could easily be the backdrop for a movie about collegiate life. The university, in fact, was the setting for the hit film "Breaking Away" about the Little 500 bicycle race, an annual fixture of Bloomington life. It's what you'd expect of a quaint town in Indiana with a courthouse square, whose population swells by 36,000 students when the university is in session. Many of the school's ivy-covered buildings were constructed at the turn of the century using Indiana limestone. There are plenty of grassy areas for spreading out your books and studying on a sunny day. "It's an absolutely beautiful campus," crows Steve Riordan, a 1989 graduate. "In the springtime, it's gorgeous."

Business students call home a nondescript limestone building that also holds the School of Public and Environmental Affairs. It contains an extensive business library and a recently renovated MBA lounge. On a nice day, students brown bag it to the second-floor patio outside. Some first-year MBAs reside at Eigenmann Hall, a high-rise dorm for graduate students two blocks from the B-school. Because demand out-strips supply, however, most grads move into their own apartments around town. Married students sometimes commute from the south side of Indianapolis because it's difficult for spouses to find work in Bloomington, which has a population of 55,000. IU does hire spouses of some MBAs, but often the work is routine or clerical.

Indiana's curriculum reflects the belief that an MBA graduate should be a generalist with the ability to make decisions. The school prides itself on being well-rounded, emphasizing both interpersonal and analytical skills through a combination of case study and lecture. During the first semester, courses are taught through lectures and classroom discussion, while the case method prevails during the second semester. In the second year, students are exposed to a mix of case, seminars, team projects, and computer simulations.

There are 13 courses in the school's core requirements, 9 of which are completed during the first year. Students can waive out of core courses, replacing them with electives, if they have previous academic or professional experience. Besides the usual array of expected courses in finance, accounting, marketing, organizational behavior, and operations, Indiana's core includes a course called Legal Concepts and Trends Affecting Business. Don't be turned off by the dull title of this course. Taught by Michael Metzger, the innovative course uses topical events, such as Exxon's disastrous oil spill in early 1989, as the springboard to explore the legal implications of business decisions. "Law has historically been undervalued in business schools," says Metzger. "Doctoral programs are becoming increasingly specialized and many business school faculty members don't have much exposure to law." Metzger's course teaches MBAs basic legal principles and examines business law from a sociohistorical perspective, touching on current events such as lawsuits against tobacco and alcohol companies.

IU students can choose from nearly 80 electives in areas such as finance, marketing, management, international business administration, decision sciences, marketing and operations, and systems management. MBAs are required to major in a functional management area or industry by taking four courses. Finance is the overwhelming major of choice, with 40% of students pursuing a concentration in that field. Marketing is next with 20%, followed by management with 16%.

Faculty members say Indiana's culture stresses teaching, though some students complain about the occasional boring professor. Oliver Heil isn't one of them. A new professor who earned his Ph.D. from Wharton in 1987, he gets rave reviews for his marketing strategy class. Heil devotes the first half of the term to marketing theory and then tests students' instincts and skills in a simulation game during the second half. As part of Professor Bruce Resnick's year-long course Applied Investment Analysis and Portfolio Management, students manage a portfolio of $120,000. They screen stocks, study companies, and monitor current events in the fall semester. By January, they put their money where their mouths—rather minds—are, making buy recommendations that they present to the class and an advisory board of IU alums working in the investment business. Despite the 1987 stock market crash, the fund has continued to show a steady return.

Computer literacy is a big priority. Effective fall 1989, students are required to have their own PCs. At the same time, new courses in management information systems and managerial communications will be added to the MBA program. Students get hands-on experience with both mainframes and PCs during orientation week when they take a crash course in spreadsheet analysis and word processing. Through Indiana's computer network, students send messages to classmates and professors by electronic mail. They also can access several databases to help them complete classwork.

Don't attend Indiana if you're not the type to join in extracurricular activities. IU views its MBA program not as a set of courses, but as a total experience, encompassing both academic and personal development. About 95% of the students join the MBA Association, the umbrella group for 14 special interest groups. Students pay $100 for a two-year MBAA membership, which also entitles them to join two other clubs for $18.75 each. Some of these, such as the Investment Club, help students network by planning field trips and bringing industry speakers to campus. Others handle the MBA newsletter, social events, a teaching evaluation report, and public relations. There are club meetings and functions at the B-school every night. "This building is jammed in the evening with a variety of activities," says B-school Dean Jack Wentworth. "It's one of the advantages of being in a small town with not a whole heck of a lot to do."

One thing they do is congregate every Thursday night at a "designated bar" chosen by the MBAA. Students try to close such popular spots as The Crazy Horse, the Irish Lion, and J. Arthur's. Not to worry. There are no classes on Friday. On other evenings, the association may sponsor theme parties where grads dress up as beach bums, Elvis impersonators, or natives of Wisconsin. (For this latter event, MBAs don flannel shirts and Brewers' caps, chatter about bowling, and swill Leinenkugel beer.) The best pizza in town can be had at Nick's English Hut, 10 blocks from the B-school. It's a dark and dingy place, stuffed with basketball memorabilia. Autographed pictures of successful IU alums are hung along the painted dark brown paneling.

Indiana MBAs plainly enjoy themselves. But they take the job search very seriously. After a student types up his résumé on a computer during orientation, it is immediately entered into the school's database. Résumé books for first-year students are only $10, while books for second-year students cost $75 each. Like other major B-schools, Indiana students are allotted points that they "bid" to interview with a particular company. The typical MBA here has between 20 and 30 interviews in the second year. These are held in one of 40 interviewing rooms in a $2 million complex built in the early 1980s.

At IU, the interview is the culmination of a series of contacts between students and companies. Every fall, the placement office sponsors a two-week program called FOCUS to introduce students to career opportunities. Each night, leading companies in a particular industry give presentations. Students are *required* to attend four sessions, choosing from such areas as corporate finance, investments, management consulting, product management, information systems, and operations. Later, companies invite students to "rap sessions" that usually begin with a videotape outlining the firm's operations and end with pep talks by operating managers and IU alumni. A cocktail reception follows the presentation.

Indiana may not be known for its placing power on Wall Street, but alumni working there are willing to spend time with IU MBAs. In the 1988–1989 academic year, the Investment Club visited trading rooms and met with partners at major securities firms. Goldman, Sachs & Company, Salomon Brothers Inc., and Morgan Stanley and Company recruit on campus.

When corporate recruiters and speakers come to IU, they stay in the Indiana Memorial Union, a stately limestone building that serves as a hotel and conference center. They often have lunch or dinner with faculty members who tip them off to promising students. Choice football tickets are part of the VIP treatment recruiters get at Indiana. "We treat recruiters like they are customers," Powell says. "You have to provide good service if you want customers to come back year after year."

Brand-name companies such as Procter & Gamble, General Electric, Ford Motor Company, Eli Lilly, Leo Burnett, Arthur Andersen, and Touche Ross like to hire Indiana MBAs. "Our people get good marks from employers," says Professor Michael Metzger. "They have a reasonable level of humility. They don't expect to be CEO in a year. They give good value for the dollar and they wear well." The $38,407 average starting pay is significantly less than that received by graduates of other top B-schools. "Students here have very realistic expectations of the business world," says Paul Santello, a 1989 graduate now working at Leo Burnett in Chicago. "They don't come out of school expecting to make $100,000 a year like people from Harvard, Wharton, and Stanford."

One reason why IU MBAs may not command high salaries is that many of them lack professional experience, practically a requirement to get into Harvard, Wharton, or Stanford. Some Indiana students complain that too many of their classmates haven't seen enough of the world. "My biggest concern about IU is the lack of importance placed on previous work experience," grouses one student who worked for five years before attending Indiana. "There are a large number of students who roll into the program with little or no experience."

Indiana MBAs can afford to earn less their first year out of B-school because they pay less for their degree. IU's tuition has historically been 50% of that charged by Michigan, but the days of rock-bottom prices are drawing to a close. The B-school recently won approval to charge more for an MBA than the university does for other master's programs. Through a series of annual increases, Indiana's tuition is expected to increase gradually over the next five years. The money will fund higher faculty salaries, longer library hours, and more graduate assistantships, says Dean Wentworth. About 40% of IU MBAs currently receive assistantships to teach undergrads or work in the placement office with Powell's high-powered staff. Mobilizing MBAs to help undergrads with their résumés, cover letters, and interviewing technique is all part of Indiana's winning strategy of finding jobs for all graduates.

Contact: Joseph A. Pica, director, MBA Program, Room 254, 812-855-8006

Prominent alumni: Edward G. Boehne, president, Federal Reserve Bank of Philadelphia; Richard L. Lesher, president, U.S. Chamber of Commerce; Frank E. McKinney, Jr., chairman and CEO, Banc One Indiana Corp.; Harold A. Poling, vice chairman and chief operating officer, Ford Motor Co.; Frank P. Popoff, CEO, Dow Chemical Co.

Indiana MBAs sound off

Indiana University MBAs are fortunate to have one of the best placement offices in the country. Placing top graduates in reputable companies *around the globe continues to foster IU's reputation as one of the best graduate business programs.—**Career development staff assistant***

*I was not alone in having difficulty finding employment due to a lack of work experience. I feel that our business placement office needs to bring in recruiters with a wider variety of needs, or Indiana should stop accepting candidates without work experience. Even with this frustration I have no regrets about getting the MBA and strongly believe that Indiana's program is among the best in the nation.—**Financial analyst***

*As a conservative-to-moderate Democrat, I realized I was among a minority of "liberal" thinkers in the school. I think a broader theory concerned with the impact and obligation that business has to society should have been more readily discussed.—**Marketing representative***

*While it is consistently ranked in the top 10 or 20, IU is not located near the major geographic centers—Wall Street (investment banking), Boston (consulting), Chicago (marketing and industry), and San Francisco (Silicon Valley). Consequently, we don't have the same volume of contacts as Harvard, Chicago, Wharton, or Stanford.—**Financial analyst***

*Because Bloomington is not a metropolitan area, Indiana works very hard to bring speakers and companies in for social functions. It works well. Some extra effort is required on our part to find time to attend. It is well worth the effort. The curriculum is an excellent combination of case study, teamwork, theory, analytical skills, and computer skills.
—**Internal auditor***

*MBA program is deserving of its high rankings. There is a real emphasis on becoming computer-literate and current material was often incorporated by the professors. A negative: the constant emphasis on development, i.e., alumni and even student contributions.—**Attorney***

*I feel I came out of the MBA program more polished and more able to succeed in the business world. Our placement program played a huge part in that growth. We began working on placement and interviewing skills, and learning about many different companies the first weeks there.
—**Marketing representative***

*They have a very personal approach to the orientation of new students by spending a very busy but organized week before classes with the new MBAs. The placement office under the direction of Dr. C. Randall Powell does an outstanding job of bringing in companies to interview and providing at least three different ways for candidates to obtain interviews with prospective employers.—**Associate consultant***

13. Carnegie-Mellon University

Graduate School of Industrial Administration
Schenley Park
Pittsburgh, Pennsylvania 15213

Recruiter ranking: 12
Enrollment: 590
Women: 21%
Foreign: 17%
Minority: 10
Part-time: 191
Average age: 25
Applicants admitted: 32%
Accepted applicants enrolled: 51%

Graduate ranking: 9
Annual tuition: $15,200
Room and board: $4200
Average GMAT score: 630
GMAT range: 400 to 770
Average GPA: 3.2
GPA range: 2.0 to 4.0
Average starting pay: $49,109

Application deadline: March 15 for fall

"If you were to imagine a business nerd, you probably would imagine him from Carnegie-Mellon," jokes Robert Barrett of the Class of 1989. Not that Carnegie MBAs have calculators dangling from their belts, but perhaps more than any other top B-school, Carnegie is something of a haven for the "quant-jocks"—the commonly used term for MBAs obsessed with mathematics and quantitative methods.

Is Carnegie a school for business nerds? Hardly. The school has significantly broadened its faculty, curriculum, and students over the years. "As the school has gotten larger, it has become more diverse," says Allan H. Meltzer, a nationally known economist and Carnegie professor. "The old image is less true today than it probably was."

Even so, you still hear plenty of talk about people who write linear programs and run lots of regressions. About 56% of its students have undergrad technical degrees in engineering and science. And students are expected to sit through a good chunk of required "quant" courses. If you have had trouble with math and calculus, Carnegie's program can be daunting. "Some courses were too difficult for students without a strong analytical background," says one 1988 graduate.

How much attention is devoted to the quantitative side? Carnegie-Mellon's own research shows that it requires more than five times the amount of class time on quantitative subjects as Harvard and twice as much as Stanford or Columbia. Even courses such as microeconomics that are not typically quantitative at other schools have a heavily mathematical bent at Carnegie. The school boasts as many electives in quantitative methods—from mind-numbing Multivariate Statistical Analysis to eye-glazing Mathematical Programming Economics—as it does in organizational analysis. That's a major reason why MBAs ranked Carnegie as the school offering the second toughest workload of the Top 20, behind only the University of Virginia.

The first year is not unlike bootcamp. Within three and one-half weeks of your arrival, you'll already be sitting down for mid-term exams. Study groups convene until 2 a.m. or 3 a.m. Students who lack a quantitative background often panic. "The sheer mass of work you have to do is incredible," adds Barrett. "You're covering material so quickly that everything around you becomes a total blur. It's probably twice the workload of your undergraduate experience."

Don't let the rigor of this program scare you away, however. Fewer than 5% of the students fail to complete the program. And while graduates describe the workload as excessive, many later concede its obvious benefits. "You're indirectly forced to prioritize, manage your time and to delegate to and rely on others," notes one 1988 graduate. "Teamwork is the only way to survive!" Moreover, Carnegie graduates overwhelmingly rated their school tops when asked, "Are you comfortable with your ability to deal with computers and other analytical tools that affect your ability to manage?"

Carnegie students face a heavy load of required courses. About 61% of the total courses a Carnegie MBA will take during his or her two other years there are required, compared with only 35% at Yale, 39% at Northwestern, and 40% at Columbia. Even so, Carnegie has come up with a few of the more novel electives offered in recent years from Managing Service and Customer-Driven Businesses to The Future of Capitalism.

The most popular among an offering of 78 electives these days is Crisis Management and Leadership in Business, taught by Gerald Meyers, former chairman of American Motors Corporation. Some 176 out of Carnegie's 208 students signed up for the course in a recent semester. One reason for the class's popularity is the quality of guest lecturers Meyers lures into the classroom: Drexel Burnham Lambert Inc. CEO Frederick Joseph; Union Carbide Corporation Chairman Warren M. Anderson; and former AT&T Chairman Charles L. Brown. Students recently rated Meyers 4.79% out of 5 for excellence in teaching.

More than most schools, the faculty at Carnegie-Mellon is at the leading edge of knowledge in their fields. The emphasis, then, is heavily on research and not on teaching. So the intellectual content of the program is high. Indeed, the school has pioneered several major breakthroughs in management theory and practice over the years, from the rational expectations concept in economics to new fields of cognitive psychology and computer science. The difference is reflected partly by the degree you get. Carnegie grads don't earn an MBA; they receive the MSIA, a Master of Science in Industrial Administration. There are neither departments nor required majors or concentration areas because Carnegie emphasizes what it calls "interdisciplinary thinking."

Despite the notable research slant at the expense of teaching, the school boasts some superb teachers and the student–faculty ratio of 4.5 to 1 is one of the lowest at the major schools. Grads strongly recommend Strikant Datar's Financial Accounting, Jerry Ross's Human Behavior in Organizations, and Robert Dammon's Corporate Finance. "Datar is a god here," crows one student. "He's got to be one of the top five professors I've ever had in my life."

Carnegie also numbers among its faculty Jean-Jacques Servan-Schreiber, former French cabinet minister and bestselling author of *The American Challenge*. In his course, Strategic Thinking in International Management, Servan-Schreiber draws analogies between military and business wars in teaching about global markets. Steer clear of Charles Kriebel's Management of Information Systems and Ramakrishna Akella's Management and Control of Manufacturing Systems unless you're a glutton for punishment. In the opinion of Carnegie students, these instructors got the lowest teaching marks of them all in the fall of 1988.

For a school with a quantitative reputation, you'd hardly think there would be much happening on the entrepreneurial side. But Carnegie boasts an entrepreneurship project course that has become the springboard for students to launch their own businesses. One of the latest: SolarCare Inc., founded by a couple of 1986 grads, markets a sunscreen on towelettes for sports and recreational use. This year a Carnegie student's business plan for a new software company beat out finalists from Harvard, Wharton, Michigan, Purdue, and Texas in "Moot Corp.," a national entrepreneurship competition sponsored by the University of Texas.

All of Carnegie's courses fit into an unusual "mini-semester" that is about seven and one-half weeks long. The eight minis over the two years allow students to take as many as 18 electives without overloading their schedules. That's almost as many electives as some schools require in total courses to graduate. With five courses a mini, that's a total of 40 courses over the two-year program. Of course, these classes are compressed to fit the mini-semester format. So a few courses, such as Production and Operations Management, extend over two mini-semesters, but Carnegie profs pack an incredible amount of learning in a single mini, too. "I don't think there's a program in the country that works them harder," says one associate dean. "We work their butts off and that's one of the comforts they have in going out into the real world. They're used to working hard and no one can work them harder than we do."

The centerpiece of the Carnegie program is The Management Game. Pioneered by Carnegie-Mellon in the 1950s, the game is a computer simulation of the soap industry, originally based on Procter & Gamble. Every second-year student is assigned to six-person teams made up of a president and a host of functional vice presidents who guide their companies through a two-year business cycle over a 15-week period.

Students even have to negotiate a labor agreement with local union leaders from the steel industry. "They crucify these kids," says Edward R. Mosler, an associate dean. "The faces around here after that first meeting with the labor reps reflect absolute shock." Companies also put together multimedia marketing campaigns that are judged by local advertising agencies. And each team has to overcome and survive a crisis—whether charges of price-fixing, employee discrimination or the dumping of toxic waste—by, among other things, meeting with local reporters.

The team reports to a board of directors that meets in one of the plush and well-appointed boardrooms of some of Pittsburgh's leading corporations, from H. J. Heinz to the Mellon Bank. On each board sits a faculty member and a handful of senior corporate executives, from the chief financial officer of Texas Instruments to a Hewlett-Packard vice president.

The board can be tough and demanding. "You're desperately trying to please your board," recalls one graduate, who reported to an unusually hard-to-please board chairman. "He'd look at every move we made with a microscope, and continually say, 'It hasn't been like this in the past. I'm not sure you're sticking to the strategy. We have to crush the competition.' We had the dominant marketshare, but he still wasn't satisfied. We nicknamed him Mr. Marketshare."

After the evening board meetings, students gather at one of the downtown bars to tell their horror or glory stories. Last year, there was plenty of talk about Mr. Marketshare. GSIA students gravitate to Chioto's, where Joe tends bar amidst a collection of Pittsburgh memorabilia. Adjacent to the old steel works in Homestead on the city's northside, this gathering hole is where students traditionally congregate for a wild celebration after final exams. The Squirrel Hill Cafe and Silky's, both a 15- to 20-minute walk from campus, are other GSIA hot spots. All three joints are favorite stops for the regular Tuesday night bar crawls (there are no classes on Wednesdays).

If you're wondering about Pittsburgh, don't. Forget the old polluted and smokestacked image of the place. It's an attractive, vibrant city of ethnic neighborhoods, the intellectual community of which is Oakland, where the university makes its home. "If there's any place where the smog is worse than Los Angeles, it's Pittsburgh," friends of Barrett told the Californian before he ventured to Carnegie. "It wasn't true. Pittsburgh has a lot of character as a city."

There's no dorm life at Carnegie. Instead, students are scattered around the city in different apartments and houses. It's wise to live within walking or bicycling distance because, as one student complained, "Parking is hell!" Once on campus, however, students tend to stay, spending vast amounts of time in Hunt Library, the university library next to the B-school, or walking and studying in neighboring Schenley Park, Pittsburgh's equivalent of Central Park. Students keep track of events in *Robber Barrons,* the weekly B-school newspaper.

Don't look for a roomy, modernistic B-school complex at Carnegie. Everything is crammed into an old, three-story, yellow brick building put up some 35 years ago. Back then, when a Carnegie class numbered all of 25 students, you might have called the facilities spacious. Now they are severely cramped. A new building, twice the size of the present one, is expected to be completed by 1992.

That's part of the reason students don't see a lot of high-profile dean, Elizabeth E. Baily, former commissioner and vice chairman of the Civil Aeronautics Board. She has been out fund raising and promoting the image of the school. Most students are more apt to know the fun-loving, chain-smoking associate dean, Ilker Baybars, with his heavy Turkish accent. Of the 150 on-campus recruiters last year for Carnegie's 200 students, technology-driven organizations from IBM and Sun Microsystems to Eaton and TRW headed the list. Last year Hughes Aircraft enticed five Carnegie grads, IBM took four, and Hewlett-Packard and Ford Motor got three each. American Cyanamid, Merck, Mellon Bank, and Strategic Planning Associates also attracted three Carnegie grads each. Despite the technology bent, 35% of all graduates headed for the world of finance. Call it the revenge of the nerds.

Contact: Susan Motz, Admissions Department, 412-268-2272

Prominent alumni: Paul A. Allaire, president of Xerox Corp.; Francois De Carbonnel, president of Strategic Planning Associates; William R. Dill, president of Babson College; Gerald C. Meyers, former chairman of American Motors; Frank A. Risch, corporate vice president of Exxon Chemical Co.

Carnegie-Mellon grads sound off

GSIA was the perfect experience for me. I am still discovering the many ways I grew and matured by being immersed for two years in that educational experience. GSIA turned a narrow-minded engineer into a business leader.—Project engineer

I started out at Carnegie-Mellon as a part-time student in the first class of part-time students to go through the program. I chose CMU because it allowed me to get an MBA from a Top 10 school while still working full-time. After I was laid off from my job, I went to the program on a full-time basis. While the program had its difficulties, I think on the whole it *was an excellent experience, well worth the substantial sacrifice of leisure time and money. I didn't apply to either Harvard or Stanford, but I have no doubt that I would have been accepted at both. Still, I do not regret having chosen CMU.—**Managing consultant***

I thought I'd give a brief list of the strengths and weaknesses of the program. Strengths: (1) finance, economics, production, and operations research; (2) analytical and computer skills; (3) consistently rated a Top 10 MBA school; (4) placement program; (5) professors with outstanding reputations among peers and at the forefront of knowledge in their fields; (6) curriculum—classes are taught in 7½-week mini-semesters in which a full semester's worth of material is covered; the student is then able to take many electives in his second year; (7) the students aren't all that competitive; and (8) Pittsburgh is a nice surprise. I can see why it was ranked quite highly by Rand McNally.

*There are weaknesses as well in: (1) marketing, organizational behavior; (2) communication skills (generally a weakness among most programs); (3) not all that many well-known among business executives; (4) not a well-established alumni network (it's about the size of two or three Harvard MBA classes); (5) teaching is uneven; and (6) the program is a little too quantitative.—**Managing consultant***

*Carnegie-Mellon has an oustanding reputation and a very good quantitative MBA program. However, it is my opinion that in trying to increase the size of the program the institution is diluting the quality of both the students and the education. I feel Carnegie is admitting too many students with marginal academic performance and no work experience. The placement office at Carnegie-Mellon was outstanding with quite a bit of personal attention given to students, good people, and a high interview/student ratio. The only weakness in placement was its inability to provide good matches in summer internships.—**Managing consultant***

*The farther removed from my MBA experience, the more I appreciate it. Because of the amount of work during the first year and its mostly quantitative emphasis, many people weren't comfortable with their MBA experience at Carnegie. During the second year, we began to realize that the seemingly excessive quantitative emphasis in the beginning was a method for helping us obtain skills important for analyzing quantitative problems. It helped me develop a framework for solving managerial problems. —**Corporate finance analyst***

*Carnegie-Mellon's GSIA is an extremely quantitative, analytical program. If you're strong in interpersonal skills to start with and you're looking to sharpen your analytical skills, I highly recommend the school. However, the administration is somewhat antagonistic and defensive about what it has to offer. Therefore, one should know what they want before attending, and keep that goal in their view.—**Production supervisor***

14. Columbia University

Columbia Business School
Uris Hall
New York, New York 10027

Recruiter ranking: 6
Enrollment: 1191
Women: 31%
Foreign: 20%
Minority: 13%
Part-time: None
Average age: 26.5
Applicants admitted: 30%*
Accepted applicants enrolled: 62%

Graduate ranking: 19
Annual tuition: $15,200
Room and board: $6500 to $9500
Average GMAT score: 635
GMAT range: 500 to 780
Average GPA: 3.3
GPA range: 2.4 to 4.0
Average starting pay: $49,397

Application deadline: April 20 for fall

You're standing on a crowded subway platform as a noisy train pulls into the station. When the doors open, the throng surges forward and you push your way into the car. Inside, people of all backgrounds and nationalities are packed tightly together. Just as you're ready to faint, your eyes glance across the car to see Henry Kravis, the leveraged buyout king, and Frank Lorenzo, CEO of Texas Air Corporation. If you could only move your hand enough to reach into your brief-case and pull out your résumé. . . .

Depending on the kind of person you are, this scenario could be a dream or a nightmare. The same holds true for the Columbia Business School. If fending for yourself in a hostile urban environment, doing combat with an army of future investment bankers, and rubbing elbows with the movers and shakers of high finance is your idea of B-school, Columbia is for you.

Ask a student or faculty member what the best thing about the Columbia B-school is, and no doubt the answer will be New York City. Ask what the worst thing is and you'll get the same reply. Like the Big Apple, Columbia offers glamor and excitement, but it is not for the thin-skinned or the faint-hearted. Only at Columbia can you attend a finance class taught by a corporate raider, rub elbows with a visiting Wall Street banker over lunch, dine at an Indonesian restaurant, and take in a Broadway show on the same day. But in the course of your travels you'll encounter a vibrant city suffering from neglect and crime.

Still, it's hard to overstate the wealth of opportunities available to MBAs thanks to its location in the leading cultural and financial center. Columbia is the kind of place where you can pick up *The New York Times* and read about the latest deal of someone who spoke to your class the day before. Just a short subway—or limo—ride away from Wall Street, the school is able to tap leading financiers and corporate executives as adjunct faculty. Many of them, including top officers from virtually all the big investment banks and financial service companies, had their own MBA passports stamped at Columbia. Their tales from the front lines of dealmaking provide a sharp contrast to the strong theoretical and research bent of the full-time faculty.

Columbia students tend to view each other first as competitors and second as business contacts. Indeed, its own grads ranked it as one of the four most competitive business schools in the country with Harvard, Chicago, and NYU in BUSINESS WEEK'S graduate survey. Although study groups are designed to foster cooperation, the kind of "we're all in this together" atmosphere common at Dartmouth or Virginia just doesn't seem to exist. MBAs are advised to pick members of their study groups with great care.

Many students grew up in New York or worked in the city before coming to school and already have a well-established social network. "Going to Columbia is like living a normal existence," says David Hofmann of the Class of 1989. "You have to lead your own life. You tend to function as you would in a work environment." Although Columbia has all the amenities of an Ivy League school, including a grassy quad surrounded by temples of learning, it is near Harlem.

There is a limited amount of student housing in Morningside Heights, as the Columbia campus and surrounding area is known, but your permanent address must be no more than 50 miles outside New York to qualify. Many Columbia B-school students live in apartments on the Upper West Side, a neighborhood filled with trendy restaurants, bars, and boutiques catering to young, upwardly mobile professionals. Columbia MBAs will often share a cab to campus in the morning, although hardier souls will take the IRT Local to 116th Street.

Since Columbia MBAs are spread all over the city and some commute from Connecticut and New Jersey, the school lacks the camaraderie often found when students live on or near campus. Other than the lounge in Uris Hall, the B-school building, there's no place for MBAs to hang out. The B-school even lost its favorite watering hole recently when the West End Bar closed down. So it's tougher to forge lasting friendships or romances at Columbia. Complained one obviously disgruntled Class of 1988 graduate: "The fellow students with whom I shared these last two years were frequently egotistical, overly competitive, self-centered yuppies whose most extreme idea of sharing is letting someone else look at their *New York Times*."

An MBA from Columbia may open the door to wealth and power, as it has for many of its prominent alumni, but be prepared to stand in line on the way to fame and fortune. The waiting starts as soon as you walk in the door of Uris Hall and press the button for the elevator, which is notoriously slow. It continues as you to try to change classes, use computers, buy sandwiches at the Uris Deli, and sign up for interviews with corporate recruiters.

It's hard to find a place in New York where you don't have to stand in line. Ask anybody who has seen a first-run movie lately. But Columbia students say some of the hassle could be avoided if the school's administration, faculty, and support staff paid attention to the lessons on service in any Marketing 101 course. So taxed were the facilities that the school reduced its enrollment by 80 students in 1988 to alleviate some crowding. Concedes former Acting Dean E. Kirby Warren, "When you're operating in an environment where there are five or six applicants for each position, you tend to treat students as a given."

Quality of life has never been one of the big attractions of the Columbia B-school, but as tuition has gone up, students have become less tolerant of cramped conditions, impersonal treatment, and mediocre facilities. That's why the Class of 1988 ranked the school, usually in the Top 10 of traditional listings, number 19. "We have let our standards slacken a little bit," says Hofmann. "A lot of other schools are biting at our heels. If we want to stay a Top 10 school, we have to address student concerns."

Warren attributes the rising discontent among Columbia students to the diminished job prospects following the October 1987 stock market crash. "When the job market was strong and the best students were getting four or five offers, nobody complained about lines in placement or going through a lottery," he says. A recent upheaval in the school's administration hasn't helped students' disenchantment with the program. In April 1988, Dean John C. Burton stepped down and seven professors resigned after the university declined to offer tenure to a candidate who had been unanimously approved by the B-school faculty. Following Burton's resignation, Vice Dean Warren was named acting dean.

To help polish its image, Columbia has recruited as its new dean Meyer Feldberg, former president of the Illinois Institute of Technology. The former head of Tulane University's business school, Feldberg raised millions of dollars for Tulane and IIT and is expected to do the same for Columbia, one of the few business schools in the nation with a deficit. "Meyer had a galvanic effect on the Tulane Business School, which was relatively sleepy within a fine university," says Ben Rosen, a noted venture capitalist and Columbia alum. "To the extent that a single person can affect a single institution, he can do it. I think he's really going to shine at Columbia."

Feldberg's arrival is good news for Columbia MBA students. He plans to build the school's reputation in other areas besides finance, to stress international management and improve the quality of student life. "Students really do have to be treated as consumers," Feldberg maintains. "The administration and faculty must be responsive to their needs."

Columbia has tentatively set aside real estate to build a residence hall for grad students in the B-school. Now it's up to Feldberg to raise the money. In the meantime, space in an existing building will be reserved as a dorm for Columbia MBAs interested in living in Morningside Heights. And Feldberg plans to make far greater use of the school's 20,000 alumni. Alums already counsel prospective students, give presentations to MBAs, and help new grads find jobs. Now they'll be asked to dig into their pockets to help their alma mater compete with its downtown rival, New York University's Stern School of Business. Thanks to a $40 million gift from Hartz Mountain Industries Chief Executive Leonard Stern, the B-school will move from its lower Manhattan quarters to a new building on NYU's Washington Square campus in Greenwich Village.

By placing a greater emphasis on international business, Columbia will not be unique among B-schools. However, it has a good shot at winning recognition in this area. Several of the school's highly respected research centers focus on international business, including the Center for International Business Cycle Research, the Center for Chinese Business Studies, and the Center on Japanese Economy and Business. At the B-school, 20% of the students are foreign, and international business is one of the most popular areas of concentration among students. Columbia MBAs are required to take five courses in their concentration.

Columbia allows MBAs to begin its program in any one of three terms each year. It is possible to complete the degree in 16 months, but most students use the summer term for an internship. Some 20 courses are required for the MBA. All but 1 of the 8 required core courses are bundled into the first two terms. As you might expect, for every elective in production or operations management, Columbia offers 5 in accounting and finance. MBAs can concentrate in any one of 11 areas of study, from accounting to public and nonprofit management. You can actually focus on investment management under a finance concentration or management consulting under a management of organizations concentration.

While most B-schools use executives-in-residence programs to make up for a shortfall of business executives in an area, Columbia views its ambitious program as a bit of real-world icing on a real-world cake. Last year, the school had six distinguished people aboard full-time, including Carol B. Einiger, former managing director of First Boston Corporation, and Douglas A. Fraser, former president of the United Auto Workers. It's rare that such programs boast women or labor leaders. Best full-time teaching bets? MBAs like Donald C. Hambrick for both the smarts and enthusiasm he brings to his business policy classes. John O. Whitney, former president of the Pathmark division of Supermarkets General, wins kudos from students for his Management of Turnarounds class.

A typical week at Columbia ends in the Uris Deli, where a weekly happy hour is held every Thursday night. After a few beers, students will break up into groups and go their separate ways, some heading down the West Side, others to the Village or Little Italy. Since there are no classes on Fridays, students use the three-day weekends to escape from the city or to work part-time.

Clearly, the highlight of Columbia's social season is the annual spring ball, an MBA version of the senior prom. Just like back in high school, it's not cool to attend the spring ball without a date. Tickets for the black-tie affair are $40 each, a bargain by New York standards for an event with an open bar, a live band, and dancing. The low ticket price allows MBAs to splurge on designer evening gowns, rented limos, and dinners at ritzy restaurants. The location of the spring ball changes each year and has included such historic landmarks as the New York Public Library, Federal Hall, and the Puck Building.

Columbia's placement office and its extensive alumni network help students gain entrance to leading investment and commercial banks and consulting firms—though Wall Street's slump has had its impact on the school. Grads heading off for jobs in the brokerage industry fell to 18.5% for the Class of 1988, down from more than 28% in 1987. Even so, Wall Street remained the second most popular destination for Columbia MBAs after commercial banking, which attracted 23% of the class. Consulting has taken up some of the slack, luring 16% of Columbia MBAs in 1988, compared with 8.9% the previous year.

Students not interested in finance and accounting have to work a little harder at Columbia. Plenty of MBAs land positions in international business and entrepreneurial firms all the time, but they often do it on their own. Rest assured, there's little danger of unemployment for the Columbia MBA—about 97% of grads have jobs by graduation. The risk is being seduced into taking a finance or consulting position that you don't really want. The peer pressure to accept one of these high-paying jobs can be overpowering. When the herd starts moving toward Wall Street, Columbia MBAs may have to use their street-fighting skills to avoid being dragged downtown.

Contact: Patricia J. Lang, dean of admissions, 212-854-5568

Prominent alumni: Peter A. Cohen, chairman of Shearson Lehman Hutton Inc.; Max C. Chapman, Jr., former president of Kidder, Peabody & Co.; Howard L. Clark, CFO of American Express Co.; Warren Buffett, chairman of Berkshire Hathaway; Jerome A. Chazen, co-chairman of Liz Claiborne Inc., William Dillard, chairman of Dillard Department Stores Inc.; Charles E. Exley, Jr., chairman of NCR Corp.; Paul M. Montrone, president of The Henley Group; Lionel I. Pincus, chairman of E.M. Warburg, Pincus & Co. Inc.

Columbia MBAs sound off

The one feature that distinguishes Columbia from the other top MBA programs is its ability to attract top adjunct professors from the business community. I was fortunate to be able to enroll in many of the small finance seminars taught by current leaders in their respective fields such as Asher Edelman, corporate raider; Richard Strickler, managing director in Morgan Stanley's M&A department; Ron Gottesman, senior vice president at Oppenheimer. On the flip side, the school faces the problem of lost identity. It's basically a commuter school stuck in Harlem without much of a cohesive campus environment.—Management consultant

Columbia Business School rests on its laurels. Because it is an Ivy League school, a certain aura of excellence surrounds it. The reality, however, is different. The professors at Columbia are, in some cases, world-renowned for their research but most accord short shrift to teaching. Many have lucrative consulting contracts on Wall Street and view the students as a bit of a nuisance. The administration tends to turn a deaf ear to the comments and grievances of students. Their attitude is that they are running a business and they want to "process" you as quickly as possible, so that they can get on to the next bunch. Thus, the atmosphere is rather like that of a factory, with scant school spirit.—Investment banker

There were some excellent professors, but the quality of the faculty was decidedly uneven. There was also a bad customer service problem, which led to low morale. The school was overcrowded and food service, building maintenance, etc. were poor. The administration was very inaccessible. The overall curriculum was not coordinated rationally. Many courses overlapped. Some individuals did the same case for five different classes or failed to bridge an important gap. The departments are quite feudal.—Marketing manager

I think Columbia as a business school could be more aggressive in helping students to explore alternate career options—entrepreneurism, high tech, health care, etc. I found the focus of classes, recruiting, and guest speakers to be too limited to traditional East Coast finance, marketing, and consulting-type jobs and people.—Career path unknown

Columbia Business School is ridiculously finance-oriented. I met students who took the required core courses, and then took exclusively finance and accounting courses. How good a general manager and people manager can these people be? The operations/production program was quite limited, giving me almost no options to take. The professors were visiting or adjuncts, and were quite boring. My education lacked because all the money was put toward finance and accounting.
—Corporate department head

15. Massachusetts Institute of Technology

Sloan School of Management
50 Memorial Drive
Cambridge, Massachusetts 02139

Recruiter ranking: 17
Enrollment: 391
Women: 20%
Foreign: 35%
Minority: 7%
Part-time: None
Average age: 26
Applicants accepted: 22%
Accepted applicants enrolled: 62%

Graduate ranking: 10
Annual tuition: $15,900
Room and board $13,200
Average GMAT score: 650
GMAT range: NA
Average GPA: 3.4
GPA range: NA
Average starting pay: $60,860

Application deadline: March 1 for fall

Harvard may have the world's most famous business school, but MIT's Sloan School of Management has the world's most famous B-school dean. Although Lester Thurow is not a household name, the author of *The Zero-Sum Society* is a celebrity in business circles. An articulate speaker and a prolific writer, Thurow has created a public image for himself as a controversial thinker and economist. Now he's trying to do the same for Sloan.

One of the first things Thurow did after becoming dean in 1988 was to change the name of the alumni magazine from Sloan to *MIT Management* and to add the CEOs of the largest 500 industrial companies to the mailing list. The decision to give the legendary Alfred P. Sloan, Jr. second billing provoked howls of protest from alumni who still view the long-time chairman of General Motors Corporation as synonymous with industrial leadership. "If you're a 22-year-old, you don't know who Sloan is," explains Thurow. "We want to emphasize that Sloan is part of MIT."

Regardless of the change, Sloan wouldn't be unhappy with Thurow's stated mission for the school he helped to endow back in 1938. Thurow is changing Sloan, a business school known for producing graduates who are quick with their calculators, into a breeding ground for a new generation of business leaders steeped in manufacturing and technology. The new mission: to help the United States recapture world leadership in manufacturing, long a neglected area of study at most business schools.

Thurow took the first major step in that direction in mid-1988 by establishing Leaders in Manufacturing, an intense, 24-month program allowing students to earn master's degrees in both management and engineering. Participants take a condensed version of the management school's core curriculum, design individual programs within one of five engineering departments, and attend a weekly professional seminar. The centerpiece of Leaders in Manufacturing is a six-month research internship at one of 11 sponsoring U.S. manufacturers, including Alcoa, Chrysler, Digital Equipment, Eastman Kodak, and Motorola.

Sloan's focus on technology and competitiveness isn't being limited to industrial companies. Thurow also has launched an International Financial Services Research Center to study how technology can be used to manage risk in the world's financial markets. Seven companies, including IBM, Citicorp, and DEC, are picking up the tab for the center's annual budget of more than $3 million.

All of Thurow's talk about MIT's mission, of course, is also designed to improve MIT's position in the B-school sweepstakes. More than half of the students admitted to Sloan and either Harvard, Stanford, or Wharton choose one of the other schools. Among employers, the MIT management school faces something of a "Catch 22." Corporations that are not technology-intensive ignore the program because of its reputation for technology, while high-tech companies overlook it because MIT has avoided marketing itself as the B-school for technology graduates.

Wherever Thurow goes and whatever he does tends to generate both excitement and controversy. Some MIT alumni and faculty now worry that Thurow's crusade to revive U.S. manufacturing may make the school less attractive to some students and corporate recruiters. If manufacturing is undervalued in the United States, how can a group of MIT graduates trained in this area help U.S. industry become more competitive? It is a question some alums have been asking.

Thurow also runs the risk of losing faculty who don't like the new high-tech, global slant. "An aggressive strategy is doomed to failure unless the faculty perceives the need for change," warns Frank Graves, principal in Incentives Research of Cambridge, Massachusetts. Alvin Silk, a management professor and former associate dean, recently left MIT for the Harvard Business School. Robert C. Merton, another highly-regarded MIT management professor, has also "crossed the river"—MIT's euphemism for defecting to Harvard. But Robert McKersie, a professor of human resources and industrial relations, says he doesn't sense any alienation among MIT faculty. "There's excitement because of the leadership," he maintains. "Under Lester Thurow, the Sloan school has crystallized a vision of what we do, what gives us a special identity. We're not going off in a new direction. These ideas have been here for some period of time." Indeed, the new mission builds on two existing strengths of the school—its technology bent and international focus.

The school's long-standing emphasis on the quantitative does scare away some prospective students and helps to attract a lot of engineering undergraduates who account for 40% of the students. But not all those who attend Sloan have plastic pen holders in their pockets and calculators attached to their belts. Sloanies are a diverse, eclectic group with an entrepreneurial bent. At least half plan to start their own businesses. Management classes also are open to students from other schools within MIT and other universities, including Harvard. One student said five Ph.D. candidates from Harvard were in his second-year information systems class.

Of all the major business schools, none can claim a higher foreign enrollment. Roughly one in three Sloan students is foreign, the greatest number from Japan, where an MS from MIT is considered a status symbol. Sloan receives about 200 applications from Japanese nationals each year and narrows these down to about 60 semifinalists. An associate dean travels to Japan to interview the semifinalists personally, particularly looking for those with outgoing personalities.

The Japanese influence is pervasive at MIT. Japanese corporations have endowed 16 chairs, including 3 in the management school, and spend about $4 million a year for access to research, much of it about Japan. But the prominent role played by Japanese corporations and students also opens a window onto Japanese culture and management style for Americans. During the 1988–1989 academic year, a group of American and Japanese students organized a two-week trip to Japan that included tours of state-of-the-art manufacturing plants.

There are many signs of MIT's science–math culture. A graduate of the program doesn't receive an MBA, but rather a Master of Science in Management. Buildings are numbered instead of named. Along with MIT's economics and political science departments, the Sloan school is housed in four buildings on MIT's East Campus along the Charles River. Many buildings at MIT have recently been renovated, including the Sloan Building. But you'd hardly call the campus picturesque.

Many students arrive at MIT via the Boston subway system's Red Line. The MIT subway stop at Kendall Square has been refurbished as part of a $250 million redevelopment project that includes a new Marriott Hotel and Legal Seafood, a favorite Boston restaurant. Erratic service on the Red Line is a pet peeve of Sloanies and recently inspired a team of students to undertake a systematic analysis of the line for a class project. The team's conclusion: until an operation has been studied closely, it's difficult to appreciate the trade-offs managers must make.

Team projects and study groups are a way of life at MIT. Even when not required to work in teams, students form study groups and divide reading among themselves. The small size of the management school helps create a friendly and cooperative atmosphere. "When you know the person sitting next to you, you're less likely to trounce him," says Jeffrey Barks, associate dean. Students are on a first-name basis with faculty and administration members, including Thurow.

Because MIT's quantitative–technical image can be intimidating to liberal arts types, prospective students should visit the campus, attend a few classes, and seek out grads to talk to them about their experiences. "A lot of people believe Sloan is for people who want to get into the nitty-gritty of technology, but when you visit the school you see the emphasis is on management," says Scott Beardsley, a 1989 grad now working as a consultant. MIT holds two open houses—in Cambridge and San Francisco—designed to woo students who have also been accepted by other top B-schools. More than half of the school's students attended an open house.

The only academic requirement to attend the school—other than an undergraduate degree—is two semesters of work each in calculus and economic theory. If you haven't sat through those classes, you should try to take them before arriving on campus. The reason: you're welcomed to campus in the first term with tests in calculus and economics. Students who flunk them must take noncredit courses to get up to speed, in addition to their regular load.

The work borders on the excessive and it is hard. In fact, incoming students are told the most important thing they'll learn is "selective negligence"—meaning figuring out what is critically important and what you can ignore. MIT's theoretical emphasis has traditionally contrasted with Harvard's reliance on case, though lately the programs have been moving closer together. Students do not receive any credit for class participation at MIT and professors do not usually call on students unless they raise their hands. More evidence of MIT's bias against competition between individuals is that grades aren't posted.

The core curriculum consists of 13 courses in the areas of applied economics, finance and accounting, behavioral and policy sciences, and management sciences. Most of them are completed in the first year. Students who have mastered any of the core subjects through previous academic or professional experience can obtain a waiver, allowing them to load up on more electives. Six of the core courses—Information Systems, Statistics, Decision Models, Accounting, Marketing, and Operations Management—rely heavily on personal computers and involve common data. Sloan has three computer labs, with hundreds of networked personal computers, an IBM mainframe, and a Prime minicomputer, open 24 hours. Before graduating, each MIT student is required to write a simple computer program in a high-level programming language. Popular classes include Manufacturing Policy, taught by Charles Fine; Decision Support Systems, taught by Robert Freund; Operations Management in the Service Industry, with Gabriel Bitran; and Industrial Economics for Strategic Decisions, with Robert Pindyck.

Sloanies also must undertake a requirement that's unusual in a graduate B-school. They have to complete a dissertation in the second year. Some students gripe that this takes up time that could be better spent looking for a job, but most are glad to have the experience under their belts when it's over. During the second year, students are required to take three electives leading to at least one concentration. Since the concentration requirements overlap, it is fairly easy to have more than one.

MIT management students play at least two games during their two years at the school. The first is Markstrat, a computer-based game popular at Wharton and other B-schools that is part of a marketing class at MIT. The object of Markstrat is to decide what is the proper price at which to sell electronic widgets. In the 1988–1989 academic year, MIT introduced a new systems dynamics game that simulates People Express, the now-defunct no-frills airline. In this game, students play CEO, deciding how many people to hire, when to hire them, and which new routes to open—and immediately seeing how profitability is affected. In 1989, the game culminated in an appearance by People Express founder Donald Burr, who played the game along with students. Burr told them that People Express failed because it lacked sophisticated computerized reservation systems, but the game revealed he hired people too quickly and lost control over the quality of service.

Most of MIT's social whirl is coordinated by the student-run Graduate Management Society, which sponsors boat cruises on the Charles, ski trips, barbecues, and a weekly "Consumption Function." At least once a year, the school's Japanese students host a karoke bar, where students croon golden oldies through a microphone, usually after several rounds of dry beer. Intramural sports such as football, basketball, tennis, and soccer are another way to let off steam. Another unusual student activity: the *MIT Management Review*, which claims to be the nation's only major business school journal run largely by students. The review helps students keep up with management research at the same time they are helping to run a business and earning tuition money.

Sloanies unwind at the Muddy Charles, a bar a couple of minutes from the management school. Since there aren't a lot of residential areas near MIT, students will often go over the bridge into Beacon Hill for drinks or dinner. The lack of off-campus housing near MIT and the school's proximity to the Red Line means that students are scattered all around Cambridge and Boston. As a result, they frequently socialize in their own neighborhoods. "The Sloan administration leaves the social side of education to students," complains one student. "School-sponsored parties are few and without much style except for when one of the professors gets a Nobel prize."

You might run the risk of being labeled a "techie" by attending MIT, but you'll have little trouble finding a well-paying job when you graduate. Grads got the fourth-highest-paying salaries to start in 1988. About 32% of MIT graduates end up in manufacturing—an unusually high percentage for a B-school. Most of the rest go to work in the service industry. Management consulting is the most popular profession for Sloanies, attracting one-quarter of the school's graduates. The field also generated the highest average starting salary without bonus—$62,900—for the Class of 1988.

Dean Thurow's decision to downplay the Sloan name and to move curriculum back to basics may have ruffled some feathers among older alumni. But greater interest seems to be building for people willing to commit themselves to the revival of American manufacturing. The regulatory-prone 1960s saw lawyers crowd top management, while the numbers folks seemed to have the edge in the 1970s when high inflation was the norm. For the 1990s, Thurow is betting that U.S. companies will need managers with a flair for manufacturing. If you're willing to make that bet with him, Sloan is the obvious place to be.

Contact: Diane Katz, director of admissions, 617-253-3767

Prominent alumni: John Reed, chairman of Citicorp; Alan Zakon, chairman of Boston Consulting Group; John Erdman, managing director of Morgan Stanley & Co.; Gideon Gartner, chairman of Gartner Group

Sloan MBAs sound off

At all times, the MIT environment continued to encourage and at times demand free thinking rather than simply repeating what had been said by others. I'm an enthusiastic supporter of the program.
—Senior manufacturing engineer

MIT is unusual in part because of its controversial thesis requirement. In my mind, it was one of the most valuable experiences in my two years there. It forced me to draw together much of what I learned and to integrate it with new, original ideas into an interesting piece of work. In fact, since I graduated I have been able to give several speeches based on the work I did for my thesis.—Management consultant

Sloan is currently undergoing a lot of change, especially with the arrival of Dean Thurow. It has a relatively large foreign student population, which provided for stimulating discussions and for less incestuous views of things American than you might find in institutions with smaller student populations. Sloan's students and teachers are very supportive and cooperative. This was a valuable experience in that we could learn that competitiveness is not the only way to achieve excellent results.
—Manufacturing consultant

Sloan has outstanding faculty who are extremely accessible. The school provided tremendous support for student-led extracurricular activites. The best part of the whole deal was getting to know our dean, Lester C. Thurow, very well. I would do it again in a second. The Sloan School is definitely for the person who knows what he wants in business. It's a "build your own" program.—Management consultant

16. University of California at Los Angeles

John E. Anderson Graduate School of Management
405 Hilgard Ave.
Los Angeles, California 90024

Recruiter ranking: 8
Enrollment: 1119
Women: 35%
Foreign: 15%
Minority: 17%
Part-time: 150
Average age: 27
Applicants admitted: 18%
Accepted applicants enrolled: 51%

Graduate ranking: 16
Annual tuition: nonresident—$7511
                  resident—$1712
Room and board: $7110
Average GMAT score: 645
GMAT range: 430 to 790
Average GPA: 3.56
GPA range: 2.2 to 4.0
Average starting pay: $45,378

Application deadline: March 19 for fall

The well-tanned youth ahead of you could easily be strolling down Malibu Beach. He's wearing the long baggy shorts favored by surfers and a tight black fluorescent T-shirt. Emblazoned on the back are the words "Black and Scholes Surf Club." A bunch of beach boys named after a pair of profs who dreamed up Wall Street's favorite options pricing model?

Welcome to UCLA's Anderson Graduate School of Management. It's a school that combines the popular mythology of California with the sometimes bewildering quantitative models of the business school world. Though just a short drive from the sandy beach, MBAs here are more likely to carry *The Wall Street Journal* under an arm than a surfboard, and Black and Scholes take precedence over Brian and Carl Wilson. There are probably as many students at Anderson who ache to be investment bankers as there are at Harvard, Wharton, or Stanford—the only B-schools that attract more applications.

Despite the 1988 crash and the fall of junk bond king Mike Milken, who ruled his empire from Drexel Burnham Lambert's Beverly Hills office, the world of finance still looks mighty attractive to UCLA MBAs. The magic degree from this school is no guarantee you'll land a finance job in Los Angeles, but the school is well known for excellence in the field and holds a spate of events to allow students to mix with local finance leaders and alumni. Besides, if that's not your bag, the Anderson School is a great jumping-off point for a career in entertainment. Where else could you attend class in the morning and drive over to Hollywood to knock on doors in the afternoon?

It's not unusual for students to follow the same path as Elizabeth Wills, who graduated from Anderson in 1989. After earning an undergraduate degree at Harvard, Wills worked on Wall Street for three years before deciding she was ready for a change. When she came to UCLA, Wills knew she wanted to do something entrepreneurial that involved finance, but she wasn't sure exactly what. The Anderson School helped her find a summer internship at a small leveraged buyout firm in Los Angeles, where she went to work full-time after getting her MBA. At first, Wills was slightly apprehensive about attending UCLA because she "had the impression it was a party school, especially when I read about the beer busts every Thursday night. But I was mistaken. I've worked harder here than I have any place else, including Harvard and Goldman, Sachs."

Like Wills, many students are surprised that a B-school surrounded by palm trees offers such a challenging MBA program. And the Anderson School does. But the main attractions are quality of life and price. UCLA is located in the California foothills in Westwood and borders Bel Air, an exclusive neighborhood whose denizens now include Ronald and Nancy Reagan. The atmosphere here is relaxed and friendly. Students catch some rays on the B-school patio while studying or plugging numbers into a spreadsheet on a laptop computer. Even outsiders end up singing Randy Newman's "I Love LA" by the time they graduate.

Although affordable housing is hard to come by in Westwood and nearby Santa Monica, tuition for out-of-state residents is a bargain at $7511. California residents pay a mere $1712 and many students qualify as state residents for the second year of the program. Like Los Angeles, the Anderson School's population is diverse, with a high percentage of women, foreigners, and minorities. More than 38% of Anderson's students are from California and a total of 60% are from the West. But one-quarter of the school's applications come from New York. "The Easterners have a sense of adventure," says Eric Mokover, director of admissions. "It takes guts to go to UCLA when all your friends are going to Wharton." Anderson doesn't place as much importance on GMAT scores as other B-schools, so be sure and mention on your application how you opened your first lemonade stand when you were six years old.

Along with sister school Berkeley, UCLA is a popular destination for the Japanese. Anderson receives tremendous support from current and former Japanese students. The bookstore does a healthy business in UCLA sweatshirts, which are status symbols in Japan, along with Louis Vuitton handbags and Gucci loafers. In spring 1989, the Tokyo alumni club underwrote a reception for students accepted by the Anderson School. These students also received a 40-page guide in Japanese explaining the mysteries of Southern California life—how to open a checking account, find an apartment, and buy a car—penned by a group of second-year Japanese students who sent off a group picture of themselves wearing UCLA sweatshirts.

Not every student admitted to UCLA gets this kind of VIP treatment, but the school competes with Harvard, Wharton, and Stanford by trying to take a personalized approach. Everyone accepted here receives a telephone call if they're in the United States and a letter in their native language if they're overseas. Student volunteers handle these hospitalities, helping to tout the school's image and organize activities. One reason is that as part of a state university, Anderson doesn't have the resources available to private schools to promote the MBA program to prospective students, alumni, and corporations.

Student participation, both in and out of the classroom, is a hallmark of the place. "Students are the most important part of the school," says Dean Clayburn La Force. They are involved in planning a new building to be constructed on the northwestern portion of UCLA's campus near the Sunset Boulevard/Westwood Plaza entrance. The seven buildings in the complex will be tied together by patios, walkways, and courtyards by early 1994. Anderson has been planning the new building for five years because its existing facilities are cramped. The B-school has no plans to increase MBA enrollment when the new building opens, but intends to expand its executive education program.

Students also organize most of the B-school's interaction with the local business community. The Association of Students and Business (ASB) sponsors lectures by prominent executives; career nights drawing dozens of firms in a particular industry such as finance, entertainment, or real estate; and "days on the job," where students turn company employees for a day. ASB's main event is an annual dinner that draws out high-level managers from local companies, students, and faculty. In 1989, they heard Carl Reichardt, chairman of Wells Fargo & Company.

At Anderson, teamwork is king—the result of a redesigned curriculum to foster greater group cooperation among students and faculty. All first-year students now take the same courses at the same time. Under the old system, students were essentially free to take the classes they wanted. Anderson divides the academic year into three quarters—fall, winter, and spring—instead of two semesters. At the beginning of each quarter, the class of 380 students is split up into sections of between 60 and 65 students. Students take all required core courses for that quarter with their section.

About half of the 24 courses required for an MBA are core courses. Eight cover areas such as finance, accounting, organizational behavior, marketing, statistics, and economics. To complete the core, students choose from one of two courses concerned with managing people—either Human Resource Management or Managing People in Organizations—and two of three courses covering technical areas such as information systems, macroeconomics and forecasting, and managerial model building. Students must take at least 8 of the 11 electives within the Anderson School. Three "free" electives can be taken in other UCLA departments. In taking electives, students can choose from disciplines such as finance, marketing, and management sciences—generally regarded as the Anderson School's three strongest areas—or from interdisciplinary areas such as entrepreneurial studies, international business, arts management, entertainment management, real estate, and not-for-profit public management.

Teaching has not been a consistent strength of the Anderson School and the structured first-year program has made disparities in teaching ability more obvious than ever. Professor Dominique "Mike" Hanssens, head of the faculty, says the B-school has responded to student dissatisfaction by removing professors from first-year core courses if they fail to measure up. You won't encounter that problem, however, when taking courses from William Yost in production and operations, Fred Weston and Richard Roll in finance, William G. Ouchi, author of the bestseller *Theory Z*, in organizational behavior, James Q. Wilson in politics, and José de la Torre in international management, especially his International Negotiations class, which meets from 8:30 a.m. to 4:30 p.m. every other Friday.

The culmination of UCLA's MBA program is a group consulting project that stretches over two quarters. After visiting a business to study a problem, a team of three to five students develops an analysis, writes it up, and then makes an oral presentation to company executives. The final task is a written document to the professor of record. Students sometimes gripe that the field study project can distract from their all-important job search, but it is crucial in helping students integrate knowledge acquired in the core courses.

As at many other B-schools, marketing and finance are the most popular majors among students. But Anderson's interdisciplinary entrepreneurial studies program, led by Al Osborne, is rapidly attracting a large following. William Cockrum's Managing Finance and Financing the Emerging Enterprise has emerged as one of the most popular courses in the entrepreneurial studies program, but many learning experiences take place outside the classroom. Through a mentor program, students can meet with successful entrepreneurs on a regular basis. The Small Business Consulting Association provides start-up ventures with management advice. Each spring, the Anderson School holds a contest whereby student proposals for new enterprises are judged by a panel of venture capitalists. The winners even take home small cash prizes—not enough to start a business, but perhaps to get your surfboard waxed.

Another interdisciplinary area on the rise at the Anderson School is international management. The school recently hired de la Torre, who spent 13 years with Insead (the famous Institut Européen d'Administration des Affaires) in France, to develop the international character of its program. Rather than creating a separate international management department, de la Torre wants to boost the international content of each functional area. "Our long-run goal is to have no international program because everything will be international," he says.

A key part of UCLA's international strategy is an MBA in international management that includes intensive language and culture study. Beginning in the summer of 1990, UCLA expects to offer a 24-month international program that will include nine months of study and work in a foreign country. During their time abroad, MBAs will attend a foreign university and do an internship with a local company. The program will initially be limited to 20 students who want to study Spanish or Chinese and will eventually include as much as 10% of the incoming class as well as French and Japanese educational and work experiences.

Anderson gets high marks from students for its interdisciplinary programs in entrepreneurial studies, international management, entertainment, arts management, and other areas. But students say the school drops the ball when it comes to placement. Although students meet with managers and executives from numerous industries through activities organized by the ASB, students think the placement office is concerned mainly with finding them finance jobs. "The recruitment and placement services are excellent for traditional business positions, but are almost nonexistent for the nonprofit and arts sectors," says a Class of 1988 grad. Adds another MBA: "There are a great many students at UCLA interested in marketing careers, but they are discouraged by the lack of support from the placement center." About 30% of Anderson grads get jobs in finance, the same percentage that end up working in marketing.

The influence of Hollywood is apparent in Anderson's annual Cabaret, a talent show featuring three hours of performances by faculty and students. Anderson MBAs are occasionally accused of being laid-back, but their competitive instincts come out in the annual Challenge for Charity, a contest between several West Coast B-schools to raise money for the Special Olympics. Following a training weekend in Palm Springs, 200 Anderson MBAs traveled to Palo Alto for three days of races, matches, and games in the spring of 1989. "We had more people at Challenge for Charity than Stanford," brags Doug Regan, a 1989 Anderson grad.

The school's location has a big influence on students' extracurricular activities. Since the weather is warm year-round, many social events take place outside, including the Thursday night beer busts held on the school patio. If Anderson MBAs don't feel like going to the beach to surf, swim, and sunbathe, they can hike and camp in a nearby national forest. In the winter, weekend ski trips are sponsored by You See LA, a club that helps students visit tourist attractions such as Disneyland, Universal Studios, and the Norton Simon museum. Like other LA natives, Anderson MBAs have problems finding an affordable place to live and a parking spot. UCLA has a limited amount of graduate student housing. Most MBAs live in Westwood and Santa Monica, beautiful but expensive neighborhoods. You need a car to survive in LA but many UCLA students take the bus to school because of the paucity of campus parking. Other students car pool and a few have been known to arrive on skateboards.

Contact: Eric Mokover, director of admissions, Room 3171, 213-825-8874

Prominent alumni: Howard W. Davis, president of Tracy-Locke Advertising; Laurence D. Fink, chairman and chief executive of Blackstone Financial Management; Lester B. Korn, chairman of Korn/Ferry International; Joan W. Robertson Spogli, managing director of Merrill Lynch Capital Markets

Anderson MBAs sound off

*I was pursuing an entrepreneurial area of study. UCLA provided me with the best support with venture capitalists, business planning, and accounting courses. Besides finance, UCLA is tops in awarding and fostering entrepreneurial achievement. It is due to connections developed at UCLA that I am employed by a unique firm that offers me everything I was looking for as a student.—**Benefits coordinator***

*There was such an emphasis on schmoozing with business people that it left little time for study. There was ample opportunity to learn about different career paths but little real teaching going on. Both the teaching and the recruiting were heavily skewed toward finance. It seemed we had to work in teams or case groups for everything.—**Sales/marketing coordinator***

*The teaching was very poor. The students were bright, motivated and, for the most part, very cooperative. The placement office had a very narrow view of business students. They held on to a rigid stereotype. Recruitment was almost exclusively limited to big firms.—**Executive intern***

*When I first entered UCLA, I didn't know what I wanted to do with the degree. The program, the company receptions, the company day-on-the-jobs helped me find out more about my options. The placement office was very supportive, offering training classes about résumés and interviewing, videotaped individualized interviews, and individual counseling sessions. Placement helped me analyze the type of career that would best suit my values and interests. In general, the students were supportive of each other. UCLA stresses group projects in which you have to learn to work together. This is especially true in the case of field study, in which three to five students study a major problem of a company, and offer analysis and recommendations through a thesis paper and presentation to senior management.—**Assistant personnel director***

17. University of California at Berkeley

Walter A. Haas School of Business
350 Barrows Hall
Berkeley, California 94720

Recruiter ranking: 16%
Enrollment: 710
Women: 38%
Foreign: 21%
Minority: 23%
Part-time: 251
Average age: 27
Applicants accepted: 22%
Accepted applicants enrolled: 46%

Graduate ranking: 14
Annual tuition: nonresident—$7700
                 resident—$1990
Room and board: NA
Average GMAT score: 650
GMAT range: 370 to 750
Average GPA: 3.56
GPA range: 2.35 to 4.0
Average starting pay: $45,083

Application deadline: March 1 for fall

It's been more than 20 years since Mario Savio led the free speech movement and students clashed with police in People's Park, but the word *Berkeley* still brings to mind images of student unrest. The Vietnam War is long over, but the faithful still find plenty of issues to take to the streets—apartheid, U.S. involvement in Central America, and the government's handling of AIDS, to name a few.

B-school students are rarely ones to protest, prompting their student newspaper to encourage them to get out and demonstrate while they still have the chance. "It is best to vent any radical emotions or opinions you have now, before you have a career to jeopardize," facetiously advised an editorial in the paper.

Even so, the MBAs of Berkeley clearly view themselves differently than their East Coast brethren. One recent poster portrayed the California MBA wearing an official Sierra Club T-shirt and "jams," armed with a portable computer, a power crystal, and a photo ID badge that reads, "President, High-Tech, Inc." By contrast, his East Coast counterpart wears the proverbial dark blue power suit, a red tie, and suspenders. He also carries an $800 briefcase "full of papers with numbers on them" and business cards that identify him as an "associate" (only 23 more years to make partner).

Truth is, being a liberal never went out of fashion in Berkeley, the city of protest east of San Francisco Bay. You'll find plenty of card-carrying members of the ACLU at the B-school, though they probably didn't vote for Dukakis. The commitment to equal opportunity that characterized America during the late sixties and early seventies is very much alive at Berkeley, simply dubbed "Cal" by students and faculty. Nearly 40% of the students are women and 23% are minorities. You can't beat Berkeley for cultural, ethnic, political, social, and intellectual diversity. More than 90% of students have work experience and they seem to know what they want—to make a difference in the world, as corny as that may sound. Failing that, they'll settle for interesting jobs with lots of freedom.

Berkeley's cutting-edge finance faculty draws many of Wall Street's future rocket scientists, but quants can afford to be a little weird, especially when they're making the firm millions of dollars a year. Many Berkeley MBAs gravitate toward high-tech companies like Apple Computer, Hewlett-Packard, and Sun Microsystems, where the corporate culture tolerates and sometimes encourages nonconformism. The thinking seems to be that the person who questions why something is done a certain way may come up with a better, more profitable way of doing it. Berkeley grads that don't land jobs in Silicon Valley often try the not-for-profit sector or go into business for themselves.

Befitting its diverse student population, Berkeley's B-School emphasizes an interdisciplinary approach to graduate business education. That's the way it has been since 1898 when UC Regent Arthur Rodgers, returning from a trip in Asia, maintained that business education should include faculty and courses from across the university. "I don't believe any other B-school has as many programs that are the products of real joint planning with other units on campus," says Dean Raymond Miles. "Others may talk about it, but we've been doing it for 90 years."

The B-school, recently named in honor of former Levi Strauss & Company President Walter A. Haas, offers interdisciplinary programs with the schools of engineering, law, public health, environmental design, and Asian studies. The joint MBA–MA in Asian studies offers special training in languages, political economy, history, and sociology for students interested in both business and Asia. To be accepted into the three-year program, a student must have a bachelor's degree and at least one year of a relevant Asian language. Dean Miles says the joint degree with Asian studies is "back to the future," because B-school founder Rodgers was convinced that California was the gateway to the Pacific Rim and that Berkeley should prepare its students to become "Pacific statesmen."

Berkeley's interdisciplinary approach has helped lure some leading faculty members away from top-ranked B-schools. Oliver Williamson recently left his post as professor of economics of law and organization at Yale to accept a joint appointment in economics and law at Berkeley. The author of *The Economic Institutions of Capitalism*, Williamson created the field of transaction economics and is considered a good bet to win the Nobel prize in economics. Sara Beckman, who spent several years as a management consultant and a program manager for Hewlett-Packard, turned down an offer from the Harvard Business School to teach at Berkeley because of the school's interdisciplinary emphasis.

The B-school's philosophy of not separating itself from the rest of Berkeley's 1200-acre campus has its downside. While sister school UCLA decided to house its B-school in a separate building, Berkeley's B-school opted to share facilities with the economics, political science, and sociology departments. When Barrows Hall opened in 1964, the B-school received three floors of the building, with long, narrow hallways and lots of doors. Classrooms are scattered all over campus. The B-school doesn't even have its own library. (Berkeley's business and management collections are part of the social science library, which is not in Barrows Hall.) The facilities are "bottom of the barrel," concedes one professor.

The good news is that the Haas School will be moving to a new 200,000-square-foot facility in 1992 or 1993. Designed by Santa Monica architects Moore Ruble Yudell, the "mini-campus" will consist of three buildings connected by bridges and surrounding a courtyard located at the eastern edge of the Berkeley campus near California Memorial Stadium. The B-school's new home will bring together the school's library, research centers, student computer labs, classrooms, faculty offices, and executive programs.

A $15 million gift from the Haas family will help fund the $40 million project, but the B-school is still raising money for the new building. This may explain the fervor with which *Cal Business*, the school's alumni magazine, describes the downtrodden state of existing facilities. The 56,000 square feet the Haas school occupies in Barrows

Hall "is the most overcrowded, outdated, and inflexible space of any major business school in the country," the magazine states. It further notes that Berkeley's B-school is operating with about one-eighth the space per student of Stanford and one-third that of UCLA. This is no doubt a touching plea for alumni contributions, but it does not paint an attractive picture for prospective students.

There's no question that Berkeley will be a better place after 1993, but it has a lot to offer without brand new facilities. Like MIT, the university is known for its strong engineering department and the B-school has traditionally emphasized quantitative skills. In recent years, there has been some movement toward the qualitative, to the chagrin of some students. Berkeley uses a combination of lecture and case study, with a heavy emphasis on group projects and student cooperation.

There are 10 courses in the core requirements covering areas such as finance, accounting, marketing, organizational behavior, economics, statistics, and information systems. Business and Public Policy, a core requirement taught by Robert Harris, is one of the most popular courses here. Berkeley's strength in this area can be traced back to the Sixties, when business and the B-school were under fire from many university students. The protests led to some soul-searching within the corridors of Barrows Hall. As a result, the B-school beefed up faculty in the political, legal and social aspects of business.

No future entrepreneur should go through the Haas School without taking Entrepreneurship, taught by Richard Holton, former dean, who was assistant secretary of commerce in the Kennedy Administration. The course is centered around a real-life start-up whose principals agree to work with students on a business plan for the company. Several members of Berkeley's finance faculty can speak with extra authority because they are actively involved in the markets. Hayne Leland is a principal in Leland O'Brien Rubenstein Associates, the firm that created portfolio insurance, a trading strategy that uses stock index futures to protect against a decline in equity prices. You'll find no shortage of outstanding teachers at Berkeley. Besides Harris, Holton, and Leland, Berkeley MBAs applaud Ken Rosen in real estate, Russ Winer in marketing, Charles O'Reilly in organizational behavior, Sara Beckman in manufacturing strategy, Fran Van Loo in nonprofit management, and Earl Cheit in business and public policy.

Along with UCLA, to which it is constantly compared, Berkeley's tuition for nonresidents is among the lowest of top 20 B-schools. At less than $2000 for California residents, it's an incredible deal. Getting a top-dollar education for a bargain-basement price prompted 1989 grad Rick Holstrom to cofound a fund-raising program where students pledge to the school 1% of their first year's salary. More than 50% of Haas School students participated in the first year of the program and 75% committed during the second year. "We decided to give a little something back to the school and it instantaneously institutionalized," Holstrom says.

When they're not raising money for their school, Berkeley MBAs are raising money for Special Olympics through the annual Challenge for Charity, an athletic competition among six West Coast schools. UCLA came out tops in athletic performance in 1989, while Berkeley tied Stanford for second and raised $22,000 for the Alameda County Special Olympics. "We take our fund-raising and charitable activities seriously," Holmstrom says.

They also take involvement seriously. Through MBA Associates, the student government body, Haas School students make their views known to faculty and administration on such issues as curriculum content, admissions, placement, and publications. MBAA serves as the umbrella organization for all extracurricular activities from the Pacific Rim Club and Women in Management to the Graduate Minority Business Association. These clubs promote a functional area of business by preparing résumé directories, organizing events that bring corporate executives and alumni to campus, and sponsoring "days-on-the-job," where students visit a company to learn about its operations.

Berkeley MBAs have a penchant for being entrepreneurial. Indeed, a team of researchers from the B-school and the university's Institute of Personality Assessment and Research began a seven-year personality study of 131 Berkeley MBAs in 1985. The findings: Berkeley MBAs were the third most creative group ever assessed by the institute, falling into what it terms the "entrepreneurial category." "The upside to that is the students are flexible, they take initiative and are willing to try new things," says Charles O'Reilly, a Berkeley professor and codirector of the study. "They are probably slightly less desirable for the corporate environment (because) they're likely to do well in situations that value creativity."

About 4% of the class of 1988 went directly to work for start-up ventures, but an extraordinarily high 24% took jobs at computer companies, which value creativity. However, an even greater number of them (28%) found employment in financial services. Consulting lured 13% of the class, while real estate provided jobs for 5%. Berkeley gets low marks from recruiters at national corporations partly because grads just don't want to leave the area. About 75% of them take jobs in California, while the other 25% go primarily to New York, Boston, or overseas. Few Berkeley students seem interested in working in Cincinnati or Buffalo. They're spoiled by the Bay Area's friendly people, good food, exciting cultural events, and mild—if a bit unpredictable—weather.

Eating ethnic is *de rigueur* at Berkeley: MBAs frequent Plearn for Thai, Blue Nile for Ethiopian, and Pasand for North Indian cuisine. MBAs don't crowd Berkeley's famed Chez Panisse restaurant every night, but they make a point of visiting it at least once. More typically, they head to Kip's or Bear's Lair for burgers and pizza. Despite the Bay Area's proximity to the wineries of the Napa and Sonoma valleys, local residents and MBAs are also beer and ale connoisseurs. Triple Rock, which serves beer brewed on the premises, is a favorite. Henry's and Raleigh's are also popular MBA hangouts. San Francisco is only 30 minutes away on the Bay Area Rapid Transit system, or BART, so MBAs often take in the night life there. Slim's, owned by rock star Boz Scaggs, was a hot club in 1989, as was DV8, where the musical theme changes every night.

Many Berkeley residents have plenty of money to spend on food because they live in rent-controlled apartments that cost as little as $200 a month. These were the hippies that stayed on after the sixties and became yuppies. Unfortunately for today's students, apartments are both hard to find and expensive. It's not unusual to pay $500 a month rent. The university only offers a limited amount of MBA housing and it goes fast.

If you're interested in Berkeley, you really have to visit it. Not only the city and school, but the state of mind. Stroll down Telegraph Avenue on a sunny afternoon, buy a tie-dyed T-shirt, sit down with a fortune teller, and stop for a cup of herbal tea at one of the health food joints. You might even feel tempted to etch your name on a petition to save the whales. Remember, though, to leave your power suit at home.

121

Contact: Fran Hill, director of admissions and student affairs, 415-642-0915

Prominent alumni: M. Anthony Burns, chairman of Ryder Systems; James A. Cronin, III, president of Tiger International; James R. Harvey, chairman of Transamerica Corp.; Paul M. Hazen, president of Wells Fargo Bank; Robert A. Lutz, president of operations at Chrysler Corp.

Haas grads sound off

*All MBAs will rave about the diversity of their classmates, but I really saw it fleshed out at Berkeley. We had all kinds—from women who didn't shave their legs to East Coast country club preppies, ex-ski racers, and a tennis club manager to dyed-in-the-wool corporate types. What I learned about the business world and various industries and occupations from my classmates will likely stay with me much longer than most of the course material.—**Human resources supervisor***

*Berkeley is an exceptional institution, especially when one takes into account the limited budget with which the administration works. U.C. Berkeley's greatest asset is its student population. Student involvement is exceptionally high in all areas of the program, whether it is academic, administrative, or social.—**College instructor***

*I was very, very impressed with our efforts as a class toward charity and community projects. As a class, we raised over $10,000 one year for Special Olympics. We also initiated a program whereby outgoing students pledge 1% of their first-year salary to the business school. This project is having a dramatic impact on the historically dormant alumni community.—**Computer sales representative***

*The school's placement center was virtually useless in offering help to older students. There were about 15 older students and none of us felt we received constructive, much less useful, information on how to obtain a middle management position. The school did not offer any counseling for older students regarding the difficulties we faced. We felt something could have been done by the school to help us adjust to the academic environment.—**Unemployed at time of survey***

*Berkeley's major weaknesses are related to its lack of alumni contributions/funding relative to other schools. It does not market its image or have the right personnel to do so. Also, the placement center is very weak. Berkeley's major strength is the commitment of the student body and the cooperation between students. They have been my greatest resource. Some of the professors are extraordinarily committed despite the fact they could probably make more money elsewhere.—**Product manager***

18. New York University

Leonard N. Stern School of Business
100 Trinity Place
New York, New York 10006

Recruiter ranking: 13
Enrollment: 3440
Women: 39%
Foreign: 12%
Minority: 7%
Part-time: 2267
Average age: 26
Applicants accepted: 29%
Accepted applicants enrolled: 55%

Graduate ranking: 22
Annual tuition: $14,226
Room and board: $9425
Average GMAT score: 620
GMAT range: NA
Average GPA: 3.4
GPA range: NA
Average starting pay: $47,047

Application deadline: April 15 for fall or October 15 for spring

Students gathered at the OTC—as the school cafeteria is commonly called—to watch the wreckage. Glum faces stared as the bright green stock quotes moved from right to left across a 30-foot-long ticker board that dominates the cafeteria. Local TV crews arrived to capture the sobering reactions. The stock market collapse of 1987 had special meaning for the students of New York University's Leonard N. Stern School of Business: as Wall Street turns so does NYU.

Squeezed between Steve's Pizza and the American Stock Exchange, the school is a key part of New York's financial community. The ticker tape in the cafeteria is but one sign of the school's focus on finance. One of the two worn buildings on Trinity place is named after Merrill Lynch founder Charles C. Merrill. The other takes its name from C. Walter Nichols, Sr., one of the founders of Chemical Bank. More than half the MBAs here pursue a finance major, and most of the visiting recruiters are from investment banks, brokerage firms, and commercial banks. On one nearby corner, an outdoor vendor even hawks suspenders for investment banker types.

So it was with good reason that students greeted the stock market's crash with great concern. Nearly a third of the 1987 graduates went to work in investment banking in 1987. When the final placement numbers came in for the class of 1988, only 20% headed off in that direction. The class's average starting salary still inched ahead by 5.3%, but it was the smallest rise in six years and barely half the jump for any of the previous five years.

As an urban school off a city street, Stern lacks the sense of community MBAs are likely to find at many other schools. After all, the campus is the sidewalk. Moreover, B-school faculty is scattered among three different buildings and 40% of the teachers have their principal offices at the main university campus in Washington Square. And the crowded facilities leave a lot to be desired. "It's easy to criticize the facilities," says one Stern MBA, "the poor lighting, the lack of fresh air, the abhorrent conditions in the bathrooms." Concedes Dean Richard R. West: "It is tougher to build community in a big, diverse school. [And] these buildings are not world-class facilities. You could have a palace with nothing going on in it. But it's hard to build good cars in a bad factory. We have a bad factory."

That's probably one of the major reasons why Stern MBAs weren't overly enthusiastic about the school in BUSINESS WEEK's graduate poll. Asked if their degree was worth its cost, MBAs were least satisified here of the 23 schools polled. When assessing the intelligence and interpersonal skills of their classmates, grads gave the school the lowest rating, too. And when asked how Stern teachers compared with others they've had in the past, MBAs ranked NYU teachers the third lowest—behind only Wharton and Columbia.

Some of these impressions could change dramatically in the near future, however. The school's antiquated plant will be abandoned in 1992 when it is expected to move into a new $50 million building at the university's Washington Square campus in Greenwich Village—mainly thanks to a huge $30 million gift in 1988 by Leonard Stern, chairman of Hartz Group, Inc. The 15-story building will unite the school's faculty in one location and provide MBA students with state-of-the-art classrooms and study halls.

Dean West, a Clark Kent lookalike whose son is studying for his MBA at rival Amos Tuck School, is using the move as the focal point for other major changes. To improve the school's overall quality, West is boosting full-time enrollment by 20% to 1200 students and cutting the size of the part-time student body by a third to 2000. Even though he plans to cut 15 teachers from the staff, West expects the overall student–faculty ratio to improve to 13 to 1, from about 16 to 1, by shrinking the undergraduate business school. West also will scrap the current MBA requirement that students take 24 courses—each class meets only once a week in one hour and 40 minutes. Instead, he'll concentrate on fewer courses—probably about 20—that meet twice a week.

These changes, expected to be in place by 1992, will make Stern a formidable competitor for top-tier students. They also will help Stern shake its image as a "night school"—the result of its 1916 roots as a satellite campus on Trinity Place for Wall Streeters who walked to class after work. Such students still account for a large part-time enrollment.

What's unique about Stern, however, isn't likely to change. It will remain a big, urban, diverse, and eclectic school with one of the best graduate finance programs in the world. Full- and part-time students also will continue to attend the same classes—something that many full-time MBAs enjoy because part-timers often bring real-life perspective to class discussions. Notes Mitchell Hecht of the Class of 1989, "I found myself taking classes at night to get certain professors, and in the evening classes you get students who are bond traders during the day who question and challenge some of the classroom theory. The level of dialogue and sophistication is pretty high." Stern also makes it easy for part-timers to switch to the full-time program. "A lot of people like the fact that you could start part-time and then switch to full-time," says Nancy Anderson, director of admissions. "Chicago and Kellogg are more restrictive on this."

Stern students are required to take 11 core courses—all of which can be waived if you've taken the same course as an undergraduate. Many of the remaining 13 courses required to graduate will fulfill "major" requirements. Stern students must major in one of seven functional areas: accounting, economics, finance, information systems, management, marketing, or statistics and operations research. You can even combine these majors with a further concentration in international business.

One thing is certain: at Stern, finance is king. A recent study of published research in *Financial Management* ranked Stern's finance department first in the nation ahead of Wharton, UCLA, Chicago, and Columbia. Stern's finance faculty alone outnumbers the entire faculty at many B-schools, including Amos Tuck. Almost 20% of the school's 250 courses are in the finance area, from Fixed-Income Securities to Venture Capital to Going Public.

While nonfinance types might initially cross Stern off their lists, the school boasts a top-notch program in international business. Don't peek in the course catalog and expect to find an overabundance of classes on global business, however. "It's more a matter of who you have in class and who's doing the teaching versus the number of courses," says West. Roughly 25% of the full-time MBAs are foreign—that's 300 people from 50 different countries from Maui to Peru, including what might be the largest single contingent at a U.S. B-school from Japan—80 Japanese students. The school even publishes a separate guide for international applicants.

Stern also boasts an internationally oriented faculty. Since 1980, more than 60% of the teachers hired by Stern didn't have a U.S. passport at one time. Sometimes that's a disadvantage because some students complain that they have had trouble understanding professors with heavy foreign accents. Even so, the Academy of International Business ranked Stern the nation's top school in 1988 for its international program. The centerpiece of the global slant is an exchange program Stern runs with 13 foreign graduate schools in 12 countries from the Chinese University of Hong Kong to Sweden's Stockholm School of Economics. Each year, 60 Stern students trek abroad for at least one semester in the fall of their second year.

Other surprises? Stern boasts a strong program in information systems. From 1980 to 1986, Stern faculty published more articles in the top five management information systems journals than teachers from any other B-school. Stern's strong showing is largely the result of a highly prolific professor, Henry C. Lucas, Jr. At Stern, unlike many other top schools, Information Systems for Management is a required, core course, not an elective.

Not-to-miss professors? Grads highly recommend Robert A. Kavesh's Social Setting of Business, Roy C. Smith's Investment Banking, and Zenas Block's Patterns in Entrepreneurship. The latter course, taught by Block, an entrepreneur himself, employs the case study approach and requires each student to write a business plan for a new venture or a case study on an entrepreneur. Students also praise both Kavesh and Smith for their real-world experience: Kavesh was at Chase Manhattan Bank while Smith is a retired senior partner from Goldman Sachs. You'll find a slew of Japanese and Korean students in a weekly seminar still taught by W. Edward Deming, the highly-regarded quality guru. Says one student of Deming and Kavesh: "Their classes are like oases in the desert." Student evaluations of teachers and classes are made public so Stern grads can attempt to avoid the worst of the lot by doing a little research.

Going to school in New York, of course, can be daunting for some. Stern tries to ease the transition by putting all its first-year students into blocks of 60 MBAs, each headed by a "Blockhead." Students keep tabs on happenings through the *Stern School Update*, the weekly calendar of lectures, beer blasts, and recruiter visits put out by the office of student affairs. MBAs also publish *Opportunity*, a poorly edited monthly newspaper that attempts to cover the school's ins and outs.

If you live outside a 100-mile radius of New York, you're guaranteed university housing—one big dorm is a 26-story, brick building at 26th Street and 2nd Avenue, a 15-minute subway ride on the #6 Express. B-school students often find themselves teamed with dental or medical grad students in rooms. While that may make for less intimacy among B-school students, it has its advantages. "You can at least go home and talk about something else," says Charles Chun of the Class of 1991. About 40% of Stern students hole up in university housing. Besides, there are the Thursday night beer blasts in the lobby of Merrill Hall at 90 Trinity. A popular MBA hangout is the local McAnn's Bar down the street at 50 Trinity Place.

Professors describe Stern students as street-savvy: not as intellectually probing as those at Wharton or Stanford, but more aggressive and street-smart. MBAs also think the school is more competitive than cooperative—only Harvard and Chicago garnered higher competitive ratings in bw's graduate poll. And when they meet Dean West at one of his four "Dean's Hour" sessions, they gripe about everything from the sublime to the ridiculous. At a recent session, West got an earful. He heard complaints about the quality of teaching as well as inconsistencies in core courses. One MBA also suggested that the school change all its doorknobs because the existing ones, combined with static electricity in the building, often gave students a bit of a jolt.

Some grads grouse about the lack of diversity among on-campus recruiters—largely financial service companies based in the Northeastern corridor. Stern draws few West Coast recruiters and few manufacturing or consumer packaging companies. Arthur Andersen, IBM, Citicorp, Chemical Bank, Merrill Lynch, and Salomon Brothers all hired 10 or more graduates of the Class of 1988.

Every spring, NYU garners a lot of media attention by releasing a survey of the top starting salaries for MBAs. In 1989, the poll showed Stern seventh among the best schools. However, bw's poll of starting pay, which includes bonuses, found that MBAs from 12 other schools scored higher starting salaries than NYU.

Contact: Nancy G. Anderson, director of admissions, 212-285-6251

Prominent alumni: Alan Greenspan, chairman of the Federal Reserve Board; Richard J. Kogan, president of Schering-Plough Corp.; Edward A. Fox, CEO of Student Loan Marketing Association; Henry Kaufman, president of Henry Kaufman Inc.; Leonard N. Stern, chairman of The Hartz Group; Marion O Sander, CEO of Golden West Financial

Stern MBAs sound off

*NYU is, unfortunately, a commuter school, which makes it quite difficult to make friends. Little housing is supplied to the students of the business school, and people tended to take apartments all over Manhattan, Queens, Brooklyn, and northern New Jersey, not near each other. Also, the school is heavily focused toward the finance and marketing majors, sometimes it seems to the exclusion of all others. This is especially prevalent in the office of career development.—**General manager***

*NYU is extremely finance oriented, therefore, marketing majors were at a disadvantage with regard to professors, curriculum, and recruiting. There was one shining star in the marketing department, otherwise, it was always a jumble when signing up for a marketing course.—**Advertising account executive***

NYU's location in Manhattan made for a stimulating and exciting environment to learn. The school was generous with financial aid (grants and scholarships). It met most of my expectations.—**Consultant**

I felt the faculty was excellent, very accessible, and better career advisors than the career office. Although the career office helps with résumés, cover letters, and interview skills, I feel they do not offer enough assistance in determining a student's area of interest. I took a job after graduating, only to find out it wasn't what I wanted and quit after 8 weeks. The career office had advised me to accept a job in the industry I found interesting without regard to what the job responsibilities were. This was poor advice.—**Career path unknown**

Like any other school, the quality of the class at NYU varied with the abilities and qualifications of each professor. Sometimes you were lucky and sometimes you weren't. NYU stresses getting a job from the start—I hated this fact while I was there, but looking back it was probably a good idea. Overall, I enjoyed attending NYU and felt the business knowledge that I learned will be helpful in the long run (certainly more marketable than a liberal arts degree).—**Big Eight accountant**

A unique aspect of the NYU program is the full integration of the part-time and full-time programs. While this enhances the "real world" perspective of the education through mixed classes, it also seems to lower the rigor of the overall program. As the school moves to its new location and redesigns the core curriculum, it will have to address the need to balance the value of part-timers with the reputation of the overall program.
—**Finance associate**

Outside the New York area, NYU has little name recognition. There is essentially no alumni network. The so-called board member for NYU alumni in D.C. won't even return my phone calls for an informational interview. School placement is aggressive about marketing students with previous Wall Street experience. Students with non-Wall Street backgrounds are shunted aside as "untouchables." The thesis option has been eliminated, which is a detriment in the employment interviewing process because interviewers often want to discuss a thesis project and ask for a copy of it as a work sample. Some classes are too large to be effective, and multiple choice tests frequently result. Several classes had more students than chairs. Closed book exams often were not proctored by anyone, thus students often cheated from each other or used books, etc. Professors almost always used the same exams semester after semester, which resulted in some students having access to old exams. As in law schools, all previous tests should be on public file. Due to these inadequacies, the expensive tuition just isn't merited. NYU does not deliver, and I would have been better served to go to any local public school at a quarter of the price.—**Financial analyst**

19. Yale University

School of Organization and Management
Box 1A
New Haven, Connecticut 06520

Recruiter ranking: 22	*Graduate ranking:* 15
Enrollment: 370	*Annual tuition:* $15,175
Women: 37%	*Annual fees:* $1250
Foreign: 19%	*Room and board:* $7075
Minority: 13%	*Average GMAT score:* 657
Part-time: None	*GMAT range:* 520 to 790
Average age: 27	*Average GPA:* NA
Applicants accepted: 22%	*GPA range:* NA
Accepted applicants enrolled: 60%	*Average starting pay:* $46,455

Application deadline: April 2 for fall

A university campus hadn't seen anything like it since the days of Vietnam. Protesting students waving placards and shouting slogans. Petitions being circulated for hundreds of signatures. Angry protest letters arriving by the dozens every day.

Another political storm to hit Yale University? Not at all. The uproar was over a new dean and how he planned to change Yale's School of Organization and Management. The protests began not long after Michael E. Levine, a lawyer and former chief of New York Airlines Inc., was tapped in October 1988 as dean of Yale's B-school. At the annual Harvard and Yale traditional football contest, Yale alums even rented an airplane to tow a banner aimed at Yale President Benno C. Schmidt, Jr. The message: "Benno—Save Yale School of Management. Send Levine to HBS."

Schmidt didn't send Levine packing to the Harvard Business School—and the protests continued into 1989. On graduation day, members of the B-school held black balloons with the message: "SOM it's not over!" Even today, many alums and some students remain bitter over Levine's redirection of a B-school that arguably offered the most unusual business education of all the prestige business schools.

The original founders of Yale's SOM envisioned a thinker's business school: small, communal, unorthodox, and steeped in theory and research. The goal was to meld private business training with broader views of the public and nonprofit sectors and groom leaders who could move comfortably from Wall Street to Washington and back. It was an experiment to humanize management education.

That any effort to change this vision led to passionate protest is in itself a sign of how meaningful the Yale experience was to its graduates. Alums share an almost religious devotion to the school and its original ideals. Future students needn't worry about finding themselves in the middle of the turbulence should they go to Yale. Campus life has returned to normal. "People see that we are prospering and that we have a good program for next year so the first-year students have decided to get on with their lives," says Levine. "Some of them now ask me if they can take part in the new curriculum. These are the same students who made me swear on my mother's grave that I wouldn't change a hair of the program."

As the smoke clears, people are finding that Levine's changes may not be nearly as revolutionary or radical as some protesting alums originally made out: at least, not yet. Today, however, students have less influence over how the school is run (they are no longer on the curriculum committee and they have a smaller role on the admissions committee) and the curriculum now offers them less flexibility. That's a big change on a campus where, as one administrator says, "Flexibility was a holy word." In the interest of creating a free-form environment, students were even permitted to postpone as many as two or three of their first-year required core courses into the second year. No other major B-school would routinely allow that to happen, and now it's no longer possible at Yale. Of the 20 courses required to graduate, students were able to select 9 or more electives. That has been cut back to 7 with the addition of 2 more mandatory courses. Students, however, can still take exams to exempt out of core courses, and they can continue to take electives from anywhere in the university, whether the Yale Law School or the forestry school.

The single most controversial curriculum change thus far is Levine's decision to scrap a first-year required class called Individual and Group Behavior that verged on group therapy. Instead, students will take a more traditional review course on organizational behavior. IGB was a common, central experience of the Yale program. Groups of eight students would gather in IGB to do role-playing in class and confront such issues as race and gender. The small size of the group and the frank, strikingly personal discussion in it formed the basis for enduring friendships. But some students found the experience unpleasant and objectionable. "I've had a student come in here and tell me, 'Look, I've spent a lot of money and seven years in psychotherapy. I don't have to do this again with amateurs,'" recalls Richard Silverman, director of admissions. IGB will now be available as one of 60 second-year electives. In the first year, students will take eight core courses as well as a new mandatory offering of Perspectives on Organization and Management that stretches over the first two semesters. Levine is teaching this latter course himself, bringing in business executives, consultants, and others as guests to spur real-world discussion and debate on the more theoretical foundation laid in the core courses.

In the second year, SOM grads will now choose from six to eight team-taught sections of a new course called Analysis of Institutions that will examine such issues as health care, control systems, or bargaining relationships. Each class will be taught by two teachers from different disciplines—an early format of Yale's program that had been set aside. Levine also has added a two-course "depth requirement" under which students must pick a fourth-semester seminar in such topics as international management, accounting, finance, or organizational behavior. The seminar will follow an earlier course in the same area taught in the third semester.

For the 1989–1990 class, Yale is relying heavily on visiting and adjunct faculty. SOM's tenure-track faculty numbered only 28 in early summer, about 16 teachers short of its goal. The reason: not knowing what direction a new dean would take, Yale has held back on faculty appointments for some time. Levine also moved SOM's entire operations research group—which teaches quality control and production systems—to another school in the university. How Levine fills these open slots will largely dictate whether the school becomes, as some alumni charge, a "second-rate imitation of the [University of] Chicago business program."

Expect more electives in functional areas such as finance and marketing—disciplines where Yale lacks strength compared to most traditional business programs. Today, organizational behavior electives outnumber those in general management, marketing, production, economics, and political analysis. Only the finance area, with about 12 electives, offers more courses than OB with roughly 10 different elective courses. "The emphasis of the organizational behavior courses will likely be broadened too," says Stanley Garstka, associate dean for curriculum. Of 10 OB electives, 7 are called experiential. They examine individual behavior rather than organizational behavior, concentrating on what motivates individuals and how people relate to group dynamics. Faculty expect fewer OB courses overall and a greater emphasis on organizational behavior in the future. One sure bet: grads recommend Greg Dees's Managing Small Organizations and Startups for effectively tying together finance, marketing, accounting, and personnel issues.

What truly makes the school unique among its prestige rivals hasn't changed. Levine, who has taught a seminar called Public and Private Management for the last couple of years, still wants SOM to remain true to its dual public–private mission. SOM graduates will continue to receive a master's degree in Public and Private Management, not an MBA. He also wants to retain its communal culture, even while giving students less influence in how the place is run.

While Harvard and Columbia are pressure cookers, SOM has been a hothouse. Instead of breeding brutal competition, the school promotes teamwork. "As an incoming first-year student, the most striking thing I found was how helpful second-year students were to us," says Sally Rubin who expected to graduate in 1990. "They counseled us on what courses to choose, helped with classwork, and gave us advice on job hunting. It's an informal, noncompetitive environment." Grading is a fancy pass-fail, and almost nobody flunks out. There's no grading curve, no rank in class, and no honors grade. The vast majority of students receive a grade of "proficient" in each class.

Given the differences in the program, how do Yale grads differ from others? For one thing, Yale has the oldest, most experienced students of any major B-school. On average, SOM entrants boast five years of experience—a year more than Harvard MBAs and nearly two years more than Carnegie-Mellon grads. More are married, with children.

In what is surely unusual for a school of business, a vast number of SOM grads tend to gravitate to nonbusiness activities. Roughly 50% come from public or nonprofit jobs with little or no business training or experience. Within five years of graduation, roughly 25% of the class works in the nonbusiness world. Yale's commitment to the nonbusiness sector is so great that it boasts the largest B-school internship fund to encourage students to forego lucrative summer job opportunities in investment banking and consulting for work in third world countries and charities. SOM grads who accept more traditional internships donate a fixed amount or 3% of their summer earnings to support these classmates. Nearly 50 students got monetary support from the fund in 1989.

They also are a diverse lot. In her IGB group alone, Rubin discovered a Japanese insurance professional, an Iran-born engineer, a Peace Corps volunteer, a joint-degree divinity student, a Wall Street lawyer, a retailer who ran the Stamford Center for the Homeless, and a Swiss engineer. Rubin, a Harvard undergrad with a master's degree in music from Yale, worked and lived in Paris as a flutist.

The maturity and diversity of the group lends to the communal atmosphere at Yale. Four out of five SOM students live in Yale's "graduate student ghetto," a square-mile enclave of lovely old Victorian homes broken into apartments. The neighborhood is a 15-minute walk from the cluster of low-rise buldings of metal and glass—dubbed Pizza Huts—that make up SOM, smack in the middle of the Yale campus.

Most foreign students end up in university dorms during their first year in the program. The bars of choice are Humphrey's and Christopher Martin's, though many SOM students simply prefer to hang out at each other's homes. Hardly a week passes when there aren't at least one to three parties to which virtually everyone is invited. The weekends begin early at Yale because there are no classes on Friday.

The social life and the grading policy are what make Yale so informal and noncompetitive. No major B-school scored better than Yale in fostering a "highly cooperative" environment in BUSINESS WEEK's survey of the Class of 1988. Yale also topped the poll in having the most friendly campus in the nation. SOM grads said they would have liked to have more than 70% of their classmates as friends, versus 40% at Columbia.

Yale grads, however, weren't enthusiastic about all aspects of life at SOM. Of all the major schools, Yale grads were least satisfied with the number and quality of firms recruiting on the campus. Though 15% of SOM grads go into public and nonprofit sectors, very few of those organizations come to campus to recruit. In fact, most of the 103 recruiting companies in 1989 are almost exclusively located in the Northeast corridor. With roughly the same number of graduates as the University of Virginia's Darden School of Business, Yale had fewer than half the number of recruiting companies and little more than a third of the interviews.

"The greatest problem we face is that people think we are a public policy school," says Nancy Bove, director of career development. "Students end up spending a lot of their time convincing interviewers that we are not a public policy school. There's also a feeling out there that this is a 'soft' school when that's not at all true."

For students seeking a nonbusiness career, Yale sponsors career days in Washington, D.C., and New York that draw representatives from such nonprofits as the American Red Cross, Children's Defense Fund, the Museum of Modern Art, and WNET-TV. Half of the 1000 correspondence opportunities Yale gets each year are from nonprofit and public organizations.

The protests over Levine's changes, says Bove, have so far had no effect on the recruiting process. Surely but slowly, even disgruntled alums are coming to accept the dean's changes. When news of Levine's plans first hit, one alum demanded that an endorsement of the school made in an admissions brochure be withdrawn. "The graduate wanted us to cease distribution of the brochure and threatened to sue us," recalls Richard Silverman, director of admissions. "Now, the graduate has changed her mind. Not only will she let us continue to use her picture, she's willing to provide another endorsement."

Contact: Richard Silverman, director of admissions, 203-432-5938

Prominent alumni: Ruth McMullin, president of John Wiley & Sons; James Firestone, president of American Express Japan; John Thornton, Goldman Sachs, London; Steve Denne, vice president of American Red Cross

Yale grads sound off

The school stands out for many reasons: its emphasis on public sector management, the diversity of incoming students, an outstanding organizational behavior department, a participative and cooperative atmosphere, the political activism and liberalism of student body, and a

strong sense of community among students and faculty. Most people enjoy their two years there immensely. The weaknesses are also apparent: a poor recruiting turnout among manufacturing companies and the public–nonprofit sector; average academics, with weaknesses in marketing; a very basic level of analytical skills among students; a divided faculty and administration on the issue of the school's mission. If I were giving advice to someone who was interested strictly in the quality of academics, my advice would be to go elsewhere.—**Product marketing manager**

SOM is a very dynamic and special place. I was pleased with the overwhelming majority of courses and professors, although the depth of exposure in health care is very shallow (that's why I did a double degree in public health). The on-campus recruiting is irrelevant to my field because almost no hospitals actively recruit. And I found the on-campus activities to be something of a circus—distrusting and unproductive. The workload (exacerbated in part by my dual-degree status) was often excessive. If nothing else, I learned effective time-management skills.—**Hospital administration consultant**

As a former graduate of Oxford University, I would never advise a friend to go there. But I think that going to Yale was one of the best decisions I've made. The diversity of students and their multidiscipline backgrounds, the mix of teaching methods, and the small size of the student body make it a gem of a place. Other special aspects of Yale are the student funded internship fund, which pays stipends for students who take low-paying public service internships.—**Museum administrator**

The teaching at Yale's SOM was generally excellent. But it was a horrible atmosphere. I just got our yearbook and have no idea how they got so many pictures of students smiling. People (many, not all) reveled in the grind, how much they were suffering, how many group meetings they had to attend. I plan to stay in touch with maybe 2 or 3 (out of 180 plus) classmates. I will never go to a class reunion, and I certainly will not consider donating money to SOM. In looking at the yearbook, my wife asked what fond memories I have of the place. "Damn few," I answered. —**University research coordinator**

Yale's career placement office is poorly organized. If it weren't for the Yale name, we'd all be out on the street. The greatest asset of the school was the student body: an eclectic and intellectually challenging group. The organizational behavior department was a major asset in fostering a sense of cooperation and understanding of interpersonal relationships. —**Corporate finance associate**

20. University of Rochester

William E. Simon Graduate School of Business Administration
Rochester, New York 14627

Recruiter ranking: 23
Enrollment: 750
Women: 30%
Foreign: 11%
Minority: 9%
Part-time: 420
Average age: 26
Applicants accepted: 38%
Accepted applicants enrolled: 35%

Graduate ranking: 17
Annual tuition: $13,500
Room and board: $5400
Average GMAT score: 596
GMAT range: 380 to 760
Average GPA: 3.20
GPA range: 2.2 to 4.0
Average starting pay: $39,990

Application deadline: July 1 for fall

When B-school students arrive at Dewey Hall each morning for class, he's waiting to meet them. He's still there when they leave in the afternoon to go home or to the library. He always wears a business suit and likes to hang his jacket over his shoulder, but he's also been known to sport a Simon School baseball cap.

The real William E. Simon doesn't spend all his time in Dewey Hall—it's only his statue that never leaves. But Simon's spirit and ideas are ubiquitous at the University of Rochester's B-school. His notion that free markets provide the best solutions to business problems is taught as gospel here. "William Simon is the last advocate of free markets and every faculty member at the school strongly supports open and competitive markets," says Dean Paul W. MacAvoy.

When donors make big enough contributions to get B-schools named for them, they typically show up for the ceremonies and leave, seldom to be heard from again. Not so with former Treasury Secretary Simon. Besides sharing the podium with other business leaders in the school's annual executive lecture series, he also has shown up at graduation to deliver an inspirational farewell speech. Whether out of devotion to the man, the school, or free-market principles, one class of 1988 grad recently named his son after Simon.

The belief that virtually every business decision, whether it concerns finance, marketing, organizational behavior, or operations, can be explained in terms of microeconomics permeates the school's curriculum. With the exception of the University of Chicago, there isn't another B-school more strongly committed to the free-market or price-theory approach than Simon.

B-schools seldom adhere so strongly to a single philosophy. Nor are they so dedicated to creating disciples to carry that message with them once they leave. "All of our senior faculty have degrees from Chicago so there's a feeling that we're more pure than other business schools," MacAvoy says.

Obviously, however, this is not an approach for everyone. Given the philosophical bent of the program, it is heavily quantitative and academically rigorous, more like Carnegie-Mellon or MIT and less like Harvard or Amos Tuck. The upshot: Rochester boasts outstanding programs in finance and economics, but you'll find fewer courses that stress on-the-job pragmatics here than at other B-schools. Moaned one 1988 grad: "Most of the material was too academic and too difficult to apply on the job."

Incoming students face a core curriculum of 10 courses designed to give them a solid foundation in economic theory and quantitative analysis. All of these classes, from Accounting to Management Science Models, are crammed into the first three quarters of the program in year one, and no one can get out of them. Rochester doesn't allow you to waive out of any core requirements—including Business Communications, a new class added in 1989. Students who need to brush up on math and computers can take a noncredit review course.

The analytical knowhow gained in the first year is then applied in most second-year electives that rely more heavily on the case study approach. You'll round out the program with 10 electives, half of them in an area of concentration. Most Simon MBAs pick finance, followed by accounting and marketing. These choices, however, belie the broad scope of concentrations offered by the school: computers and information systems, business environment and public policy, entrepreneurship, operations research, operations management, and organizations and markets.

None of these areas is taught in a vacuum. Several professors teach in more than one department and all adhere to an interdisciplinary approach to instruction. Former Dean William H. Meckling, who still teaches, has been a pioneer in agency theory, which analyzes how economic principles govern the behavior of individuals and organizations. Charles Plosser teaches economics, statistics, and finance. Jerold Zimmerman teaches accounting and organizational theory, while Ross Watts teaches almost as much in finance as he does in accounting.

Are you worried that your eyes might glaze over when people start talking about multiple linear regressions? Everyone from Dean MacAvoy on down earnestly believes that economic theory is not something you read about in a textbook and forget about when you leave B-school. "There's nothing more practical than theory," is an expression you'll hear more than once if you attend the Simon School. The intellectual curiosity in the air at Dewey Hall is contagious.

The finance and accounting areas have dominated the Simon School's relatively short history. Faculty members here edit three top academic journals—the *Journal of Accounting and Economics*, the *Journal of Financial Economics*, and the *Journal of Monetary Economics*. Along with a Carnegie-Mellon professor, Simon's Karl Brunner founded the Shadow Open Market Committee in 1973. This group of academic and business economists acts as a watchdog over the Federal Reserve Board by holding meetings and issuing policy statements concerning U.S. monetary policy. Dean MacAvoy is himself a well-known economist who conjured up the phrase "voodoo economics" for George Bush when Bush opposed Ronald Reagan for the Republican nomination for the president. MacAvoy served as an economic adviser to President Ford and to Bush when he was vice president.

Best teaching bets: Cliff W. Smith, Jr. has collected 4 of the last 10 superior teaching awards for his classes in finance and economics. "He has an incredible knack for taking complex, subtle issues and expressing them in layman's terms," says John Jukowski, class of 1989. His Financial Intermediation elective is a Simon School highpoint. Ray Ball is another perennial favorite of B-school students. A leading researcher, Ball teaches the introductory core course in accounting.

Like Cornell's Johnson School, the Simon School is located in upstate New York, which has more in common with the Midwest than with New York City. In many ways, Rochester is a company town, home to Eastman Kodak Company, Xerox Corporation, and Bausch & Lomb. You'll find great appreciation and plenty of corporate financial support for the arts, from the university's world-renowned Eastman School of Music to the Rochester Philharmonic Orchestra. Photo buffs find the International Museum of Photography at the George Eastman House a joy, while art lovers hang out at the university's Memorial Art Gallery.

The Simon School is part of the university's main or River Campus, located on the banks of the Genesee River about three miles from downtown. Most of the MBA action occurs in Dewey Hall, one of four stately, columned buildings on the Eastman Quadrangle. Even though it is close to downtown, the U of R's red brick buildings and a nearby public park and golf course provide a collegiate environment. The intellectual atmosphere of the Simon School is anything but stuffy.

There is no undergraduate business program at Rochester, so most of the resources here can be lavished on the MBAs and Rochester's strong Doctor of Philosophy program. The best place to study: the management library on the third floor of the university's Rush Rhees Library, located at the head of the Eastman Quad. MBAs say it's one of the quietest places on campus, where you can find anything you'll ever need for a paper or presentation.

While finance and economics dominate, Rochester also is positioning itself as an ideal place to study information systems as well as how to manage technology in the manufacturing process. Like his friend, MIT Dean Lester Thurow, Dean MacAvoy is convinced technology can help revitalize American industry and that B-schools have an important role to play in this process. Where MIT and Rochester part ways is that the Simon School believes assembly line automation must be considered within the context of a company's financial strategy. "Right now the shop floor is being run for automation, not for financial efficiency," MacAvoy says. "We can do better than the technocratic approach at MIT with our combination of market smarts and hands-on problem solving."

Since its founding three years ago, the Simon School's Center for Manufacturing and Operations Research has made a name for itself for relating manufacturing decisions to corporate financial and marketing strategies. In 1988, Xerox gave the school $5 million for faculty research in manufacturing and computer information systems. Xerox also began interviewing Simon School MBAs for jobs as production managers for the first time in 1988.

Whether Xerox will find many takers remains to be seen. Right now, only 6% of Simon School grads go to work in operations management. A whopping 64% land finance positions, while 12% head off into marketing. Most of the companies that recruit at the Simon School are either based locally or in New York, Boston, or Chicago. It is possible to land a position in California or Florida, but you'll be fighting the odds. About one-fourth of the class of 1988 ended up in New York City, where the school actually takes students for interviews. In 1988, corporate recruiters did about 1300 interviews at the school with each student averaging about 10 interviews.

Despite the renown of its faculty in financial research circles, the Simon School lacks the public recognition of Chicago and MIT, other B-schools known for their analytical expertise. In its 25-year history, the Simon School has had only two deans—Meckling and MacAvoy. Meckling's strength was being Mr. Inside, selecting faculty members with talent and building the program. By contrast, MacAvoy's mandate is to market the B-school to the world at large. Naming the school in honor of Simon has improved Rochester's visibility, but work still needs to be done. "A lot of people in the business community haven't heard about us," says Professor Cliff Smith.

Given the high number of quants roaming around Dewey Hall, it's no surprise that Simon MBAs don't spend a lot of time partying. However, since there are no classes on Fridays, students will stop by the Elmwood Inn for a beer or two on Thursday nights. During the day, students grab a bite at the Hillside Restaurant in the Susan B. Anthony dormitory, where the fare is a cut above the traditional dorm steam table.

Most students live within a half-mile of the university and return to River Campus in the evening to use the computing center and the library. The Graduate Business Club organizes coffee and donut social hours, parties with beer and pretzels, and picnics. The GSB also sponsors CEO seminars as well as business breakfasts and luncheons that in 1989 drew the likes of Robert Callander, vice chairman of Chemical Bank; Frank Zarb, chairman and CEO of Smith Barney; Peter Flanigan, managing director of Dillon, Read & Co.; and Charle Hugel, chairman of Combustion Engineering.

Assuming they have the free time, Simon MBAs have plenty of opportunity to participate in winter sports such as ice skating and downhill and cross-country skiing. In cooperation with the city of Rochester, the university operates a heated ice rink next to campus. There are also numerous intramural teams in basketball, squash, and racquetball. The Zornow Sports Center includes both indoor and outdoor tennis courts, a 24-meter swimming pool, and Nautilus exercise equipment. Once the snow melts, Simon MBAs head to the nearby public golf course and practice their putting in anticipation of the annual MBA golf tournament held at Cornell in nearby Ithaca.

Rochester winters are harsh, making some students wonder why they ventured so far north for an MBA. Humor seems to serve as the best antidote to the cabin fever known to set in after many winter nights holed up in the computing center or library. On one occasion, students were greeted by the statue of William E. Simon wearing a Halloween mask while another time he was immodestly clad in a pair of white boxer shorts with little red hearts.

Contact: Priscilla E. Gumina, director of admissions, 716-275-3533

Prominent alumni: Leonard Schutzman, treasurer of PepsiCo; Frank G. Creamer, Jr., executive director of Citicorp Real Estate Inc.; Ronald A. Homer, CEO of Bank of Boston; Alan Hasselwander, CEO of Rochester Telephone Corp.

Simon MBAs sound off

*The faculty is on the cutting edge of research in their respective fields. Because of the emphasis placed on research, however, they are not always as enthusiastic about communicating this research in the classroom.—**Junior analyst***

The Simon School is currently working to improve their marketing program. Since the school's reputation has primarily been earned in the area of finance, less attention had been traditionally given to marketing. In my second year, I saw many efforts being made to recruit new marketing faculty and elicit the interest of more high-powered marketing companies in recruiting students. I received a great deal of individual attention in my two years there and have made friendships which I'm sure will continue for years to come. The alumni network is strong, as is the school's involvement in city and university affairs. I give the program an A!—**Senior marketing research assistant**

I did not do enough research on the different philosophies of business schools. I assumed I would be taught management skills and would cover a broad base of topics. Simon did not stress people management skills at all.—**Financial analyst**

The Simon School MBA program was perfect for me. Because it had a research/analytical approach, we learned how to thoroughly think through a problem from scratch, rather than learning a cookbook solution to the problem.—**Consumer insights assistant**

The professors are at the leading edge in their fields, especially in finance, accounting, and organizational theory. For this reason, the quality of class discussion and learning was exceptionally good. It was the accessibility of faculty and their quality, which led me to attend the Simon School. It was a great experience.—**Senior analyst**

CHAPTER 6

THE RUNNERS-UP

All the attention generated by Top 20 rankings tends to obscure a fundamental reality in the world of graduate business education: There are a slew of other excellent institutions that grant the MBA. Yet, few applicants have much of a sense for these other schools. Because of the frenzy by applicants to get into a Top 20 B-school, the others are somewhat obscured from view.

BUSINESS WEEK picked the schools that are profiled in this chapter as the next best bunch on the basis of their showing in our corporate recruiter survey as well as their standing with B-school deans and others in the know. You'll find some familiar names here, like the University of Texas at Austin and the University of Southern California—schools that over the years have popped in and out of Top 20 rankings. You'll also find some less known treasures, like Washington University's Olin School of Business in St. Louis and Case Western Reserve's Weatherhead School of Management in Cleveland—schools that could break through the top-tier barrier in the near future.

Some of these schools are just as selective as some of their elite counterparts in the Top 20. The University of Washington's B-school in Seattle, for example, accepts only one in three applicants, a level of selectivity that makes the school as choosy as Indiana University or Carnegie-Mellon. And the average undergraduate grades of Washington students equal those at Columbia University.

BUSINESS WEEK lists this group without an actual ranking.

The Hidden Twenty

	Full-time enroll-ment	Total MBA cost	Starting pay	Jobs by gradua-tion
Case Western Reserve (Weatherhead)	334	$25,000	$35,000	65%
Georgetown	202	25,600	41,027	65
Michigan State	396	12,696	33,000	80
Ohio State	258	13,536	33,606	85
Pennsylvania State	302	15,388	38,000	87
Purdue (Krannert)	285	11,600	39,800	89
Southern Methodist (Cox)	160	19,770	37,000	45
Washington (Olin)	266	26,000	36,592	85
Univ. at Buffalo, SUNY	355	9,200	32,000	81
Univ. of Florida	190	12,228	32,700	80
Univ. of Georgia	120	9,700	34,500	78
Univ. of Illinois at Urbana-Champaign	247	15,572	38,481	80
Univ. of Iowa	285	12,472	31,000	50
Univ. of Minnesota (Carlson)	300	16,000	33,740	75
Univ. of Notre Dame	250	22,500	36,300	75
Univ. of Pittsburgh (Katz)	285	14,400	35,000	82
Univ. of Southern California	659	26,892	38,071	87
Univ. of Texas at Austin	1,212	7,200	40,116	80
Univ. of Washington	376	21,372	34,300	65
Univ. of Wisconsin—Madison	525	15,524	NA	NA

Case Western Reserve University

Weatherhead School of Management
Cleveland, Ohio 44106 °

Enrollment: 1026	*Annual tuition:* $12,500
Women: 33%	*Room and board:* $5800
Foreign: 9%	*Average GMAT score:* 567
Minority: 5%	*GMAT range:* NA
Part-time: 692	*Average GPA:* 3.05
Average age: 26	*GPA range:* NA
Applicants admitted: 66%	*Average starting pay:* $34,806
Accepted applicants enrolled: 49%	

Application deadline: June 1 for fall

You might not expect to find one of the country's most innovative B-school programs in a Rust Belt city like Cleveland, but check out the Weatherhead School at Case Western Reserve University. Perhaps because of its location and its relatively small size, Weatherhead is pioneering new ideas and programs in business education.

"Innovation in management education isn't really occurring at the Top 20 schools," contends Scott S. Cowen, Weatherhead dean. "It's happening at the next level of schools because things like this can rapidly propel you into the Top 20."

It's hard to think of a school that has more dramatically changed its curriculum in more creative ways than Weatherhead, which takes its name from a local entrepreneur. With an entering class of only 120 full-timers, the school promises a small, intimate learning experience. Now it's also promising one of the most distinctive MBA programs. Cowen is organizing core courses around broad themes, tying courses overall to skill development, and tailoring the MBA program to take best advantage of the strengths and weaknesses of individual students.

The students who arrive here in 1990 will immediately find themselves in a core required course dubbed Management Assessment/Development. It has a dull ring to it as many core courses do, but in this class each student will be evaluated for strengths, weaknesses, and personal skills. Professors will test you for leadership potential, for entrepreneurship, for decision making. You'll take sitdown tests, but your presentations will also be videotaped to see how they can be improved. Then, the student, consulting with faculty, will develop a tailor-made learning plan for the remainder of the two-year program.

Every course at the school has been audited, not for just the discipline-based knowledge it may impart in such fields as finance or marketing but more importantly for the skills it attempts to develop in students. If you're weak in quantitative methods, you'll be steered to courses that teach those skills better—whether they are in marketing, finance, or operations. If you're weak in communications skills, you'll pick courses that will emphasize that area regardless of their subject matter. It's far more refined than this, of course, since the faculty at Weatherhead has broken down skill development into 72 separate categories, from your ability to sell ideas to your skill in using computer modeling.

That's not all. In the first year, you'll take a pair of what Cowen is calling "perspective courses" that cover material that transcends the traditional B-school disciplines. Example: technology management, which doesn't really belong in any single department, will be team-taught by three professors from different disciplines.

You'll also become a member of an "Executive Action Team" of 12 students who will work with a host executive in the area who will serve as team mentor. Students will be paired by common interests, weaknesses, and experience. The mentor may bring the team into his or her organization to meet with managers in marketing and production. How does this differ from the typical study group? Team members won't be studying for a particular course. Instead, they'll be sharing their own different learning programs, figuring out how to work together, and exploring the sponsoring organization's way of business life.

Besides these three required courses and the team assignment, you'll have 11 more typical courses. But even here there's a big difference. Weatherhead faculty have been redesigning these core courses to overlay certain intellectual themes. "When you take accounting," says Cowen, "you are not going to just learn accounting, you're going to learn it in the context of several underlying themes." They include: the global economy, understanding the cultural settings in which managers function, social responsibility, and how to adapt to change and technology. With prior experience or an exam, you could waive 6 of these 11 classes and graduate in 12 months. Otherwise, you typically choose 6 electives from nearly 100 courses offered by a full-time tenure-track faculty of about 65. Best bets: N. Mohan Reddy in marketing, Robert Kauer in finance, and Vasu Ramanujam in management policy.

Another Weatherhead strength: its mentor program. Like SMU's B-school, Weatherhead matches students with executives from such companies as AT&T, TRW, Eaton, and McKinsey who serve as mentors throughout the length of the program. And in virtually every course here, students are organized to do projects for companies in the Cleveland area. More than 400 managers and executives annually volunteer their time in class projects, lectures, clubs, or mentorships.

What about Cleveland? This is, after all, the Rust Belt. You obviously won't find an intellectual climate such as in Ann Arbor or Berkeley, or a setting with the dynamics of a Chicago or New York. But Cleveland can surprise. The B-school took over a new, modern building in 1989 and completely renovated an older facility next door so that the two buildings are linked on the fourth, fifth, and sixth floors. It sits in a park-like campus in Cleveland's University Circle section on the eastern edge of the city. Once a rough, high-crime area, it has gone through major gentrification.

University Circle is home to the city museums of art and natural history. For drinking and eating, MBAs favor The Greenhouse, a restaurant bar on Murray Hill Drive, just a five-minute walk from campus, and Canterbury Ales, also within walking distance. Students get together for two school-wide picnics a year and frequent faculty and student softball games. And on the last Thursday afternoon of each month students meet for the latest party in a "survival series" where beer, pizza, and subs help attract a good crowd to the atrium of the new building.

Weatherhead obviously isn't on the tip of everyone's tongue. There's little brand-name identity to the program and little national recognition. Some 88 companies came to recruit on campus in 1989, with the biggest single recruiters being National City Bank (4), Ameritrust, BP America, TRW, Ernst & Whinney (3 each) and Eaton (2). In 1988, Weatherhead grads captured starting salaries that ranged from $25,000 to $72,000.

Contact: Terri Justofin, director of admissions, 216-368-3761

Georgetown University

School of Business Administration
Washington, D.C. 20057

Enrollment: 202
Women: 36%
Foreign: 25%
Minority: 13%
Part-time: None
Average age: 26
Applicants admitted: 41%
Accepted applicants enrolled: 40%

Annual tuition: $12,800
Room and board: NA
Average GMAT score: 600
GMAT range: 540 to 670 (mid 80%)
Average GPA: 3.13
GPA range: 2.67 to 3.63 (mid 80%)
Average starting pay: $41,027

Application deadline: May 1 for fall

When Melanie Hayes started looking at B-schools, she knew she wanted to go somewhere that specialized in international business. The Institut Européen d'Administration des Affaires (Insead) in Fountainebleau, France, was her first choice. But after visiting Georgetown's B-school, Hayes concluded she didn't have to leave the United States to study global management.

Georgetown versus the prestigious Insead? It seems an unlikely comparison, especially since Georgetown's MBA program is only eight years old and just recently gained accreditation. MBAs didn't even have a student government or a talent show until the 1988–1989 school year.

Yet the B-school already is making a name for itself in international business under the leadership of Dean Robert S. Parker, a former McKinsey & Company partner. His mission: to catapult Georgetown to Top 10 stature and carve out a niche as the nation's premier school for international management. He faces tough competition, but benefits greatly from the halo effect of an excellent university and from having established high admissions standards.

International business is more than just a fad at Georgetown. Each course, whether it's accounting, marketing, or production, is taught from a global perspective. The core curriculum includes a mandatory Global Environment of Business course. One of every four MBAs here is from outside the United States, and nearly three-fourths of the students speak a second language or have lived abroad. "We offer a general management program that focuses on working with and managing people of all cultures, not just Americans," Parker says. "We don't want anyone without a global perspective."

The urbane dean's focus seems a natural for Georgetown, home of the elite School of Foreign Service that trains diplomats from all over the world. The school offers MBAs an elective in International Business Diplomacy. Business types can also take courses in the highly regarded School of Language and Linguistics or choose from electives in culture, history, and social and economic development through Georgetown's Arab, Asian, Latin American, or Russian area studies programs.

Georgetown's location in the nation's capital obviously provides MBAs with a window on the relationship between business and government—another major theme that runs through the program. Just as NYU students study securities analysis with and under people who do it for a living on Wall Street, Georgetown students have the advantage of learning how government and business interests collide from adjunct faculty working at the U.S. Treasury, the Federal Reserve Board, the Small Business Administration, and the U.S. Senate Banking Committee. "One of the great things about being in Washington is that you can run down to the SEC to do research on a company," says Hayes of the Class of 1989. To promote greater understanding between private and public sector leaders, Georgetown has established a Center for Business–Government Relations.

"Quant jocks" need not apply here. About 57% of MBAs majored in social sciences as undergrads and another 15% have undergraduate degrees in humanities. In keeping with the university's liberal arts bent, MBAs are trained as generalists and must take a communications course. Georgetown loads 13 courses into the core, including a year-long ethics course that befits this Jesuit institution's tradition of emphasizing moral values.

Once you're through the core, you then select 6 electives from the 28 offered by the B-school or elsewhere in the university. Best bets? John Dealy, former president of Fairchild Industries, wins fans with his capstone course in businesss policy as well as an elective on mergers and acquisitions. Stanley Nollen's Managerial Economics, Pietra Rivoli's Financial Management, and Reena Aggarwal's Investment Analysis also draw good reviews.

Like the MBA program, the building that houses the B-school unites history with modern ideas. Built in 1795, Old North is the oldest surviving university building. It was renovated six years ago and contains two case-style classrooms and a state-of-the-art computer lab. Most students live off-campus in townhouses in the cosmopolitan neighborhood filled with trendy bars, foreign restaurants, and tony boutiques. The private homes are quite expensive, but less luxurious townhouses are shared by groups of students or yuppies just starting out on the Hill.

Georgetown itself is a wonderful playground for young adults. There are cocktail parties in the MBA lounge in Old North and groups of students often head over to The Tombs for thick, crusty pizza and beer after an exam. There's no shortage of things to do in D.C., which is why students tend not to hang around Old North when classes are over.

Despite the small size of the program, the B-school still splits incoming students into more intimate groups of 40 each. Parker wants to increase the graduating class to 160 during the next few years while at the same time boosting admissions standards. He believes he can do that without sacrificing the personalized attention MBAs get here.

In keeping with the global slant, placement helps find international jobs for U.S. graduates—whether they want to work here or go overseas—as well as for foreign students who want to return to their home country, or work abroad or in the United States for an American corporation. In 1989, 35 organizations came on campus to interview and only 65% of the MBAs had job offers when graduation rolled around. Those low numbers reflect the downside of enrolling in a new MBA program. Still, you also have to realize the school graduated only 73 MBAs in 1989 and that the on-campus recruiters are top-drawer companies, including Arthur Andersen, Bell Atlantic, Citicorp, McKinsey, Procter & Gamble, and Johnson & Johnson. With Parker's consulting connections, you know this part of the program has to improve dramatically.

Contact: Nancy S. Driscoll, director of admissions, 202-687-4200

Michigan State University

Graduate School of Business Administration
215 Eppley Center
East Lansing, Michigan 48824

Enrollment: 496
Women: 33%
Foreign: 16%
Minority: 5%
Part-time: 100
Average age: 25
Applicants accepted: 35%
Accepted applicants enrolled: 45%

Annual tuition: nonresident—$6348
resident—$3270
Room and board: $3700 to $4500
Average GMAT score: 564
GMAT range: 460 to 720
Average GPA: 3.26
GPA range: 2.8 to 3.96
Average starting pay: $33,000

Application deadline: Rolling admissions

East Lansing, Michigan, is about as far away from Wall Street as an MBA can get. Downtown is a short strip of storefronts eight blocks long and one block wide. The main drag, Grand River Avenue, was the old Indian trail from Grand Rapids to Detroit. Neighboring Lansing, home to looming smokestacks and red brick factories, is part of the industrial heartland. Manufacturing, from General Motors' expansive Buick–Oldsmobile–Cadillac complex to tiny tool and die shops, dominates the area.

About the only deal-making that goes on in these parts is when the MBAs at Michigan State University try to eke out a few more bucks from their employers. The environment has its effects on the culture of the university's B-school, where there are as many courses in materials and logistics management as there are in finance. But don't expect a drab, Rust Belt looking campus.

What will immediately impress you here is both the unexpected beauty of the campus and the size of it. "Shockingly beautiful" was the way *The Chicago Tribune* described it. The Red Cedar River flows through the handsomely landscaped and tree-lined grounds. The buildings may be a bit of a hodgepodge, from the classic red clay brick and slate roofs to rectangular slabs of concrete that look like old IBM punch cards. And there's lots of activity on the massive 2100-acre campus that overflows with 42,000 students. Over 24,000 bicycles are registered on campus.

Indeed, incoming MBAs tend to gripe about the difficulty of just knowing how to get around the place in the first few weeks. While brick and sandstone Eppley Center is home to undergraduate and graduate business students, many administrative services are centralized. So MBAs have to navigate their way around campus to different offices for everything from financial aid to placement. Registration in "The Pit"—a facility for intramural sports—is a common and unifying nightmare for new students. Under construction is a new B-school building that will more than double its space.

The MBA program, with less than 400 full-time students, is vastly overshadowed by a mammoth undergraduate business program with more than 6000 students. It imposes a huge demand upon faculty time so that some MBAs find it difficult to meet with faculty outside the classroom. Fully half of the students arrive here direct from their undergraduate colleges without work experience. "We are a state school that behaves like one so we do not discriminate against the young and inexperienced," says Bruce Coleman, director of the MBA program. Michigan State admits applicants four times a year so you don't have to wait until September to begin the program.

For business undergrads, the school also offers a shortcut: by waiving core requirements, you could gain your MBA in only one year. You'll have to give up your summer and the possibility of an internship, but a third of Michigan State's MBAs obviously think it's worth it. Otherwise, it would be a typical two-year program, though it starts late, September 20, and ends later than most, with graduation on June 10.

If you lack a BA in business, you'll take what's called a "pre-core" program of basics. Then you move to the seven required courses in the core curriculum, and about five in your area of major concentration. That leaves you with two free electives to be taken anywhere you'd like in the university. Some of this work may be at night. The full- and part-time programs are combined so that full-time MBAs sometimes take evening courses (about 20% of the classes begin in late-afternoon or at night).

Some grads are surprised by the amount of quantitative work, though few complain that the workload is excessive. Typically, a full load amounts to three classes a quarter, each a two-hour session meeting twice a week for a nine-week term. You take three quarters a year in the regular two-year program. Judging by the electives, accounting and marketing tend to be king (each with 18 offerings).

Classes worth waiting in long lines for? Owen Irvine's Macroeconomic Models and Jack Allen's Food Marketing Systems, which features a guest speaker from the corporate world at every class. If you're at Michigan State, you owe it to yourself to squeeze into Eugene Jennings's Supervisory and Executive Development, the most popular elective for nonmanagement majors. Jennings is a widely quoted observer of the business world, and a lively professor in the class.

Those who haven't given up on American manufacturing might be keen to look into Michigan State's master's degree in materials and logistics management. The program spans both the management and marketing departments in covering what Dean Richard J. Lewis calls "a complete systems approach" from procurement of materials to manufacturing and shipment to the final consumer. Some 60 students are signed up for this unusual program, sponsored by the big three automakers, Dow Chemical, 3M, and Domino's Pizza.

Aching to run a hotel or restaurant someday? You might try another unusual offering: an MBA with a major in hotel or restaurant management. The B-school offers this one with the university's School of Hotel, Restaurant and Institutional Management, which uses the university itself as a laboratory. After all, Michigan State houses 26,000 students and has one of the largest feeding systems in the nation.

You won't find the competition cut-throat, either. "I like the attitude of my fellow students," says Vic Black, who will graduate in 1990. "We are competitive with each other, but we're also willing to help each other out." That extends to study groups and spills into an active social scene. There's the annual MBA picnic at Lake Lansing Park, and every Thursday afternoon grads pick a local bar to drink and chat (Zeke's at the new Holiday Inn, Bennigan's in Okemos, or Olga's downtown are the favorites).

Some students complain that the placement office doesn't do a good enough job in attracting a national audience of recruiters. Still, about 120 companies came to Michigan State last year to interview MBAs and offer jobs with salaries that ranged from $18,000 to $100,000. The single largest group of MBAs (24%) headed for the automotive and mechanical equipment industries, while 11% went into accounting.

But, then, this is the industrial heartland.

Contact: Bruce P. Coleman, director of MBA program, 517-355-7604

145

Ohio State University

College of Business
1775 College Road
Columbus, Ohio 43210

Enrollment: 451
Women: 29%
Foreign: 14%
Minority: 12%
Part-time: 193
Average age: 25.5
Applicants admitted: 37%
Accepted applicants enrolled: 53%

Annual tuition: nonresident—$6768
resident—$2679
Room and board: $3460
Average GMAT score: 579
GMAT range: 380 to 720
Average GPA: 3.25
GPA range: 2.40 to 4.00
Average starting pay: $33,606

Application deadline: Rolling admissions

Imagine a university that puts so much trust in its MBA students that it plans to turn over $5 million of endowment money for them to invest. The closest most B-school students come to managing money is when they try to balance their personal checkbooks. Yet Ohio State University is hoping to cultivate some future Warren Buffetts. Whether the students will someday be able to outperform Buffett, one the world's most famous investors, is another matter.

Even so, when MBAs in 1988 managed $1.5 million in fake Monopoly money, their investment portfolio matched the performance of the Standard & Poor's 500 index—something that many professional money managers have had trouble achieving. In 1989, students were expected to get the task of investing real money. The novel, hands-on venture has improved the visibility of Ohio State, whose program is overshadowed by such top Midwest B-schools as Michigan and Indiana. B-school Placement Director Kim Lux received several calls from companies that wanted to interview students who helped manage the equities portfolio. Merrill Lynch, Shearson Lehman Hutton, and Prudential-Bache came up with internships for MBAs in the investment program.

All the attention was greatly welcomed here. "One of the things our MBA program lacks is national publicity," says Ken Keeley, director of the MBA program. "We're better than people think we are, but they don't hear about us." That's partly because there's little to differentiate the school from its B-school brethren. Although it is one of the nation's top schools in operations and logistics management, finance and accounting are also strong departments.

People tend to overlook Ohio State partly because only 140 full-time students are in each graduating class, less than half those at Michigan and Indiana. The smaller program helps promote a strong sense of camaraderie among students that can be comforting on a campus with 55,000 students. But it doesn't help spread the word about the B-school's program, and it also hurts Ohio State in the placement area. Some companies aren't willing to make the trip to Columbus because they cannot fill more than a day of interviews. Cincinnati-based Procter & Gamble, for example, recently stopped recruiting on campus because it could not fill its interview schedule.

Ohio State wants to increase the size of its MBA program to 250 students a year, but the B-school's facilities are already overcrowded. The College of Business is currently housed in Hagerty and Page Halls, though Ohio State is seeking to raise $30 million for a new B-school facility.

Ohio State splits its incoming class of 140 MBAs into four groups of 35 students that pass through the 15 courses in the core curriculum together in classes of 70 students each. You then get to choose 9 electives from among 74 offered by the B-school. Ohio State has as many advanced courses in operations and logistics (7) as it has in marketing. The most (21) are piled up in management and human resources. A third of your electives must be taken in one of nine areas of emphasis that include insurance and risk, international business, and real estate. In all, 24 courses are required to graduate.

You also have the opportunity to develop concentrations in hospital and health service administration, sports administration, pharmacy and health care, and agricultural economics by signing up for courses in other OSU departments. If you come here, grads say you shouldn't miss David Cole's seminar in financial institutions or Roger Blackwell's course in consumer behavior. Applied Marketing Planning, taught by Peter Dickson, is another favorite.

In many of these courses, group work and team spirit are emphasized. Consider the investment management program, under the supervision of finance professors Stephen Buser and Anthony Sanders. Students in a finance elective are assigned to one of several teams that help manage an equities portfolio inherited from the previous class. One team is responsible for monitoring the portfolio's performance and reporting to the university treasurer. Other teams work with securities dealers, evaluate investment services, coordinate guest speakers, and handle media and public relations.

Like most B-schools, Ohio State has an active MBA Association, which holds an annual MBA follies. The 1989 follies at the Olde Grandview Inn included a formal dinner, skits, musical numbers, and a mock awards ceremony. MBAs who were always late for class received cheap watches. Another student was recognized for the dubious achievement of breaking his foot and indefinitely extending his handicapped parking sticker. (Parking is hard to come by on the Ohio State campus.) The MBA Association also holds a picnic twice a year and sponsors an annual golf day that pairs MBAs with executives from Ohio companies that recruit at the B-school.

Nearly all MBAs live off campus in Columbus, where a one-bedroom apartment can be found for between $350 and $400 a month. The Avenue and Zeno's are the drinking establishments favored by Ohio State MBAs, while Max & Erma's serves up the best hamburgers in town. Columbus, the capital and largest city in Ohio, may not spring to mind as one of the best places to live in the United States, but students and residents swear by the quality of life here. More than 30% of the Class of 1989 took jobs in the Columbus area and another 17% found employment in other parts of Ohio.

About 200 companies recruit at Ohio State, offering MBAs starting salaries that ranged from a low of $24,000 to a high of $60,000 in 1988. The biggest recruiters: Bank One of Columbus, Huntington National Bank, National Bank of Detroit, Arthur Andersen, Ford Motor Co., NCR Corp., and GTE Corp. Finance is the most popular industry choice of MBAs, taking 37% of the graduating class, followed by marketing with 20%, and operations and logistics with 12%.

Students say the placement office needs to do a better job of attracting national companies, especially in consumer products marketing. "The school has yet to establish a national reputation," says Jennifer Crites. "Time and money have to be spent to make finding a job a little easier."

Contact: Mary Rose, coordinator of MBA admissions, 614-292-8511

Pennsylvania State University

College of Business Administration
University Park, Pennsylvania 16802

Enrollment: 302
Women: 26%
Foreign: 15%
Minority: 14%
Part-time: None
Average age: 25
Applicants accepted: 30%
Accepted applicants enrolled: 49%

Annual tuition: nonresident—$7694
     resident—$3850
Room and board: $3100
Average GMAT score: NA
GMAT range: NA
Average GPA: 3.2
GPA range: 2.55 to 3.65 (mid 80%)
Average starting pay: $38,000

Application deadline: June 30 for fall

Before deciding where to get his MBA, Paul Lindsay took a week during a recent summer to check out five schools. Penn State was his last stop. As he walked through the door of the College of Business Administration, the receptionist said his name. "I had the feeling they were waiting for me," Lindsay says. After a student took him out to lunch, Lindsay spent an hour each with the admissions and placement directors.

All B-schools claim to take a personal interest in their MBA students, but at Penn State it's not a hollow promise. The small size of the program—no more than 160 in each graduating class—allows administration and faculty members to get to know students well. Each incoming class is divided into four sections of 40 (instead of the giant classes of 90 that typify the Harvard experience) who take core courses together. There is only one section in each core course and the average class size in elective courses is 12.

Penn State's MBA program requires total immersion. MBA students are accepted only in the fall and must spend two academic years in the program. The school does not accept part-time students and there are no commuters. All students live within five miles of the B-school. Penn State likes to say that it is equidistant from everywhere, but it's also in the middle of nowhere. The school is smack in the center of Pennsylvania, off Interstate 80. Pittsburgh is 120 miles west and Philadelphia 150 miles east. Other than Penn State's sprawling 5032-acre University Park campus with 30,000 students, there's nothing much else here. That means there are few distractions from study and few opportunities for internships or part-time jobs during the school year.

What sets the program apart is its emphasis on communications. Learning how to write a convincing business report or give a dynamic multi-media presentation is never an afterthought. Penn became one of the first schools to make communications a required component of the MBA program 14 years ago. To graduate, students must take a year-long Managerial Communications course for which they receive three credits. So effective is the program that GTE Corporation has been known to ask the Penn State MBAs it hires to teach presentation skills to other employees. "The amount we spend on communications is unique," says Merlin Ritz, admissions coordinator. "A lot of other schools have looked at our program and they say they can't afford it."

The key course is taught by an interdisciplinary team of professors who assign students to write business memos and letters and to make individual and group oral presentations. Each presentation is recorded on videotape so students' progress can be monitored throughout the year. "It's painful the first time you see yourself on videotape, but you get tough fast," says Joan Curley of the Class of 1989. An annual high point is when the class splits into consulting teams that are given 72 hours to study a business problem, develop a solution, and make a case presentation. The winning teams present their recommendations to a panel of presidents and CEOs of major companies.

There are 13 courses in Penn State's core curriculum, including the year-long communications course. Penn State tells prospective MBAs to expect between 50 and 70 hours of work a week during their first year, but students say it can approach 90. After taking 10 core courses in the first year, you'll have another 3 in the second. The curriculum doesn't offer much flexibility, but it gives students a solid foundation in business. After you meet the requirement to take at least 3 electives in one of 13 areas of emphasis, you have only 2 free electives. The B-school offers 78 advanced courses. To graduate with honors, students must complete a professional paper that is the equivalent of a master's thesis. Penn doesn't lack for good teachers. Dan Toy has won a following among students for his Quantitative Analysis for Marketing Decisions. J. Randall Woolridge wins high marks for two courses, Financial Decision Processes and Security Analysis.

One hidden strength is business logistics and transportation—the distribution of products after they are manufactured—in which Penn State is considered one of the top schools. Thanks to the marketing department's Institute for the Study of Business Markets, the B-school is renowned for its expertise in business-to-business marketing, an area many other schools are only beginning to discover. Penn State has recently taken advantage of the university's strength in engineering by adding a manufacturing option in 1989 for students with undergraduate degrees in engineering.

Most of the B-school's social life revolves around the MBA Association, which holds several formal events, a Halloween party, bowling outings, and tailgate parties before football games, where MBAs sit together to cheer on Penn State's Nittany Lions. If you've never been to a game in Beaver Stadium surrounded by 80,000 screaming fans, it's hard to imagine the devotion grads here have to their alma mater. Alumni loyalty recently inspired Merrill Lynch and its chairman, William A. Schreyer, who has a Penn State BA in commerce and finance, to donate $1 million to establish a global management chair in Schreyer's name.

Some students escape to Stone Valley Recreational Area for boating or fishing on a 72-acre lake. Rather than spending time in bars or restaurants, students save money by attending parties given by classmates or organized by MBAA. "The first year you are so busy the only social things you have time for are those that fall naturally," says Curley of the Class of 1989. Lindsay agrees. "Most first-years come here with a new set of golf clubs but the first year is so overwhelming, everything like that gets pushed aside," he says.

The hard work pays off. Nearly 90% of students have jobs by the time they graduate. University Park may be out in the boondocks, but corporate America recruits heavily here. Recruiting companies (170) actually outnumber the 160 MBAs Penn State graduates each year. About a quarter of grads go to work in finance, the same number that find jobs in marketing. Recruiters luring the most MBAs are IBM, Ford Motor Co., Mobil, Digital Equipment Corp., Xerox, Procter & Gamble, and 3M.

Penn State MBAs aren't forgotten when they hook up with one of these top firms. Not only do administrators know your name when you arrive on the doorstep, they also remember you when you're gone.

Contact: Merlin C. Ritz, admissions coordinator, 814-863-0474

Purdue University

Krannert Graduate School of Management
West Lafayette, Indiana 47907

Enrollment: 285
Women: 25%
Foreign: 12%
Minority: 10%
Part-time: None
Average age: 26
Applicants admitted: 29%
Accepted applicants enrolled: 50%

Annual tuition: nonresident—$5800
resident—$1916
Room and board: $4500
Average GMAT score: 595
GMAT range: 550 to 780
Average GPA: 3.3
GPA range: 2.8 to 4.0
Average starting pay: $39,800

Application deadline: April 15 for fall

If you're not from these parts, you immediately have to know that Frank Perdue, chicken salesman extraordinaire, has nothing to do with Purdue University or its School of Management. That's important because it's somewhat unnerving, if typical, for out-of-towners to ask if the scrawny CEO of Perdue fame is affiliated with the school.

Yet, the unpretentious, down home style he portrays in his famous television ads neatly captures the spirit of this small, conservative university town. "If you're looking for an Ivy League, John Kennedy type of sophistication, that's not us," says Stephen J. Resch, director of placement. You'll feel a sense of belonging here. "You walk down the street and strangers say hello," says Brian Vos, a 1989 graduate who now works for Gallo Winery in California. "You go to the dry cleaner without enough cash and they tell you, 'Don't worry about it. Pay me next time.' People here are so open and trusting."

You can spot the seven-story Krannert Building, named after the founder of Inland Container Corporation, on the southeast edge of the university's stately 1565-acre campus. In a sea of red brick buildings, it is a massive block of white concrete with narrow strip windows that run up and down. The top floor is packed with computer equipment, while the ground floor is home to a French provincial drawing room that serves as the student lounge. In what is a Krannert ritual, graduate students and some faculty gather in this room at 9:30 a.m. for coffee after the first-period class.

The B-school is linked via underground tunnel to a pair of adjacent graduate dorms as well as the Purdue Memorial Union, a popular spot for a quick and cheap lunch. It's also only a block away from Chauncy Hill Mall, where grads sometimes meet at Quincy's for drinks, or stop in at Garcia's Pan Pizza, Toogies' cookies, and Penquin's ice cream. Almost a second graduate lounge is Harry's Chocolate Shop, an old, weathered place with scribblings on the walls where students migrate after exams. Many grads live off-campus where you can get a one-bedroom apartment for as little as $250 a month. You can park in the Grant Street garage just across from the B-school for only $15 a year.

West Lafayette isn't exactly the most exciting place in the world. "There are few distractions here," adds Vos. "You don't have a beach, and you don't have a lot of culture other than what the school provides. So your focus in on school." Chicago is 120 miles to the north, while Indianapolis is 70 miles to the south. For biz grads, there's an annual picnic and the softball game on Intramural Field near the Purdue Airport on Groundhog Day, even when there's snow on the ground. Big Ten football and basketball games are *de rigueur*.

Students here don't receive the MBA. They get a Master of Science in either industrial administration or management—a difference that reflects the program's emphasis on technical and analytical training. About 60% of the students have undergraduate degrees in science or engineering. There's also a major difference in these two master's degrees. The MS in industrial administration is granted when you complete Purdue's equivalent of the marathon, a frantically paced run to get a graduate degree in 11 months. (The University of Pittsburgh and Southern Methodist University offer the same type of program.) The MS in management is the traditional two-year program that permits a concentration in operations, finance, or another functional area of management.

In year one, your first two semesters are crammed with 11 required core courses. "The first semester is a real trial," says Elizabeth Bostwick, who graduated in 1989. "The program puts you through a lot of quantitative exercises." At the same time, the school claims it is one of only a handful where students must fulfill a written communication requirement as part of a first-semester managerial policy report course. More than half the students here also find themselves in one or more consulting experiences with real companies. In case study courses, half your grade is based on class participation.

In the second year, another 5 core courses are thrown in. That leaves you with 6 electives, 4 of which are generally consumed by one of 8 "options," or majors, from accounting to strategic management. You can increase your load of electives by waiving out of some core courses. Krannert offers only about 75 electives, a sore point among students who believe the school should hire more faculty to offer a broader array of courses. An additional 18 courses, however, are offered to students who study operations management—one of Purdue's major strengths. Dean Ronald Frank is building upon this reputation with a relatively new Center for the Management of Manufacturing Enterprises. He also expects a new "option" in manufacturing—a joint program with Purdue's engineering department.

Krannert is one of the few B-schools to offer an MS in human resource management, a track that delves into company staffing and selection, compensation, and human resource planning. The program adopts an interdisciplinary approach with courses from the university's economics, sociology, psychology, and communications departments. About 22 students graduated with this degree in 1989.

Grads who go through this program get to see a bit more of one of Krannert's best teachers, Chris J. Berger, a specialist in organizational behavior. Arnold C. Cooper wins student plaudits for his courses in strategic management and entrepreneurship, as does Carolyn Woo, who is known for challenging her students to back up statements in class. "She'll force you to develop a logical thought process," says one fan. Grads also favor John McConnell and Robert Johnson for finance courses.

Krannert grads have little reason to complain about the placement office. Each student gets about 15 on-campus job interviews—and 3 offers, up from 1.2 five years ago. In 1989, about 148 companies came to recruit MBAs and 90% of the class had job offers by graduation day. Despite the manufacturing focus, more students head for finance (35%) and marketing (22%) than operations and engineering (20%). General Motors, Ford Motor, Otis Elevator, Hewlett-Packard, Air Products & Chemicals, and IBM hire the largest number of Krannert grads.

Contact: Ward D. Snearly, associate director of master's program, 317-494-4365

Southern Methodist University

Edwin L. Cox School of Business
Dallas, Texas 75275

Enrollment: 541	*Annual tuition:* $19,770
Women: 25%	*Other expenses:* $1000
Foreign: 5%	*Room and board:* $8500
Minority: 3%	*Average GMAT score:* 565
Part-time: 380	*GMAT range:* 490 to 740
Average age: 25.5	*Average GPA:* 3.17
Applicants accepted: 47%	*GPA range:* NA
Accepted applicants enrolled: 65%	*Average starting pay* $36,384

Application deadline: November 1 for spring/May 15 for fall

Just a few years ago, the idea of having a mentor to provide career advice and counsel was a hot idea. Some corporations even launched formal programs to encourage apprenticeships as a method of executive development. After all, it's helpful to have someone to rely upon for unbiased counsel and help.

Want a mentor? Here's a B-school that will actually help align you with one. The Edwin L. Cox School of Business has this down to a science. At an orientation reception before classes begin in August, students mingle with the group of 100 business executives in Dallas who have volunteered to pitch in. You're even handed a book of biographies on the mentors to help you choose from one to three of them.

Soon after, the pairings begin. The vice president of human resources for Neiman-Marcus? A managing partner of Touche Ross? The general manager of Lehndorff-LGB Minerals? A vice president of Arco Oil & Gas? All of them and more will meet with MBA protégés on a regular basis, offering everything from advice on how to handle the tough workload of this program to future careers.

It's an unusual feature of an unusual MBA program. Like the programs at the University of Pittsburgh and Purdue, the Cox School offers the chance to get an MBA in one year. The compressed trimester schedule begins in late August and culminates in the same month the following year. The pace is obviously frenetic, but students are willing to put up with it because they can get an MBA in nearly half the time. "About 80% of my classmates are here because we can get in and out of here in a year," says James Lerdal, a 1989 graduate who now works for Texas Commerce Bank. "It's very rigorous. It's jumping from test to test. Last semester there was one 12-week stretch where I didn't have a weekend to myself."

Named after a Dallas oil and gas entrepreneur, the Cox School enrolls only 160 full-time students a year. So you're assured a rather intimate, if grueling, MBA experience. "SMU is a relatively small school so every aspect of university life is more personalized," says Arden Showalter, director of placement. And it's all in the land of Dallas. "People used to view Dallas as the Emerald City, but that's not so anymore," says Philip J. Miller, director of MBA programs. The economy of Texas, suffering from low energy prices and a banking crisis, wiped out any image of Oz. A dropoff in applications in 1988 caused some concern at the school, but Miller says they were back to normal in 1989.

This is a 48-hour program, with 33 hours of the teaching in core courses. Each required class puts the emphasis on five key issues: international business, ethics, database management, written communications, and leadership. Students can choose up to 15 electives from an array of 75 in six functional departments, the lion's share offered in finance. Many of these courses are in the evening, combined with the part-time program. You can take electives outside the Cox School, though that's pretty difficult because the rest of the university is on a different schedule. Owing to its Texas locale, Cox also boasts a bevy of courses in oil and gas.

Everyone gets a dose of "Stiebernomics"— that's what grads call the core introductory economics course deftly taught by John Stieber, a man known for bad jokes and pithy lessons on life. George Hempel's Financial Intermediaries saw lots of sober-looking folks from Texas's troubled banking community tell about their struggles to turnaround the loss-plagued S&Ls. Also try to get Richard Bettis for your required Business Policy course or sign up for his Global Strategy elective.

SMU also offers the typical joint-degree program in law and business. Less typical, however, and more innovative is its program granting a master's in the fine arts from SMU's Meadows School with the MBA from Cox in just two years. The program, restricted to about 15 new students a year, offers an ideal educational background for an administrative job in the art world. In the program's final semester, you're assigned an internship with a museum, orchestra, or zoo. Last year's graduates flocked to jobs at such places as the Philadelphia Orchestra, the Dallas Symphony, the Fort Worth Opera, and the Bosch in Germany.

When you're not in the classroom, the grassy campus is inviting enough to study outdoors. The university's affiliation with the Methodist Church means that virtually all drinking must be done off campus. That's no problem at all for SMU MBAs who don't have classes on Fridays. One Thursday evening ritual: margaritas on the patio at "OTB"—short for On the Border, a Mexican restaurant and bar only a short drive from Cox.

The university's tree-lined, 60-acre campus is set in the middle of University Park, an affluent residential area five miles from downtown Dallas. The two-year-old, $17-million Cox School is a horseshoe-shaped building with an open courtyard in the center. Undergraduate and graduate business students have separate wings and dedicated classrooms in the three-story brick building. Few SMU grads live on campus. Most make their home in "the village," a residential area of apartment complexes about a half-mile away from campus.

Wherever you live, you'll likely stay there for the entire year because most students lack the time for summer internships due to the one-year program. True, some students arrange short work–study pacts with local companies, such as Trammell Crow, Frito-Lay, Dr. Pepper, and American Airlines. They can even gain credit for them as a "Directed Study." But it's certainly not the norm. So expect to lose the opportunity of a summer internship if you go to Cox.

Students also gripe that the academic workload is too heavy to allow them to conduct a job search as graduation nears. Some 55 companies, mostly the regional offices of major companies and Dallas-headquartered firms, recruited on campus last year. Where did they end up? The single biggest group (17%) went to work in commercial banking, while 15% headed for real estate. MBAs here won starting salaries from a low of $26,000 to a high of $68,000 in 1988. For graduating from a one-year program in troubled Texas these days, that's not bad at all.

Contact: Audrey Randuk, assistant director for admissions, 214-692-2630

Washington University

John M. Olin School of Business
One Brookings Drive
St. Louis, Missouri 63130

Enrollment: 570
Women: 30%
Foreign: 6%
Minority: 8%
Part-time: 304
Average age: 25
Applicants admitted: 50%
Accepted applicants enrolled: 39%

Annual tuition: $13,000
Room and board: $7000
Average GMAT score: 602
GMAT range: 500 to 730
Average GPA: 3.2
GPA range: 2.3 to 4.0
Average starting pay: $36,590

Application deadline: December 12/May 15/July 15 for fall

If a business school were a hit record on the Billboard charts, the John M. Olin School of Business would arrive there with a bullet. Washington University's B-school is a hidden treasure among the 20 second-tier schools. Like Duke University only a few years ago, it stands ready to break into the top ranks of the nation's best business schools. Why? It has the two crucial ingredients: the money and an aggressive dean bent on making a difference.

The money came in 1988 when the John M. Olin Foundation gave the school a $15 million grant—enough loot to get the school to name itself after the former chairman of Olin Corporation. The school expects others to match that grant by 1992. All that cash will go toward building the program's quality since it already boasts a modern $13.5 million home in John E. Simon Hall, which opened in 1986.

The dean came in Robert L. Virgil, who has been working hard to improve the place for the past 12 years. The faculty now numbers 48, up from only 5 a dozen years ago. Back then, there were no international students, virtually none of the full-time MBA candidates had work experience, and the average GMAT for admitted students was 520. Today, 70% have one to two years of experience and the average GMAT of an admit is higher than those at Texas, Minnesota, or Southern California. Virgil has even lured tenured faculty to Olin from Dartmouth, Chicago, and Yale.

"It's a small school striving to be the best it can," says Jennifer Plumley, a 1989 graduate who now works with McKinsey & Co. "So there's a real energy and feeling of upward growth. There's a lot of pride in how far the school has come and where it's going." Adds Patricia Masidonski, director of placement, "We know we are on the threshold and everyone is working to break through."

Before you rush off to apply, however, remember that Olin is still a school making the climb. One telling measure that it isn't quite there is the school's selectivity. Roughly 50% of those who apply get in and more than half of those decline the invitation. All the Top 20 schools and a good number of the Runners-Up are far more choosy. Indiana, Michigan, and North Carolina, for example, accept only 30% or fewer of their applicants. If your heart is set on working at a McKinsey or a Goldman Sachs, you'll have to organize your own job search as Plumley did to gain her job.

Still, at Olin you'd find one of the best-designed B-schools in the world with one of the more underrated faculties. Inspired by the architecture of the universities of Oxford and Cambridge, the school is housed in a slate-roofed building of red granite trimmed with limestone. The first-floor classrooms in Simon Hall look out on an enclosed courtyard, a favorite gathering area. Last year the student newspaper picked the B-school's library as the best place on campus to study. "It was a curse and a blessing because it attracted law, engineering, and other students," laughs Virgil.

Although Simon Hall—the largest single building on Wash U's Hilltop campus—houses Olin's undergraduate business program and its larger part-time program, MBAs describe the atmosphere as small, close-knit, and informal. "You get to know just about everybody else in class," says one student. "Professors around here know your name and they take the time to talk with you in and out of the classroom."

In class, you'll find yourself moving through what Olin calls a "modular schedule." Translation: different core courses vary in length. You can waive some of these classes by exam, and you can also take evening classes designed for part-timers if you prefer. Unlike the first year, which is fairly rigid and offers no opportunities for electives unless you've gained a waiver, students pick 8 classes of their choice during their second year. No one is required to declare a major area of study or a concentration. One of most popular of some 51 electives is Operations Strategy taught by Dean H. Kropp. Grads also favor Morton Pincus's Financial Accounting and Scott M. Davis's marketing courses. Armand C. Stalnaker, who teaches Strategy Formulation and Implementation, emerges as a role model to some students. He oftens ends classes with personal advice and recommendations of books to read.

Standard fare in this program is the "Tycoon Game" played by all first-year students the week after finals in early May. It's the same management simulation game played out by Dartmouth's MBAs (see profile on the Amos Tuck School). Another major annual event is the John M. Olin Cup competition in which students defend their position on a topic of importance to American business.

Like most smaller programs, Olin can't provide the breadth of course offerings that larger institutions routinely offer. Olin offers 9 finance electives, compared to 41 at New York University. On the other hand, there's an informality and friendliness here that's hard to find at large urban schools. Once a month, the dean invites 10 MBAs over to lunch in the faculty club. Every Friday afternoon, MBAs and faculty join together for a keg party to swap stories and jokes. "It's a great chance to sit down and have a beer with one of your favorite teachers," notes one student. MBAs hang out at the Hi-Pointe Cafe, a crowded spot across from campus, and Blueberry Hill, a bar loaded with a collection of antique jukeboxes and movie posters.

There's another unusual difference at Olin. The school goes so far as to guarantee students a summer internship. Some MBAs even convert those internships with local companies into part-time jobs. Virgil figures that about 20% of the full-time students work afternoons at such firms as A.G. Edwards or Anheuser-Busch. Most second-year MBA classes meet from 8:30 a.m. to 1:30 p.m. to allow flexibility.

Arriving on campus last year were 113 recruiting companies that interviewed 2151 MBAs. Olin grads took jobs that paid from a low of $21,000 to a high of $77,000 to start. Arthur Andersen hired the biggest chunk of Olin grads last year with 10; May Co. and Procter & Gamble each took 4; while Exxon, Ralston Purina, and Trammell Crow got 3 each.

With brand-name corporations like those hiring its MBA grads, Olin arrives among the best hidden B-schools with a definite bullet.

Contact: Jean Milburn, director of admissions, 314-889-6315

University at Buffalo, State University of New York

School of Management
206 Jacobs Management Center
Buffalo, New York 14260

Enrollment: 821
Women: 37%
Foreign: 26%
Minority: 3%
Part-time: 466
Average age: 24
Applicants admitted: 29%
Accepted applicants enrolled: 56%

Application deadline: June 15 for fall

Annual tuition: nonresident—$4600
resident—$2150
Room and board: $3990
Average GMAT score: 567
GMAT range: 350 to 730
Average GPA: 3.2
GPA range: 2.18 to 3.92
Average starting pay:$32,000

Buffalo, New York, has an image problem. Factory closings and layoffs over the past decade have dealt a blow to the local economy, painting a picture of an industrial city whose time has passed. Even Buffalo's once-thriving financial services industry has been trimming staff due to the savings and loan crisis. And etched in everyone's memory is the infamous "Blizzard of '77," a raging storm that dumped more than 56 inches of snow on Buffalo in less than a week. It's a reminder of how chillingly cold a winter in this city can be.

So why would any sane person want to go to a B-school in Buffalo? Because you'll discover an outstanding graduate business school here that offers a quality MBA at only a fraction of the cost of other major schools. If you're a New York resident, you'd pay only a sixth of what the B-schools at Cornell University or the University of Rochester demand. Even nonresidents can get an MBA from the University at Buffalo, SUNY, for a third of what it costs at more prominent upstate New York schools.

Students lured here by the savings will find a B-school devising ways to serve as a catalyst for the reemergence of the Buffalo economy and to reach out to the international business community. A Center for Industrial Effectiveness, a joint venture between the business and engineering schools, dispenses technical and managerial advice to struggling local companies. Since 1987, the center claims to have helped save 5665 jobs and create another 600 positions, working with such companies as Dunlop Tire & Rubber and Harrison Radiator.

Students go through their MBA paces in the Jacobs Management Center, a modern red brick building on the university's North Campus in Amherst. Built in 1985, the $4.9 million center includes 70,000 square feet of classrooms, office space, meetings rooms, and a computer center. Like most facilities on the Amherst campus, the center is connected by walkways to neighboring buildings, forming a corridor known as "The Spine," which protects students from the elements.

Even though the B-school building is relatively new, the growth in the number of undergrads majoring in business has created a space shortage. "The school isn't large enough for the student body," complains Jim Zielinski, a 1989 grad. "There aren't enough areas for MBAs to work on projects, and the graduate lounge is always busy."

You'll find that few of your classmates bring real-world experience to the program. Only 20% of the MBAs here have work experience: a severe drawback to informed debate in the classroom but a potential advantage to applicants who want to attend a quality B-school direct from college. Yet, Buffalo is pretty selective: Like the B-schools at Columbia or Chicago, Buffalo rejects for admission more than 7 out of every 10 applicants.

If you pass that screen, you'll have to accumulate 60 credits of work to get the MBA here. That translates into 13 core courses that eat up 36 credits and 8 electives that account for the rest. MBAs can use some of their electives to specialize in one of 10 areas that include health care systems management, and management information systems. Most students leave UB, as the university is often called, with an "option" or major in finance, but international business is gaining favor and popularity.

For the more typical classroom fare, grads highly recommend Philip Perry's Financial Institutions and Brian Ratchford's Product and Promotion, fascinating courses taught by dynamic teachers. You can hardly go wrong by signing up for classes with Frank Krzystofiak, Jerry Newman, or Ronald Huefner. All of them have won awards for teaching excellence within the SUNY system.

Buffalo sponsors a unique MBA program in China and has graduated three classes of Chinese students who spend three semesters in Dalian, China, where they are taught by Buffalo and Chinese faculty. The Chinese students come to Buffalo for their final semester. A handful of American MBA students also can spend a semester in Dalian, though in 1989 upheaval in China forced their early return.

When MBAs take a break from studies in Buffalo, they tend to go off campus for rest and recreation. They head over to Molly's Pub for beers and a game of darts or over to the Marriott, Garcia's, or Coulter Bay for drinks. Buffalo Bills football games and Buffalo Sabres hockey contests are popular ways to unwind, while Niagara Falls, just 20 miles from Buffalo, is a popular destination for foreign students. Most students live off-campus, where apartments can be had for as little as $200 a month.

When students get ready to leave this program, they're not always happy with the B-school's placement office. In 1989, some 80 companies came to campus to recruit Buffalo MBAs. The leading recruiters are the Big Eight accounting firms, Xerox, Ford Motor, Marine Midland, and Manufacturers and Traders Bank. About a third of the MBAs find jobs with the accounting firms, while 22% go into finance and 14% head for marketing positions. Grads complain that not enough resources are being devoted to placement to attract more recruiting companies to campus. One problem is the B-school's mostly regional appeal (half its grads stay in western New York). The other problem is Buffalo itself. Unlike Rochester, home to such corporate giants as Xerox, Eastman Kodak, and Bausch & Lomb, the Buffalo economy is still groping for a strategy to attract new businesses. "We produce more MBAs than Buffalo can absorb, and there are a lot of small to medium-sized companies that cannot afford to hire our students," says Larry Michael, director of placement.

Buffalo may have a hard time enticing the Street's blue chip investment bankers to campus. But if the B-school succeeds in helping to nurture entrepreneurial start-ups and making the remaining manufacturing concerns more competitive, it could help itself in the process.

Contact: Arlene Bergwall, assistant dean, 716-636-3207

University of Florida

Graduate School of Business
301 Business Building
Gainesville, Florida 32611

Enrollment: 190
Women: 42%
Foreign: 10%
Minority: 2%
Average age: 27
Part-time: None
Applicants admitted: 20%
Accepted applicants enrolled: 50%

Annual tuition: nonresident—$6114
resident—$2116
Room and board: $4195
Average GMAT score: 600
GMAT range: 470 to 740
Average GPA: 3.3
GPA range: 2.6 to 4.0
Average starting pay: $32,700

Application deadline: April 1 for fall

After spending four years in public accounting, Richard Visman was ready for a change. The Canadian-born Visman not only wanted to switch careers, he also yearned for a dramatically different lifestyle. How to accomplish both in a single stroke? He went for his MBA at the University of Florida. After graduating in 1989, he captured a marketing job with Barnett Banks in Jacksonville.

In opting for this sunny enclave of palm trees and warm winters, Visman isn't alone. Each year, many out-of-state MBA candidates decide to take advantage of both the lifestyle and the university's reputation in the Southeast. More than 60% of the university's MBAs take jobs in Florida, most of them in the booming areas of commercial banking and health care. "People are attracted to Florida's MBA program for a number of reasons, including price," says Sandra S. Kramer, who recently resigned as MBA program director to return to teaching. "But most people come here because they want to live in Florida."

Along the way, of course, they're also getting a top-flight MBA from an excellent school with particularly strong programs in accounting, finance, and health care. The university's B-school has a lot in common with its rival to the north, the University of Georgia in Athens. Both schools offer small, regional MBA programs with top-rated faculty. Both schools are also part of large state universities with sprawling lush, green campuses. While Gainesville is much larger than Athens, it still retains the feel of a college town. All these attributes permit a high standard of selectivity at Florida, surprisingly higher than most Top 20 schools, including Wharton, Michigan, and Cornell. The B-school accepts only one of every five applicants.

That's quite a change from a decade ago when Florida founded its Graduate Business School in 1979. Then, the MBA was little more than an extension of the undergraduate business degree—up to 80% of the MBAs had no work experience and had majored in business as undergrads. Today, only 35% of Florida's 190 MBAs have an undergraduate business degree and 70% have a year or more of work experience. The average GMAT score here is now 600, better than many of the schools on BUSINESS WEEK's Runners-Up List.

These vast improvements largely reflect the achievements of Dean Alan G. Merten, who recently resigned to become dean of Cornell's Johnson School of Management. His departure and the recent exodus of several other key administrators cause some concern about the program. The school hadn't found a successor to

Merten or Kramer as of early July, 1988. And in 1988–1989, the school was without a placement director, which caused considerable grumbling among students.

The B-school is housed in a complex of three buildings, known as "The Triangle": Bryan Hall, Matherly Hall, and the Business Administration Building. Though MBAs share the space with 2500 undergraduate business students, they have their own computer labs and other facilities. One benefit of Florida's MBA program is its small size. There are about 50 students in the first-year core courses and as few as 10 students in second-year elective courses. The class size encourages greater class participation and cultivates closer relationships among students and faculty.

Students must complete 60 credits worth of courses in a traditional four-semester program to get the MBA. The core curriculum is loaded with 14 courses, the vast majority packed in the first year when you'll juggle 6 courses worth 16 credits each semester. "They deliberately give you too much to do during your first year so you learn how to manage your time," says Sheila McGuigan, a 1989 grad.

In the second year, MBAs develop a concentration by taking three courses in 1 of 12 areas that include law, real estate, international business, and health and hospital administration. Nearly one of every three MBAs jumps on the finance track, while 20% specialize in health service administration. Gaining greater prominence are Florida's marketing and decision and information sciences departments. The B-school also offers joint-degree programs with the College of Health Related Professions and the Nijenrode, The Netherlands School of Business. The latter program allows you to spend your full second year studying in The Netherlands.

For those who stick close to home, grads say you shouldn't go through this program without taking classes from Virginia Maurer in business law, Richard Romano in economics, and Arnold A. Heggestad in banking. Heggestad's investment banking course is a favorite because he lures to his classroom leading corporate speakers from Kohlberg Kravis Roberts, Barnett Banks, and Marriott. In marketing, sure bets are Barton A. Weitz and John G. Lynch, Jr.

At many B-schools, the MBA Association allows students to participate in curriculum development, admissions, and placement. But at Florida, the group is little more than a social club for first-year students. The association is greeted with apathy by second-year MBAs trying to find jobs. "When students are spending 90 hours a week on school and maybe working part-time or spending time with their families, it's hard to find the time to get involved," Visman says.

When MBAs do get together, they grab a quick bite at Burrito Brothers, an informal spot across from the B-school. Danny's, in downtown Gainesville, is a popular watering hole. The Purple Porpoise and Calico Jack's are on the wild side for some of the button-down types in the B-school, but they are Gainesville hot spots nonetheless. The closest beach is about 80 miles east of the campus.

Only about 45 companies come to Gainesville each year to interview MBAs. In 1988, they offered jobs to MBAs that paid from $22,500 to $50,400. Besides the Florida banks, Andersen Consulting, Harris Corp., Ryder System, Ford Motor, and AT&T are the big recruiters. The Big Eight accounting firms come to campus to recruit graduates of Florida's Fisher School of Accounting, a separate school within the College of Business Administration.

Contact: Patricia M. Cumming, assistant director for admissions, 904-392-7992

University of Georgia

College of Business Administration
Brooks Hall
Athens, Georgia 30602

Enrollment: 120
Women: 33%
Foreign: 19%
Minority: 6%
Part-time: None
Average age: 25.5
Applicants accepted: 33%
Accepted applicants enrolled: 47%

Annual tuition: nonresident—$4875
resident—$1839
Room and board: $5500
Average GMAT score: 580
GMAT range: 500 to 660 (mid 80%)
Average GPA: 3.3
GPA range: 2.72 to 3.78 (mid 80%)
Average starting pay: $34,500

Admissions deadline: Rolling admissions

The old South meets the new at the University of Georgia's B-school. On a campus that could have been the setting for *Gone with the Wind*, MBAs study finance, accounting, insurance, real estate, and management information systems—all growth areas in Georgia's dynamic service-based economy.

Rhett and Scarlett would feel right at home on UGA's 532-acre campus, with its antebellum architecture, tree-lined walkways, and fiery-colored azalea bushes. Located 70 miles northeast of Atlanta, Athens calls itself "Georgia's classic city"—and with good reason. People joke that there are probably more Greek columns here than any place except the original Athens.

The reverence for history found at UGA is the kind most people associate with New England. Georgia is no Harvard, but its College of Business was founded in 1912 and began offering graduate classes 11 years later. Tradition, however, hasn't prevented the B-school from changing. In the early 1980s, the MBA program was overhauled to allow MBAs to specialize among a mind-boggling array of disciplines.

To begin with, Georgia offers two versions of its MBA: a two-year program for students who did not major in business as undergraduates and a one-year program for those who did. One-year types, however, must take five courses during a summer term. MBAs in the two-year program arrive in the fall take a total of 50 hours of required core courses during three 10-week quarters. The electives kick in during the second year when you can choose from 25 "sequences" to follow in many differing fields. You can pursue a sequence in investment management in the finance department or organizational communication in the management group. Or you can pick one of the three novel paths offered with other areas at the university: media organization management, with the Henry W. Grady School of Journalism; textile management, with the College of Home Economics; or pharmacy care administration, with the College of Pharmacy.

By taking two sequences, students can pursue an interdisciplinary approach in preparing for a career. MBAs keen on joining the information systems department of an insurer can enroll in the risk management and insurance sequence along with an MIS sequence. "The sequence approach during the second year is different from what you'll find any place else," says Melvin Crask, director of graduate programs. "Before we redesigned the curriculum, there was almost no specialization allowed.

This left us open to criticism so we decided to also give them training in skills they can use pretty quickly."

Many courses here adopt a hands-on approach. In Personal Selling, students learn the basic steps of selling and engage in role-playing exercises captured on video. "Some of the academic people scoff at a class in selling but they've never been out in the real world," says Guy Gray, a 1989 grad who sold cars before coming to Georgia for his MBA. "Regardless of what you're going to do, it never hurts to have some know-how in terms of selling."

Accounting, finance, and management are the strongest departments at Georgia in terms of faculty research. But the insurance, legal studies, and real estate areas have strong student followings. Hugh O. Nourse gets rave reviews for the enthusiasm and dedication he shows in his corporate real estate asset management course, which is taught entirely by case study. James J. Musumeci, who teaches finance, is also a favorite of Georgia MBAs. Fred Stephenson, who won the 1988 outstanding teaching award, describes himself as a "frustrated comedian," but his witty approach grabs students in transportation and distribution courses.

The 120 MBAs here—a third of them in the one-year program—make up a minuscule part of the 25,000-student population at the university. They're also overwhelmed in the B-school by 4500 business undergrads. Most MBA classes are held in horseshoe-style classrooms in Caldwell Hall, a modern building located next to maze-like Brooks Hall, a Greek Revival structure, where faculty and administrative offices are housed along with several classrooms. The B-school has outgrown its facilities and will probably begin work on a new building within the next five years. The biggest obstacle to new facilities is aesthetic, says Don Perry, MBA program director. "There is a lot of opposition to cutting down an oak tree and putting up a building," Perry says. "All the trees and flowers help make this a beautiful campus."

Many college towns brag about their quaint downtown shopping area and their historic homes, but Athens is right up there with the best. Besides Greek Revival architecture, the town of 60,000 is also known for music. MBAs often frequent the 40-Watt Club, where rock groups R.E.M. and the B-52s both got their start. O'Malley's, an old mill on the Oconee River that has been converted to a bar, is a favorite dancing hangout of B-school students. The social event of the year is the MBA Bash, a formal event held at the lush state botanical garden located a few miles off campus.

More than 20% of MBAs take jobs in Atlanta and more than half stay in the Southeast after graduating. Finance, marketing, and operations are the most popular career destinations. As at most B-schools, starting salaries here vary greatly depending on the amount and type of work experience an MBA brings to his or her new employer. Georgia MBAs without work experience averaged starting salaries of $30,100 while those with two to three years of work behind them garnered $38,700.

Some 50 companies, including Arthur Andersen, Federal Express, Barnett Banks, Texas Instruments, and Eli Lilly, come to Athens to recruit MBAs. Given the predominance of service companies in the state's economy, many job opportunities are in sales and retail financial services, which often don't pay the salaries that MBAs expect. "A lot of Georgia businesses are mad because they can't afford our MBAs," says Crask. Despite the old-fashioned Southern charm that reigns at Georgia, MBAs here are just as hard-nosed about the bottom line as they are anyplace else.

Contact: Don Perry, director of MBA program, 404-542-5671

University of Illinois at Urbana-Champaign

College of Commerce and Business Administration
1206 South Sixth Street
Champaign, Illinois 61820

Enrollment: 247
Women: 28%
Foreign: 13%
Minority: 9%
Part-time: None
Average age: 24
Applicants admitted: 37%
Accepted applicants enrolled: 44%*

Admissions deadline: May 1 for fall

Annual tuition: nonresident—$7966
resident—$3286
Room and board: $3850
Average GMAT score: 610
GMAT range: NA
Average GPA: 4.4 (out of 5.0)
GPA range: NA
Average starting pay: $38,481

When the Chicago Cubs need a steady hand in the bullpen, they bring up a promising young player from the Iowa Cubs in Des Moines. Chicago's business community also has a farm team for MBAs—the University of Illinois. If you've ever wanted to work for Arthur Andersen, Leo Burnett, Kraft, or First Chicago, there's a well-worn path along Interstate 57 from Champaign to Chicago. The only more direct route to a job in the Windy City is to attend the University of Chicago or Northwestern's top-rated Kellogg School of Management in Evanston.

Along with other state universities such as Indiana and North Carolina, Illinois offers a lot of bang for the buck. But its MBA program has always trailed those other institutions in stature because it has long been a stepchild to a far larger undergraduate program in business, although that is changing.

Illinois is undergoing a dramatic overhaul, updating and expanding its curriculum, upgrading the facilities, and boosting the size of the student body, faculty, administration, and staff. The changes reflect a desire to become a bigger player on the MBA scene as well as a chance to develop a more innovative curriculum.

MBA students share space with undergrads in Commerce West and David Kinley Hall. But the university has been renovating the Survey Building, a Jacobean-style structure built in the Victorian era that will reopen in 1990 as the exclusive home of the MBA program. "We're trying to send the message that this is a preprofessional program," says Jane Nathan, director of the MBA program. "We hope the feeling of the MBA program will be closer to an executive workshop than an undergraduate class." Meantime, Illinois has set aside two-tiered classrooms in Commerce West for MBAs as a first step toward separating the two programs.

During the next five years, Illinois plans to double the size of the MBA program from 250 to 500 students by adding 50 students each year. The class size in the core courses will increase from between 45 and 50 students to between 60 and 65. To help serve the expanded student body, Illinois is hiring 10 new faculty members in the fall of 1990 and is adding an assistant placement director and assistant director to the MBA program, as well as more secretaries and support staff. "We need more bulk, as coaches say about their athletes," says Professor David Whetten. "More students will mean more electives, a larger presence within the college and a bigger pool of graduates for recruiters to interview. There are some who like intimate classes in the core, but that's the tradeoff you have to make."

Some of the most crucial changes are occurring in the curriculum. Four themes now stretch over the 12 required core courses of the program: information, integrity, innovation, and internationalization. The school also has added two required, though noncredit, workshops in the first year, one in computer competency and the other in oral and written communications. And the school is establishing greater links with nearby companies to supplement the business basics with real-world learning.

All but 2 of the core courses are in the first year of the program, while students are required to take 6 electives in their second year. You don't have to declare a major or concentration here. Students can take all their electives in one area or spread them out. The B-school offers 95 electives in 11 areas, including international business and entrepreneurship.

One of the B-school's most popular electives is in the organizational behavior area. Called simply Power and Influence, the course attracts students with a wide variety of career goals. It is taught by Gerald R. Salancik, who is admired by students for his no-nonsense style and his practical advice on how to master corporate politics.

Illinois grads bring that savvy to some blue chip corporations such as General Motors, Ford, Dow Chemical, Whirlpool, Motorola, and Eli Lilly, all major recruiters here along with accounting's Big Eight. In fact, in BUSINESS WEEK's corporate recruiter survey, Illinois rated higher than the B-schools at Yale, North Carolina, Purdue, and the University of Southern California. About 80% of the MBAs find jobs by graduation.

Illinois alumni show lots of loyalty to their alma mater, often helping new grads find jobs. A group of alums at advertising agency Leo Burnett even contributes artwork, photos, and graphics for the alumni magazine, *Commerce*, making it the slickest B-school mag in the country. And an annual event is the MBA trip to Evanston for the Northwestern–Illinois basketball game, an outing that includes sessions with alumni, tours of the Chicago futures and options exchanges, shopping along Michigan Avenue's Miracle Mile, and drinking and dancing at jazz bars and rock clubs until the wee hours.

Closer to home, MBAs favor Gully's Riverview Inn for drinks—especially on Thursday nights because no classes are scheduled on Fridays. For the best burgers in town, students go to Murphy's. In between classes, MBAs will often grab a bite at Newman Hall. "It's the closest place to Commerce West that serves food and the prices are cheap," says Jill DeForest of the Class of 1989.

The campus is an oasis of culture surrounded by miles of farmland. The Krannert Center for the Performing Arts pulls in the likes of opera star Luciano Pavarotti and rock group Bon Jovi. The campus also is home to the World Heritage Museum's extensive collection of ancient art. Even so, you'll find more sports lovers than museum goers. The MBA Association sponsors tailgate barbecues before football games that bring the faithful out to watch the Fightin' Illini and its mascot Chief Illiniwek, replete with warpaint and feathered head gear. When they can't watch athletic events at Illinois, MBAs vigorously compete in intramural sports. They work on their curve ball in the hopes that next summer they'll be playing on Arthur Andersen's softball team in Chicago's Lincoln Park.

Contact: Jane Nathan, director of the MBA Program, 217-244-1452

University of Iowa

College of Business Administration
Iowa City, Iowa 52242

Enrollment: 550
Women: 35%
Foreign: 12%
Minority: 5%
Part-time: 265
Average age: 27
Applicants accepted: 40%
Accepted applicants enrolled: 60%

Annual tuition: nonresident—$6236
resident—$2020
Room and board: NA
Average GMAT score: 590
GMAT range: 390 to 790
Average GPA: 3.33
GPA range: 2.25 to 4.0
Average starting pay: $31,000

Application deadline: July 1 for fall, November 15 for spring

Wharton may have its Follies and Dartmouth its Tycoon Game, but the high point of the year for MBAs at the University of Iowa is neither a show nor a game—it's a pig roast. Each fall, some 400 students, faculty, staff members, and their families converge on Professor Eleanor Birch's farm for ribs, beer, and volleyball. In these parts, it's an MBA tradition.

To the 60% of MBAs who come from Iowa, Birch's hospitality doesn't seem out of the ordinary, but the sense of community within the B-school is striking to out-of-state students. Originally from Michigan, Cindy Knight opted to study at "UI" after visiting Iowa City, a town of red brick Victorian homes and leafy streets. "I really feel comfortable here," says Knight, Class of 1989. "I don't think twice about going out at night and walking around by myself." "If you stop people to ask directions, they'll probably invite you into their car so they can drive you there," says Paul Boynton, another 1989 grad. And in Iowa City, you'd get in without a second thought.

There's a memorable line in the hit movie "Field of Dreams" that rings true for those who come to the Buckeye State. At one point in the film, Shoeless Joe Jackson asks, "Is this heaven?" "No," comes the reply, "it's Iowa!" "People make Iowa what it is," says Willis R. Greer, Jr., who took over from Birch as associate dean for graduate programs. "It's a good place to live and a good place to study. The students are straightforward and honest and the faculty members reflect those values."

Think of the word *Iowa* and you're apt to visualize those cornfields that surround the baseball diamond in "Field of Dreams." For sure, lots of corn gets planted around here. But the state also boasts two outstanding state universities: Iowa State in Ames is known for agriculture and engineering while the University of Iowa has achieved recognition in medicine and liberal arts. The world-famous Iowa Writers Workshop is held at UI each summer.

Iowa's B-school has been a well-kept secret except to those who read scholarly journals. A recent article in the *Review of Business and Economic Research* ranked Iowa's faculty twelfth in terms of research. And the faculty's expertise in finance and economics has led to some influential government appointments. Finance Professor Susan M. Phillips returned to Iowa in 1987 after serving as chairman of the Commodity Futures Trading Commission.

Until recently, MBAs needed 62 hours (credits) to graduate if they lacked the undergraduate course work or professional knowledge necessary to waive courses.

This put the B-school in an awkward position since the state does not permit graduate students to take more than 15 hours a semester. "We had a two-year program that students couldn't get through in two years," Greer says. So the school reduced the required hours to 60 in the fall of 1989. Of the 45 hours in the core, 22 are for foundation courses that may be waived. A student with an undergraduate business degree could get an MBA in as little as 38 hours.

Many MBA programs evenly divide the core courses and electives. But at Iowa the heavily quantitative core accounts for three-fourths of the course work needed to graduate. The 15 hours of electives can be taken in one of seven areas of concentration, though you're also free to explore courses outside the MBA program. At the B-school, MBAs favor marketing classes with Peter Riesz, chairman of the marketing department. The MBA Association's teacher of the year award recently went to Paul Lansing, an industrial relations and human resources professor.

While it is improving its curriculum, Iowa's B-school is trying to get state funding for a new building. So crowded is Phillips Hall, the six-story B-school building, that only three-fourths of the MBA courses are held there. Iowa hopes to begin work on a new $40-million B-school building in 1990.

The big-name CEOs seldom trek to Iowa to address the students. But a good number of vice presidents come here through the school's John R. Hughes lecture series, named in honor of the former Hills Bank and Trust Company president who was shot to death in 1985 by a farmer who had mortgaged his crops to the bank. In 1989, the series drew executives from McDonald's Corporation, Kansas City Southern Industries, and U.S. West. The school also draws upon such Iowa-based companies as Amana, Maytag, Winnebago, and HON Industries for speakers and support.

Iowa MBAs complain that placement isn't nearly as good as it could be. For one thing, the school lacks its own placement facilities, using instead the university's centralized operation. For another, only 80 companies come to campus to recruit (versus more than 300 at Indiana), and only half the MBAs here have jobs by graduation. Many Iowa grads become corporate financial analysts, but consulting is the most popular choice—one of three MBAs go that route. Among leading recruiters of graduates: Arthur Andersen, Kimberly-Clark, AT&T, Deere & Co., and the General Accounting Office's Kansas City branch.

Unless you've visited Iowa City, it's hard to imagine just how charming this college town is. With a population of 60,000, including 30,000 students, Iowa City is the state's answer to Michigan's Ann Arbor or Wisconsin's Madison. By Iowa standards, housing in Iowa City is pricey: $350 for a one-bedroom apartment. Ninety percent of MBAs live off-campus, either in apartment complexes or Victorian homes that have been divided into apartments.

The campus sits on a bluff overlooking the Iowa River and intermingles with the downtown area. During fall and spring evenings, musicians play guitars and portable keyboards along a downtown pedestrian mall—a favorite place for MBA students to stroll. On Thursday nights, the MBA Association holds parties at Fitzpatrick's, the B-school's unofficial student union. When the weather is warm, students sit at the outdoor bar and eat grilled ribs, burgers, and chicken. The ribs at Fitzpatrick's are good, but they don't come close to those cooked over an open fire at Birch's farm.

Contact: Jana Wessels, director of admissions, 319-335-1037

University of Minnesota

Curtis L. Carlson School of Management
271 19th Avenue South
Minneapolis, Minnesota 55455

Enrollment: 1800
Women: 34%
Foreign: 12%
Minority: 5%
Part-time: 1500
Average age: 26
Applicants accepted: 50%
Accepted applicants enrolled: 65%

Annual tuition: nonresident—$8000
resident—$5350
Room and board: $5000
Average GMAT score: 610
GMAT range: 450 to 790
Average GPA: 3.35
GPA range: 2.70 to 4.0
Average starting pay: $33,740

Admission deadline: April 1 for fall

Carlson is hardly a household name, but it will be if the University of Minnesota's B-school has its way. The school named itself for local entrepreneur Curtis L. Carlson in 1986 after he launched a university fundraising effort with a $25 million gift. The three-year capital campaign raised $364.7 million, with the Carlson School's share of this bounty a whopping $40 million.

Carlson, who built a small trading stamp firm into a $3 billion travel and entertainment concern, is not Lee Iacocca. And the B-school here is no Harvard. But backed by that huge treasure chest, the management school is charting a course to gain national prominence and break into the ranks of the Top 20. Rather than devoting the resources to bricks and mortar, Carlson is using the loot to woo top faculty and students throughout the country, to generously fund academic research and student scholarships, and to strengthen its placement operations.

Like Washington University and other B-schools on the move, Carlson faces a sticky problem in its upward climb: to carve out a national reputation requires a national student population. About 60% of Carlson MBAs are from Minnesota and about 65% stay in the state after they graduate. "The school needs to increase its pool of applicants and it needs to attract students from outside Minnesota who will eventually relocate and talk about the school across the country," says Holly Parker, a 1988 grad who works for Pillsbury.

To help bring them here, the B-school has significantly upped the ante on personnel. It has recently enticed top professors in strategic management, accounting, and marketing from Northwestern's Kellogg School, Carnegie-Mellon, and the University of Washington. It has created 18 new professorial chairs since 1986, bringing the total number of endowed faculty positions to 23. Having lost its dean recently to the Conference Board, the school also is searching for a new leader.

If you're willing to bet on a rising B-school star, you'll find that Carlson offers two MBA programs: the typical two-year regimen of 20 courses and an accelerated option of 14 courses for students with undergrad business degrees. In the regular MBA program, you'll be required to take 8 of your 12 core courses in the first year. In the second year, you can take 3 courses in one of six areas of concentration. There are three free electives.

You'll find that the curriculum strengths of the school tend to reflect the focus of the Twin Cities' business community. The area is home to marketing powerhouses such as General Mills and Pillsbury as well as computer makers Control Data Corporation and Cray Research, and Carlson boasts strong tracks in information systems management as well as marketing. The Carlson school considers the Minneapolis–St. Paul business community to be its laboratory. Many MBAs sign on for internships or part-time jobs. A field study requirement also puts students into 14-week-long consulting projects for these firms. "The driving force of the Carlson School is the corporate community's long tradition of participating in public life, which allowed us to raise $40 million in three years. We talk a lot about the private–public partnership around here," says acting Dean Tim Nantell. "Every CEO in town is on our board of overseers and they all show up for every meeting and participate. It's an amazing thing to watch."

The foreign takeover binge of American companies is leading to a new emphasis on international business. After Pillsbury was acquired by British-owned Grand Metropolitan in 1988, the new British chairman of Pillsbury told the school it needed to do more in the international area. "This community is crying out for international management training," Nantell says. So Carlson has added a few international business courses and is looking to hire faculty to develop a concentration in international management. Carlson joined B-schools at NYU, Michigan, and Berkeley in an international program that runs a student-for-student exchange with foreign B-schools.

"The faculty is stronger in research than teaching, but teaching is still above average," says Jim White, a 1989 grad. "What the school is trying to do is change the structure and make teaching an important part of a professor's position," he adds. Grads recommend Richard Cardozo's Entrepreneurial Studies and Kenneth Roering's Strategic Marketing. Process, Technology, and Innovation, taught by Gary Scudder, gets enthusiastic endorsements as does virtually any statistics course taught by Christopher J. Nachtsheim.

Typical of urban schools, the MBAs are scattered around the Twin Cities area and tend to have their own lives away from school. Outside of classes and MBA Association events, the only time MBAs regularly get together is on Thursday nights at Bullwinkle's, a bar about two blocks from campus. A winter in Minneapolis–St. Paul can sometimes make you feel like the Abominable Snowman. It gets cold here, really cold. But even the parking garages are heated so cars don't freeze and virtually all the campus buildings are linked by tunnels and skyways. And you'll find the Twin Cities one of the most hospitable locales in the nation. The corporate largess that has benefited the B-school extends to social services and culture. The area boasts 100 theaters, more than any other city except for New York, and more than 100 art galleries and museums.

Twin Cities' corporations recruit heavily here, accounting for many of the 186 companies that interviewed MBAs for jobs in 1988. "Since the majority of students want to stay here, the job-hunting is very competitive," says Karen McLaughlin, who will be graduating in 1990. "Starting salaries are lower for Carlson grads because the companies know they've got a captive audience." Andersen Consulting, General Mills, 3M, and Norwest Banks are major recruiters here.

Students say the placement office needs to do a better job of bringing to campus more out-of-state recruiters. If the school is successful in boosting its reputation and prestige, that will be an easy task indeed.

Contact: Sandra Kelzenberg, MBA Office, 612-624-0006

University of Notre Dame

College of Business Administration
Notre Dame, Indiana 46556

Enrollment: 250	*Annual tuition:* $11,250
Women: 25%	*Room and board:* $4500
Foreign: 15%	*Average GMAT score:* 570
Minority: 5%	*GMAT range:* 450 to 710
Part-time: None	*Average GPA:* 3.25
Average age: 24	*GPA range:* 2.5 to 4.0
Applicants admitted: 55%	*Average starting pay:* $36,300
Accepted applicants enrolled: 50%	

Application deadline: May 15 for fall

Instead of sending insider traders and other white-collar criminals to prison, maybe the government should make them earn an MBA from Notre Dame. While many other B-schools have suddenly discovered ethics, Notre Dame has considered moral and ethical questions in all its courses ever since it began offering an MBA more than 20 years ago.

Part of the reason can be traced to its history. Founded by the congregation of the Holy Cross in 1842, Notre Dame still retains its identity as a Catholic institution. Even within Notre Dame's B-school, it's difficult to forget you're attending a Catholic university. Wherever you go on campus, you can see the administration building's huge, golden dome topped by a statue of the Virgin Mary.

While ethics are woven throughout the curriculum, it is also a major theme of the required Government–Business–Society course. Taught by the Reverend Oliver F. Williams and John W. Houck, the course examines such things as labor relations, environmental issues, and equal opportunity for women and minorities. "An ethical issue is never black or white," says Larry Ballinger, director of Notre Dame's MBA program. "We try to make students aware of the ethical and moral dimensions of business issues and help them to develop their own set of standards. We're not trying to convert them to Catholicism."

As part of Notre Dame's commitment to developing artistic and intellectual values in its MBAs, the same course exposes students to music and literature—a revelation of sorts for some undergraduate business majors. "We have a fantastic art museum right here on campus but I would never have stepped inside if it weren't for Professor Houck's class," says Colleen McElroy, a 1989 grad. "But I learned that if I want to be successful in business, I have to know something about culture."

Notre Dame can also claim a head start in another growing area of study at most B-schools: international business. It became the first American university to offer a four-year degree in foreign commerce in 1917. When the B-school's Hurley Building was constructed in the 1930s, an eight-foot revolving globe and maps of the seven continents were placed in the foyer of the two-story, E-shaped Gothic structure. Notre Dame has not lost interest in the global dimensions of business. International business remains a required course, and the B-school offers a specialization in global business that includes a semester abroad at Notre Dame's London Centre.

The MBA here comes in two flavors: the regular two-year program and a three-semester abbreviated MBA for students with an undergraduate degree in business.

The two-year program consists of 60 credits taken over four semesters, with admission only during the fall semester. There are 13 core courses, 1 management elective, and 5 free electives. The three-semester program consists of 42 credits and begins with the summer semester. By taking 3 to 5 courses in one of six areas, you can gain a specialization, such as finance or marketing, but it is not required. One of the most popular electives at Notre Dame is Entrepreneurship, taught by a consultant who works with small businesses in the South Bend area. In the course, students are divided into groups of five and assigned to solve a business problem for a local business with sales of about $1 million to $20 million a year. Other favorites: Frank Reilly's Securities Analysis, William Wilkie's Buyer Behavior, and Gary Kern's Data Base Management.

Besides its emphasis on ethics and international business, what makes the school distinctive is its small size. MBA students number 250, including 70 in the three-semester program, and there are about 50 faculty members. While that assures an intimate learning experience, at Notre Dame it also means resources are somewhat slim. There's neither a separate library nor a dedicated placement facility for MBAs. MBA classes are held in the Hayes-Healey Center, which was built as an attachment to the Hurley Building in 1968.

A highlight of the year is the Notre Dame MBA Case Competition, an event squeezed between spring break and Easter. Funded in part by Johnson & Johnson, the contest brings teams of MBAs from other schools on campus to compete in analyzing and presenting a case to a panel of academic and corporate judges. Several lecture series and an executive-in-residence program bring corporate executives, entrepreneurs, and labor leaders to campus each year.

If Catholicism is the religion of the University of Notre Dame, sports is the religion of Notre Dame, Indiana. "School spirit is a tidal wave here. It makes you want to be part of it," says McElroy of the Class of 1989. In addition to going as a group to watch the Fightin' Irish play football, MBAs participate in intramural basketball, ice hockey, and volleyball. Some MBAs spend the whole year practicing for "bookstore basketball," a tournament held on courts outside the bookstore.

When MBAs aren't watching or playing sports, they're hanging out at bars with names like Coach's and The Linebacker. Bridget's, about one mile south of campus, is another popular watering hole. On campus, MBAs gather at the bar run by the alumni association Thursday and Friday nights.

About 100 companies come to recruit MBAs here, which isn't bad considering there are only 140 students in a graduating class. Most of the firms are from the Midwest and the Northeast. The B-school counts on local alumni associations to help MBAs get interviews with companies in California, Texas, and Florida. The strong sense of loyalty Notre Dame grads feel toward their alma mater is definitely a plus for MBAs. About 70% of MBAs have jobs by the time they graduate. Many students find work in Chicago with Arthur Andersen, Leo Burnett, or First Chicago. Ford, General Motors, Dow Chemical Company, and Eli Lilly are also major Notre Dame recruiters. And the B-school has a special relationship with Whirlpool Corporation, about an hour away in Benton Harbor, Michigan. The company employs several interns each year and is a frequent recruiter.

Contact: Joyce Manthay, MBA admissions coordinator, 219-239-6500

University of Pittsburgh

The Joseph M. Katz Graduate School of Business
276 Mervis Hall
Pittsburgh, Pennsylvania 15260

Enrollment: 1055
Foreign: 20%
Women: 31%
Minority: 6%
Part-time: 770
Average age: 26
Applicants accepted: 46%
Accepted applicants enrolled: 60%

Annual tuition: nonresident—$14,400
resident—$8100
Room and board: $8800
Average GMAT score: 590
GMAT range: 490 to 750
Average GPA: 3.3
GPA range: 2.4 to 4.0
Average starting pay: $35,500

Application deadline: March 15 for fall

From the outside, the Katz School of Business looks more like the contemporary headquarters of a high-tech corporation than an educational institution. The only ivy around this striking glass and steel building hangs from the nearby centerfield wall of the old Forbes Field, once home to the Pittsburgh Pirates and Steelers. Dean H. J. Zoffer jokes that he should exchange his building with PPG Industries in town because the company's structure looks more like a university building than his own.

But that's not the only surprise for students who come to "Pitt." Katz offers a first-rate MBA in a unique 11-month program. That's right. A virtual two years of study crammed into 11 tortuous months. When AT&T Chairman Robert E. Allen came to campus to deliver the graduation address last year, he called the program "the intellectual equivalent of swimming the English Channel underwater."

At times, that's exactly how students feel. "It's an intense experience," says Nick Grasberger, a 1989 survivor who now works for H. J. Heinz Co. "You typically have six or seven courses a term, and you can go through a textbook in 7 weeks instead of 14." While your friends are still on the beach, you're showing up at Katz for five days worth of orientation two weeks before Labor Day. The first of three 14-week terms begins about August 20. The last one doesn't end until August 1.

On Wednesday at 8 a.m., small groups of students gather on the third floor of Mervis Hall for the dean's weekly "Donut Hour." "In the first term, they complain about the pressure and the difficulty of managing their time," says Zoffer, Pitt's engaging dean for 21 years. "In the second term, they still wonder what they committed themselves to. In the last term, the complaints turn to placement or whatever."

Packed into those three terms is a whirlwind of activity: 17 required courses in the core curriculum and 7 electives. Some classes meet throughout the term; others last only seven weeks. The practical effect of the shorter program is that you lose out on 2 electives. You also lose the opportunity of a summer internship. Indeed, that's the major drawback to the program. For the career switcher or someone with little work experience that is a considerable negative. If you're trying to convince H. J. Heinz to hire you for a marketing job despite your financial background, a summer job at Procter & Gamble makes the task a lot easier.

What you get, in turn, is the chance to participate in what Zoffer calls a "living laboratory." More than most B-school deans, Zoffer has been adept at luring corporate executives to his five-year-old building to sit and chat with students. Two or three times each month, Zoffer hosts an Executive Briefing in which CEOs from major Pittsburgh corporations talk for 40 minutes on the challenges and frustrations of the job and then field student questions. After each session, a handful of students head for the University Club for a private lunch with the chair of Alcoa or Mellon Bank.

Each spring, over a dozen corporate executives come to campus for the American Assembly Dialogue. Pitt MBAs set the agenda for the off-the-record discussions that have attracted the likes of a varied group of big-time chieftains from "Ted" Turner of Turner Broadcasting System Inc. to Richard A. Zimmerman, chairman of Hershey Foods Corporation. The real-world thoughts of visiting CEOs provide a good balance to all the learning in Pitt's tiered, horseshoe-shaped classrooms. Katz offers students up to 65 electives, the most popular of which is Interpersonal Skills for Managers. A key part of the program is its emphasis on how to use information as a strategic resource. Katz boasts an impressive computer lab filled with $6 million worth of hardware and software. Electives in management information systems outnumber those in finance, marketing, human resources, and international business.

Student evaluations of teachers are not made public at Pitt, so you'll need to do some homework to know who to avoid. Pitt MBAs, however, highly recommend anything taught by Thomas L. Saaty, Robert Nachtmann's Corporate Finance, and Anil Makhija's Capital Markets. Saaty, who has published joke books, brings theatrics to quantitative methods. "Classrooms overflow when he's teaching and other professors come in to listen to his lectures," notes one MBA fan.

Some of the most rewarding electives are "project courses" that allow students to consult with corporations on actual problems. Pitt MBAs have helped to forecast trends in entertainment behavior for Eastman Kodak Company and helped design a management information system for Barclays Bank. Special programs? If you're really an academic masochist, Pitt offers the MBA in double-degree programs with a master's in management information systems (18 months) or health administration (two years), and even a Master of Divinity with the Pittsburgh Theological Seminary.

Most students, of course, find one 11-month degree program tough enough to handle. The B-school doesn't schedule classes on Wednesdays so there is a mid-day week for study. But Pitt loads up that day with optional workshops and executive briefings. There's also a Significant Film Series in which such famous flicks as "All Quiet on the Western Front" and "Caine Mutiny" are shown to students during lunch. Each film comes with a lecture on how the movie portrays relevant business issues.

Students gravitate to the basement of Mervis Hall for lunch at Clara's Cafe. As you might have guessed, Clara runs the joint, even reprimanding the dean for grabbing too big a piece of cake for lunch. For drinks, the MBAs favor Zelda's, which serves up pizza and is only one block from the school, and Doc's Place, the Yuppie watering hole in Shadyside some two miles away. Most students choose private housing near campus in the rather charming Oakland section of Pittsburgh.

Pitt isn't for everybody. "If you want to go to Wall Street, you probably shouldn't go to Pitt," adds Grasberger. "You don't have Goldman Sachs coming here to recruit." In 1989, about 90 companies interviewed at Katz. Ford Motor hires more Pitt MBAs than MBAs from any other school except Harvard. The automaker took 13 in 1989. Starting salaries and bonuses in 1988 ranged from a low of $20,000 to $87,000.

Contact: Kathleen Riehle, director of admissions, 412-648-1700

University of Southern California

Graduate School of Business
University Park
Los Angeles, California 90089

Enrollment: 1344
Women: 34%
Foreign: 11%
Minority: 19%
Part-time: 685
Average age: 27
Applicants accepted: 36%
Accepted applicants enrolled: 56%

Annual tuition: $13,446
Room and board: $6080
Average GMAT score: 590
GMAT range: 390 to 750
Average GPA: 3.4
GPA range: 2.3 to 4.0
Average starting pay: $38,071

Application deadline: April 1 for fall

No one ever accused the University of Southern California's business school of producing "quant jocks" or "digit heads." If anything, some joke that the place is a "soft" school where the "touchy-feely" folks go. Corporate recruiters arrive at USC's doorstep thinking they'll find more students interested in human resources because of the reputation of the B-school's organizational behavior (OB) group. And they are usually surprised to find that few students are interested. Some recruiters deliberately ask technical questions of USC grads to make sure they aren't "softies."

"It's something of a mismatch," says Glenn Payne, placement director. "The students come in and like to take courses from these (OB) folks, but they don't major in that area because the job market doesn't dictate it." Like students at other schools, most of the MBAs at USC line up for the hard-core finance and accounting courses. But those who take advantage of a top-notch OB program are exposed to some of the sharpest and most articulate management thinkers in American business. Among them: Warren Bennis, something of an institution himself in OB circles, James O'Toole, the witty and irreverent author of *Vanguard Management*, and Edward Lawler, who runs the school's Center for Effective Organizations.

When you look through the school's catalog, however, you'll find that of the nearly 120 electives, the lion's share is in accounting, with 37 advanced courses. This is because USC grants both a Master of Accounting and a Master of Business Taxation. The management and OB group offers more electives (18) than marketing (13), though finance and economics are second only to accounting in the number of advanced classes (26).

USC actually offers two different programs for full-time MBAs: a 50-unit MBA for students with undergraduate business degrees that can be completed in a year and a half and a two-year, 64-unit program for those without. The first year is crammed with required core courses, while in the second, students typically select a "track emphasis" in one of many disciplines.

First-year students without undergraduate degrees in business are clustered in teams of five each and placed in USC's management internship program. Here the students work with executives at local companies on assigned industry problems. The projects, with such firms as Lockheed, KLM Royal Dutch Airlines, Rockwell International, and Toyota can last up to nine months. "One of the things we've tried to emphasize over the years is a blending of theory and practice," says Dean Jack R. Borsting. "This project is part of the core and an important part of that goal."

Grads give high marks to USC faculty for their accessibility. "Even when they didn't have faculty hours, they always welcomed you to come by and many of them gave you their personal phone numbers," says Diane Fulginiti, who graduated in 1989. In BUSINESS WEEK's graduate survey, USC faculty fared less well on being at the leading edge of knowledge in their fields. Clearly not in this category, however, is Dennis Draper, whose Introduction to Finance and Futures and Options courses typically start off with a topical event that is used to introduce the day's lecture or discussion. "He's energetic, has a great personality, and he's in tune with what's going on in the business world," says one student admirer. The same is true of Caren Siehl's Managing Behavior in Organizations, the basic OB course that even provides lessons on how to manage your boss. Grads also recommend Phillip Birnbaum's course in competitive strategy and Peter Ritchken's class in futures and options.

Perhaps the most widely discussed and all-encompassing elective is Joseph Vinso's Advanced Financial Analysis—a course in which you dissect the financials of a public corporation, projecting sales and profits and analyzing investment opportunities. Vinso wins great reviews, even though he's tough. "At times, you feel like strangling him because he makes you do so much work," says Fulginiti of Vinso. She turned in a 200-page paper for the course.

The B-school sits in the middle of the 150-acre urban campus, a cluster of three buildings, including the I. M. Pei-designed Hoffman Hall. The facilities are cramped, however, and the dean has recently told faculty that the B-school is suffering a $3 million deficit. Across the street is the Los Angeles Coliseum, home to the Los Angeles Raiders. It's a cozy, park-like campus in a lousy neighborhood just south of downtown L.A. "You don't walk out alone at night," says one graduate, "or you'd be asking for trouble." Even so, many students rent nearby apartments which come a lot cheaper than the more desirable spots closer to Santa Monica beach, about 20 miles away. A limited number of on-campus dorms and apartments are available, but you have to apply early to get in. A family student complex for married students features 215 furnished studios, one-, and two-bedroom apartments.

What's a USC student like? "The students I admired or developed friendships with are some of the finest people I've ever met," said one graduate. "Another segment seemed to have social skills learned from 'Dynasty' or 'Dallas.' They were extremely self-interested." Maybe so, but there's plenty of social interaction at USC. Before every home football game, there's a company-sponsored barbecue. There's also a student–faculty football game in the fall (the faculty won in 1988). Students often unwind at Traditions, an on-campus bar that opens at 4 p.m. every day.

In 1989, 135 companies came to recruit on campus, offering jobs that paid starting salaries that ranged from $25,000 to a high of $70,000. The big recruiters were Wells Fargo Bank (8), while Hewlett-Packard, Arthur Andersen, Ernst & Whinney, First Interstate Bank, and Hughes Aircraft each recruited 4.

Contact: John D. Hammett, director of admissions, 213-743-7771

University of Texas at Austin

Graduate School of Business
Austin, Texas 78712

Enrollment: 1212	*Annual tuition:* nonresident—$3600
Women: 30%	resident—$768
Foreign: 12%	*Room and board:* $4409
Minority: 12%	*Average GMAT score:* 590
Part-time: None	*GMAT range:* NA
Average age: 26	*Average GPA:* 3.4
Applicants admitted: 48%*	*GPA range:* NA
Accepted applicants enrolled: 54%	*Average starting pay:* $40,115

Application deadline: March 1 for fall

Many MBAs graduate from the prestigious private universities in debt to the tune of $40,000. They spend years paying off their loans. And a good number of them rush into investment banking and consulting, only because they can't afford not to. That doesn't happen at the University of Texas at Austin. You probably cannot find a better bargain in a quality MBA education anywhere in the world.

Whether you're jetting in from Des Moines or Kuala Lumpur, you'll find it hard to beat the out-of-state tuition. Indeed, many nonresidents often find it cheaper to study at Texas than their own state universities. And a resident of the Lone Star State can get an MBA here for less than the cost of the books alone at the Harvard B-school. What about that cliché, "You get what you pay for"? Sure, there are some drawbacks to Texas, but any way you slice it, the program is an incredible bargain.

As a huge, sprawling state university, Texas offers a large faculty and a broad program overflowing with diversity and resources. Programs in accounting, information systems, marketing, and technology are strong. A distinguished faculty often gets this school into research-oriented Top 20 rankings. Some 350 corporations come here annually to recruit the graduate students.

Yet the sheer size of the place, with a total university student population of 48,000, makes it a dramatically different experience. "You're not going to have your hand held here," notes Scott Hull, who graduated in 1989 and now works for Quaker Oats. "There is not a staff to provide everything for you. Our ratio of advisers to students isn't nearly as good as it is at other schools." Grads say the alumni network also lacks strength because the B-school staff is too small to marshal it into an advantage. Budget cuts in recent years haven't helped matters, either.

Along with the more than 1200 MBA students here, there are 9000 undergraduates who converge on the collection of four buildings that form the B-school. The complex is on the south end of the 300-acre campus, not far from the central mall or the famous tower that houses part of the main library. A modern glass-and-concrete six-story building with a mall-like atrium is home to the graduate school of business. Among the modern, tiered classrooms is one that could have made the set of "Star Trek." Dubbed "Classroom 2000," the room boasts personal computers for 48 students and a gee-whiz electronic instruction center that allows professors to flash lessons on a huge screen in the front of the classroom. MBAs who pursue a concentration in information systems management, one of the major strengths of the B-school, take most of their classes in the room.

High-tech types might immediately think of heading for a B-school near Boston's Route 128 or California's Silicon Valley, but Texas is carving out an ambitious program that innovatively brings together management and technology. One of the best reasons to come here is George Kozmetsky, former B-school dean and a technological wizard who co-founded Teledyne. Kozmetsky is behind a new university-backed technology incubator that puts a roof over the head of high-tech start-ups and helps them get off the ground. MBAs play a role in critiquing their business plans as part of a course. Kozmetsky, who teaches Creative and Innovative Management, routinely shepherds his students to 6 of the more than 30 laboratories on campus to meet and mingle with science and engineering graduate students.

While resources are increasingly being devoted to technology management, accounting remains king at Texas. Nearly a third of the B-school's tenure-track faculty of 151 teachers reside in the accounting department, which offers a two-year Master of Public Accounting degree as well as a five-year CPA–MPA. You have lots of options in this program, from developing a specialization in finance or marketing to not concentrating in any single field at all. But you'll have few decisions in the highly structured first year, when the school piles on 33 hours of required core courses. You can waive some by exam or previous coursework and graduate earlier. Otherwise, you're likely to sweat out a few summer classes. A third of the MBAs attend summer courses, losing the opportunity to do an internship. In the second year, only one integrative course is required. The remaining eight courses can be chosen from the B-school's more than 170 electives (though some grads gripe that it's difficult to get into some popular classes). Three of the eight courses can be taken outside the B-school.

Students hand some of the best teaching grades to Leigh McAlister, a leading authority on marketing and sales promotion; Keith Brown, known for his Wall Street and finance savvy; and Frank Cross, a witty professor with a Harvard Law degree who teaches the business law core class. Says Hull of Brown, "He's funny, brilliant, and makes it a joy to go to class."

Also a joy is Austin, a lively state capital in the hill country of central Texas. MBAs go to Lake Austin for windsurfing, water skiing, and boating. For a night out, Texas grads venture off to Sixth Street, a popular Austin strip loaded with bars, live bands, and restaurants—Tex-Mex and barbeque. For cheap beer and a game of pool, you can't beat the Crown & Anchor Pub at 29th and Speedway, just 10 minutes from the school. A half-dozen times a semester, MBAs gather at local bars for "Think and Drink" parties, although grads concede that "Drink and Think" would be a more appropriate description for these bashes.

The strength of Texas's accounting program brings the Big Eight firms here in full force. In 1988, for example, Arthur Andersen recruited 50 Texas MBAs alone. At least a third of the more than 300 students who graduated in May of 1989 took jobs with the accounting firms, mostly in their consulting arms. The oil companies have also been major recruiters at Texas. Mobil International has recruited more MBAs here than at any other B-school in the nation.

And when MBAs take out their calculators to compute the cost–benefit ratio of their degree, the answer is typically a no brainer. Against the low cost of a Texas MBA, an average starting salary of $40,000 looks mighty good.

Contact: Robert Sullivan, associate dean, 512-471-1711

University of Washington

Graduate School of Business Administration
110 Mackenzie Hall
Seattle, Washington 98195

Enrollment: 456
Women: 29%
Foreign: 17%
Minority: 8%
Part-time: 80
Average age: 28
Applicants accepted: 34%
Accepted applicants enrolled: 60%

Annual tuition: nonresident—$6474
resident—$2601
Room and board: $4212
Average GMAT score: 607
GMAT range: NA
Average GPA: 3.27
GPA range: NA
Average starting pay: $34,300

Application deadline: March 15 for fall

Here's a school that doesn't work at being unique. It makes no pretensions about what it offers: a simple, quality MBA program without the bells and whistles others try to sound. "We're not a school that goes in for fads and fashions," explains Alfred N. Page, dean of the B-school of the University of Washington. "We work through the middle of the mainstream. It's an almost conservative look at business education."

Yet, the B-school can rightly lay claim to being one of the most selective schools among the Runners-Up. Indeed, it's as choosy if not more so than a few of the Top 20 schools, including Michigan, Indiana, and Rochester. Why? For out-of-state students, the city of Seattle has as much pull as the B-school. "Most of us are recreation nuts, and within an hour of this place you have skiiig, biking, and kayaking," says Ann Harris, director of the MBA program. In these parts, they call it the "Rainier Factor"— meaning that Mount Rainier and other nearby recreational spots provide a lifestyle that helps the school lure quality students and faculty.

Indeed, MBAs from other top schools often ring up the head of placement here asking for advice on how to relocate with a Seattle-based company. "I tell them it rains a lot and the salaries are low," laughs James Peters, director of placement. In 1989, there were up to 25 MBAs from Chicago who wanted to come out to work up some kind of reciprocal placement agreement beween the two schools.

The university itself is in a park-like setting with a combination of classic old buildings and generally nicely styled new ones. Everywhere it's green. In the spring, cherry trees bloom along the main corridor of the campus. Around the east perimeter of the grounds are the shores of Lake Washington, the residence of the graduate sailing club. Looming in the background are the majestic Olympic and Cascade Mountains. Balmer Hall, a four-story stucco building housing the library and classrooms, and Mackenzie Hall, the faculty and administration center, form the focus of the B-school on the upper campus. Across the street stands Lewis Hall, home of the executive education program.

MBAs hike through the rain forest on the Olympic Penninsula or climb Mount Rainier. A fixture of MBA life here is the salmon bake—about 100 grads recently consumed 40 pounds of salmon barbecued on the grill on the shores of Lake Washington. The Thursday evening ritual, dubbed TGIT (Thank God It's Thursday), sees most MBAs pick one of the several microbreweries in town to swill such tavern-brewed beers as Ballard Bitter, Pyramid, and Henry Weinhard. Nearly as popular as the local brew is the local espresso. MBAs like the outdoor porch of Cafe Roma on University Avenue for its espresso. MBAs also like to trek into Vancouver, British Columbia, for weekends, or to Portland. When in Seattle, you might live in the university's graduate housing, but most students reside off campus.

The natural beauty surprises most first-time visitors to Seattle. New students are often amazed by how friendly, outgoing, and diverse they find their classmates to be. "I expected a lot of little Alex Keatons walking around, but I was amazed at the number of people who did very different things, including working for the Peace Corps," says Janet Wu, of the Class of 1990. They come to enter as plain vanilla a program as you'll find. You'll go through a rigorous, quantitative first-year core that offers little flexibility. There are no electives in the three quarters of the first year unless you can waive out of some of the 13 core courses. All told, you need 24 courses to graduate. There's also a research requirement in lieu of a thesis in an area of interest, whether marketing, international business, or finance. For the adventurous, Washington offers six international exchange programs that allow you to spend a quarter abroad in the Pacific Rim or Europe.

In the first year, you'll be in class roughly four hours a day, Monday through Thursday. Grads say you need to do about two hours of prep work before a class, plus another two hours of homework after it. Students are grouped into cores of 45 each and attend the required courses together. Washington tries to maintain a 50–50 balance of lecture and case study. Most of the work in the first year falls on the individual, while the second year tends to be dominated by group work. In either year, "You can get tired of the format," says Jim Clute, of the Class of 1989.

There are a few professors here of whom students never tire. For the core courses, grads say you can't beat Bruce H. Faaland's Quantitative Methods and Gary C. Biddle's Financial Accounting. The former was voted the 1989 teacher of the year by students, while the latter is known for his entertaining style and dry sense of humor. Richard W. Moxon's International Business Environment and Philip K. Kienast's Negotiations draw rave reviews, too. The school employs 100 full-time tenure-track faculty, including those who teach the 1400 business undergraduates and the Ph.D. program. The number of accounting electives (25) is more than double those in marketing (12).

Until recently, MBAs would go to a centralized university placement office, and the school helped no more than 30% of its students gain summer internships. The new center, occupying an entire floor of Lewis Hall, opens in January 1990. About 120 companies arrived on campus to recruit the 190 or so members of the Class of 1989. In 1988, Hewlett-Packard hired 10 Washington MBAs. Arthur Andersen took the second biggest group, while Boeing, Seafirst, and Weyerhauser all tied by taking 6 each. Grads nailed down starting salaries that ranged from $25,000 to $65,000. Recruiters, however, complain that the majority of Washington MBAs can't be pried away from the area. "The students gripe that there aren't enough employers coming out to recruit them," says Peters. "The employers gripe that the students they want to recruit don't want to leave Seattle." Up to 65% of the graduates (some 41% enter the program from the area) stay here, even though salaries tend to be $5000 to $7000 less than most other U.S. cities.

So why do so many MBAs—even from other schools—want to come here? That wonderful lifestyle.

Contact: Leighanne Harris, director of MBA program, 206-543-4660

University of Wisconsin—Madison

School of Business
1155 Observatory Drive
Madison, Wisconsin 53706

Enrollment: 740
Women: 38%
Foreign: 19%
Minority: 8%
Part-time: 215
Average age: 27
Applicants admitted: 40%
Accepted applicants enrolled: 70%

Application deadline: June 15 for fall

Annual tuition: nonresident—$7762
resident—$2617
Room and board: $3815
Average GMAT score: 592
GMAT range: NA
Average GPA: 3.31
GPA range: NA
Average starting pay: $34,700

Madison, Wisconsin, might have more socialists per capita than any other town in America, but you'll find no shortage of capitalists at the university's graduate school of business in this radical hotbed.

Still, in the pair of B-school buildings atop the campus's Bascom Hill, there's an unusual, eclectic approach brought to business education. Like other B-schools within strong liberal arts universities, Wisconsin is reaching out to other departments on campus, trying to raise money for interdisciplinary seminars that would relate the humanities to business. "Why shouldn't MBAs study Shakespeare?" asks Dean James C. Hickman. "You could look at *King Lear* as a failure in management succession."

Madison's tolerance of alternative viewpoints provides a fertile environment for scholarly research within both the university at large and the B-school. A recent article in the *Review of Business and Economic Research* ranked Wisconsin first among all public B-schools in the amount of pages published in 14 leading academic journals.

Of course, that's not always a good sign for students because it may well indicate that the professors are far more interested in research than they are in quality teaching. It's telling, perhaps, that while the B-school's own efforts to market itself are lackluster, its marketing department has been ranked number one in research among all public B-schools. Indeed, the B-school's graduate bulletin looks like it was run off on a high school mimeograph machine and its alumni magazine is less exciting than many high school newspapers.

But while this school is short on gloss, it does guarantee students a solid, quality MBA education that is improving all the time. These days, Wisconsin is beefing up the MBA program by tightening admission requirements, introducing a new curriculum and building a new B-school building. In the fall of 1989, the B-school dropped a one-year version of its MBA to focus on the traditional two-year program. The improvements may cost students an additional $1000 a year in tuition starting in the fall of 1989.

You need 54 credits to gain the Wisconsin MBA, 39 of them consumed by required core courses. A revamped core curriculum features four newly created courses that reflect the challenges of managing the twenty-first-century corporation: International Perspectives; Decision Information Systems; Political, Legal, and Ethical Environments, and Innovation and Technology Management. "In order for the United States to remain competitive, we are going to have to produce a different kind of manager," says Jack Nevin, chairman of the marketing department. "Our new MBA program is a major change in that direction."

After completing the core, you'll have only 15 credits left for advanced coursework unless you've been able to waive out of some classes. If you select a concentration in one of 11 areas of study, you could find yourself left with only two remaining electives. One out of every five MBAs major in finance, while 16% of them enroll in the marketing concentration.

Most MBA classes are held in Commerce, a dull five-story yellow brick building constructed in the 1950s. The business library, offices, and additional classrooms are in Bascom Hall, a Greek Revival building with a statue of Abraham Lincoln in front. In the summer of 1990, Wisconsin expects to break ground for a new $26.3 million B-school facility. The view from atop Bascom Hill is one of the best on the Madison campus. Looking down State Street, you can see the state capitol. But trudging up the hill on a brutal winter morning isn't the most pleasant experience you'll have.

Although faculty members must "publish or perish" at Madison, some students say they still give MBAs personal attention. "The faculty is first-rate and very responsive to students," says Aaron Kennedy, a 1989 grad. "When they are teaching a class or talking to you they don't seem like all they have on their minds is their latest research project." In recent years, the school's teacher of the year award has been won by Randy Dunham, who teaches organizational behavior; Gil Churchill, a market research expert; accounting guru Jerry Weygandt; and Roger Formisano, who teaches principles of risk management.

Despite its national reputation for research, Wisconsin remains a regional school. About 70% of the MBA students are from the state and half of the graduating class remains in Wisconsin. Where Madison differs from other regional programs is in its ability to attract large consumer products companies to recruit. Quaker Oats, Oscar Mayer, General Mills, and Pepsico all hire Wisconsin MBAs for marketing jobs. Other major corporate recruiters who come to campus are Ford, 3M, and Kimberly-Clark.

The placement office makes a special effort to expose MBAs to opportunities with small business and not-for-profit organizations. In addition to a Career Fair that attracts 100 large companies, Wisconsin holds a Small Business Career Day that brings in about 20 small- and medium-sized enterprises. "It's easy to get caught up in the glitz and glamor of the biggest 500 companies," says Karen Stauffacher, director of career services. "We try to make students aware of other opportunities."

Like its rival—Ann Arbor, Michigan—Madison is a very liberal, cosmopolitan community. Locals joke that Madison, with its resilient co-ops and communes, is still stuck in the year 1968. But there's no denying that Wisconsin is the land of beer, brauts, and Badgers, the name of the school's sports teams. Popular MBA hangouts include the Brauthaus, which specializes in the dish its name implies, and the Kollege Klub. When the weather warms, MBAs trek to the Memorial Union to drink beer and wine on the terrace overlooking Lake Mendota, a favorite spot for canoeing. Wisconsin is no UCLA, but a resort mentality prevails here during late spring and summer when temperatures climb to the 80s and 90s.

During the late 1960s and early 1970s, Madison was one of the most radical college campuses in the country, along with Ann Arbor and Berkeley. The Left is still alive in Madison, but capitalists are firmly in control of the B-school.

Contact: E. James Blakely, associate dean, 608-262-1555

CHAPTER 7

ACCREDITED B-SCHOOLS ...
AND HOW TO SIZE THEM UP

What if you can't make it into a top-ranked school? Or maybe you just want to attend a school closer to your home or job. If you aim to get your MBA from a school that's not a household name, consider whether it's accredited by the American Assembly of Collegiate Schools of Business (AACSB). About 700 institutions offer MBAs, but only a few more than a third of them meet the group's standards. Some large schools don't, including 3 of the nation's 10 largest schools by enrollment—New York's Pace University, Fairleigh Dickinson University in Rutherford, New Jersey, and Pepperdine University in Malibu, California.

As corporations become savvier recruiters of MBA talent, they are giving more weight to the AACSB seal. Hewlett-Packard Company, for instance, refuses to pay tuition for employees who attend unaccredited schools. "We want an employee to get an MBA from a school that we would feel comfortable hiring from," explains a company official. And a number of foundations hand out fellowship money for minorities and female students only to schools who have earned the AACSB okay. Another key consideration: "Recruiting companies use accreditation to decide whether they will visit a particular campus," says Ronald Frank, dean of Purdue University's School of Management.

The AACSB's imprimatur could be especially important to part-timers who switch schools when their employers relocate them. Many B-schools will only accept transfer credits from accredited schools. Beware of schools that claim to be accredited, but lack the seal

180

of approval by the AACSB. This accreditation group is considered by many in the business school world to be the most credible. Some business schools are accredited by regional or other groups that fail to set standards that are important to business school students.

Accreditation by the AACSB requires that 75% of the faculty teach full-time and that 75% hold doctorates—standards that help to ensure a basic level of teaching quality. Programs that overly rely on teaching by retired executives run the risk of having classes composed of corporate war stories, not leading-edge learning. Accreditation also requires that the Ph.D.s are spread across the departments of a business school to ensure professionalism in all critical courses. A school that routinely accepts students with poor undergraduate records and very low scores on the Graduate Management Admission Test isn't likely to be accredited. Neither is one with an inadequate library or poor computer facilities.

When a business school meets the AACSB's approval, it must offer quality programs in all areas—undergraduate, graduate, full-time, and part-time. A substandard part-time MBA program would prevent the full-time program from qualifying for accreditation. And when an accrediting team visits a school, it even meets with the students on campus. Typical questions: "Can you get in to see the faculty when you want? Do you have sufficient access to computers? Are the classrooms too crowded?" Each school's accreditation also comes up for renewal every nine years.

These are all reasons why accreditation is important. Still, it is hardly a Good Housekeeping Seal of Approval. Some accredited schools, say the critics, offer students an education that may well fall below that offered by some of the unaccredited schools. Roughly 60% of the 251 AACSB-approved schools, for example, admit half or more than half of those who apply for admission to them. Some of these B-schools, including Boise State University, the University of Tennessee at Chattanooga, and Virginia's James Madison University, open their doors to 9 out of every 10 applicants. That's hardly the kind of selectivity reflective of a quality school.

On the other hand, the lack of the AACSB seal isn't automatically a sign of a "second-rate" institution. Some fine schools have deliberately foregone accreditation. Yale's School of Management is one good example. By all accounts, Yale offers one of the best business school educations in the country. But it has long viewed its program as "nontraditional" because it integrates public- and private-sector initiatives. For years, Yale has neither pursued accreditation nor expressed an interest in it. Today, however, the school is actively considering the issue partly because, without the AACSB seal, it has lost out on some fellowship money for students.

Yale isn't the only excellent school without accreditation. The same is true of the American Graduate School of International Management in Glendale, Arizona, popularly known as Thunderbird. Founded in 1946, the school is widely recognized for its graduate program in international business. It attracts such major corporate recruiters as Citicorp, BankAmerica, General Motors, American Express, Sears, IBM, and General Electric. *The Journal of International Business Studies* recently ranked Thunderbird the number one international business master's degree program. Even so, the school lacks AASCB accreditation.

Generally, however, accreditation shows that a B-school cares about the quality of its program. Its absence should spur applicants to look more closely at an institution's curriculum and faculty. If you're investing in that precious passport, be sure it will take you where you want to go.

There's no sure formula that determines a quality school, but the following institutions have received the AACSB's seal of approval and jumped a few other hurdles that make them excellent institutions. To squeeze through this screen, these institutions had to meet two criteria applied by BUSINESS WEEK: that they be selective enough to turn away at least half their applicants and that student GMAT scores average 590 or more. You can obtain for free a complete list of accredited schools from the AACSB, 605 Old Ballas Road, St. Louis, Missouri 63141. Or you can purchase a complete list with details on the best of them from BUSINESS WEEK. (For a copy, send a check for $3.95 to BUSINESS WEEK, MBA Survey, 1221 Avenue of the Americas, New York, New York 10020, 39th Floor, Attn: Celeste Whittaker.)

Emory University
School of Business
Atlanta, Georgia 30322

Enrollment: 239	*Annual tuition:* $12,890
Women: 29%	*Room and board:* $7400
Foreign: 15%	*Average GMAT score:* 600
Minority: 8%	*GMAT range:* 410 to 760
Part-time: None	*Average GPA:* NA
Applicants accepted: 40%	*GPA range:* 2.7 to 4.0
Average starting pay: $40,000	*Jobs by graduation:* NA

Application deadline: April 15 for fall

Small, intimate MBA program with a superb reputation and a strong candidate for the BUSINESS WEEK Runners-Up list. This Methodist-affiliated university has turned out some 2000 MBAs since 1954 with an emphasis in general management. Grads concentrate in accounting, finance, management, or marketing. Encourages teamwork and mutual support, has close relationships with local business community.

Georgia Institute of Technology
College of Management
Atlanta, Georgia 30332

Enrollment: 175	*Annual tuition:* nonresident—$5598
Women: 30%	resident—$1896

Foreign: 20%   *Room and board:* NA
Minority: 8%   *Average GMAT score:* 610
Part-time: None   *GMAT range:* 420 to 780
Applicants accepted: 30%   *Average GPA:* 3.2
Average starting pay: NA   *GPA range:* 2.1 to 4.0

Application deadline: August 1 for fall

Based in mid-town Atlanta on 300 acres of wooded campus, the institute has been turning out MBAs since 1945. Claims strength in accounting, financial services, human resources, computer integrated manufacturing, and information systems.

Contact: Ann Johnson Scott, assistant director of graduate studies, 404-894-2604

Rensselaer Polytechnic Institute
School of Management
Troy, New York 12180

Enrollment: 174   *Annual tuition:* $12,000
Women: 28%   *Room and board:* $4790
Foreign: 24%   *Average GMAT score:* 605
Minority: 8%   *GMAT range:* 510 to 780
Part-time: 49   *Average GPA:* 3.15
Applicants accepted: 45%   *GPA range:* 2.5 to 4.0
Average starting pay: $37,200   *Jobs by graduation:* 63%

Application deadline: March 15 for fall

The B-school is one of the surprising secrets at America's oldest technological university. Focus is on small classes and close faculty–student interaction. Maintains strength in the technical aspects of management.

Contact: Barry Taylor, director of student programs, 518-276-6853

Tulane University
A. B. Freeman School of Business
New Orleans, Louisiana 70118

Enrollment: 485   *Annual tuition:* $12,580
Women: 23%   *Room and board:* $8000
Foreign: 20%   *Average GMAT score:* 593
Minority: 9%   *GMAT range:* 420 to 750
Part-time: 164   *Average GPA:* 3.0
Applicants accepted: 45%   *GPA range:* 2.0 to 4.0
Average starting salary: $35,400 *Jobs by graduation:* 40%

Application deadline: May 31 for fall/December 1 for spring

Boasts summer abroad program in Paris for first-year students, small classes, and a strong and loyal alumni network. B-school housed in new Goldring/Woldenberg Hall on the 110-acre campus in a residential area in uptown New Orleans.

Contact: Julie S. Dolan, assistant dean for admissions, 800-223-5402

183

University of Arizona
Graduate School of Management
Tucson, Arizona 85721

Enrollment: 540	*Annual tuition:* nonresident—$3844
Women: 31%	resident—$990
Foreign: 10%	*Room and board:* $2200
Minority: 17%	*Average GMAT score:* 595
Part-time: NA	*GMAT range:* NA
Applicants accepted: 34%	*Average GPA:* 3.3
Average starting pay: NA	*GPA range:* NA

Application deadline: June 1 for fall

Contact: Diana Vidal, director of admissions, 602-621-2169

University of Massachusetts at Amherst
School of Management
Amherst, Massachusetts 01003

Enrollment: 382	*Tuition:* nonresident—$189/credit
Women: 44%	resident—$68/credit
Foreign: 35%	*Room and board:* NA
Minority: 5%	*Average GMAT score:* 590
Part-time: 170	*GMAT range:* NA
Applicants accepted: 29%	*Average GPA:* NA
Average starting pay: $32,000	*GPA range:* NA

Application deadline: March 1 for fall

Contact: Richard Asebrook, director of MBA program, 413-549-4930

Wake Forest University
Babcock Graduate School of Management
7659 Reynolds Station
Winston-Salem, North Carolina 27109

Enrollment: 390	*Annual tuition:* $9850
Women: 33%	*Room and board:* $3680
Foreign: 9%	*Average GMAT score:* 600
Minority: 5%	*GMAT range:* 500 to 700
Part-time: 190	*Average GPA:* 3.1
Applicants accepted: 43%	*GPA range:* 2.4 to 3.8
Average starting salary: $31,688	*Jobs by graduation:* 85%

Application deadline: May 15 for fall

Yet another intimate program employing an "experiential" and case study approach to MBA education. Claims strong tracks in banking, financing, marketing, and international business. Expects new B-school building on 350-acre campus in 1991.

Contact: James Garner Ptaszynski, director of admissions, 800-722-1622

Index

Arizona:
American Graduate School of International Management (Thunderbird), 181–182
University of Arizona, 184

California:
Stanford University, 2, 4, 7, 9, 18, 24, 25, 26, 27–36, 78–81
University of California at Berkeley (Haas), 3, 25, 26, 27–36, 118–122
University of California at Los Angeles (Anderson), 20, 25, 27–36, 113–117
University of Southern California, 7, 27–36, 139, 154, 172–173
Connecticut:
Yale University, 11, 25, 27–36, 128–132, 154, 181

Florida:
University of Florida, 139, 158–159

Georgia:
Emory University, 182
Georgia Institute of Technology, 182–183
University of Georgia, 139, 160–161

Idaho:
Boise State University, 181

Illinois:
DePaul University, 20
Loyola University, 20
Northwestern University (Kellogg), 7, 10, 15, 17, 19, 20, 21, 22, 24, 25, 26, 27–36, 38–42
University of Chicago, 7, 14, 19–20, 21–22, 25, 26, 27–36, 88–91, 154
University of Illinois at Chicago, 20
University of Illinois at Urbana-Champaign, 139, 162–163
Indiana:
Indiana University, 25, 27–36, 93–97, 154
Purdue University (Krannert), 27–36, 152, 180
University of Notre Dame, 139, 168–169
Iowa:
University of Iowa, 139, 164–165

Louisiana:
Tulane University, 183–184

Massachusetts:
Bentley College, 20
Harvard University, 3, 4, 5, 7, 8, 18, 24, 25, 26, 27–36, 43–47
Massachusetts Institute of Technology (Sloan), 25, 26, 27–36, 108–112
University of Massachusetts at Amherst, 184